dies in Management Science
and Systems

Volume 17

Series Edito

Burton V. Dea

*Department of Organization and Managemen
San Jose State Universit
San Jose, California, U.S.A*

NORTH-HOLLANI
AMSTERDAM • NEW YORK • OXFORD • TOKY(

APPLI   Stu

Applied Expert Systems

Edited by:

Efraim TURBAN

School of Business
United States International University
San Diego, CA, U.S.A.

and

Paul R. WATKINS

School of Accounting
University of Southern California
Los Angeles, CA, U.S.A.

1988

NORTH-HOLLAND
AMSTERDAM ● NEW YORK ● OXFORD ● TOKYO

© Elsevier Science Publishers B.V., 1988

ISBN: 0 444 70489 2

Published by:
Elsevier Science Publishers B.V.
P.O. Box 1991
1000 BZ Amsterdam
The Netherlands

Sole distributors for the U.S.A. and Canada:
Elsevier Science Publishing Company, Inc.
52 Vanderbilt Avenue
New York, N.Y. 10017
U.S.A.

PRINTED IN THE NETHERLANDS

PREFACE

During the last five years we have witnessed the emergence of a new computer technology - Expert Systems (ES). The number of commercially available systems have grown from a few dozen five years ago, to a few thousand today. The CRI directory of ES [1] lists several hundred systems, and so does the list by Walker and Miller [2]. Companies such as du Pont, Bell Telephone, GTE and Xerox have each developed hundreds of systems. Sales of the most popular shells (such as EXSYS, INSIGHT 2, M.1 and Personal Consultant) are reaching the 10,000 mark. Dozens of books have been written on the theory of expert systems and on the many tools that can be used to build them quickly and inexpensively. Artificial Intelligence languages, such as LISP and PROLOG, have close to 50 commercial dialects and variants. Almost none of these products existed five years ago. From just a tiny research-oriented venture a few years ago, expert systems now is one of the fastest-growing segments of the computer industry.

Applied Expert Systems is a volume which was designed to keep the reader abreast of some of the latest developments in the applications of experts systems. It brings to light several innovations which could result in an increased rate of expert systems applications in industry, military and government. The carefully selected and refereed papers represent the efforts of about 30 scientists and practitioners in several countries.

This volume shows also the great potential of expert systems, the diversification of applications, the benefits and some of the problems and the issues involved in a successful application of the new technology. It could benefit researchers, practitioners and students alike. Finally, the volume contains over 400 items in its lists of references.

The volume is divided into two major parts which we titled as applied methodologies and practical applications. Each part includes several papers whose highlights are described next.

Part I: Applied Methodologies

While attempting to apply expert systems to commercial situations, people encounter several issues which are generic in nature. The lessons acquired in such situations and the methodologies developed to handle them are of an utmost importance to an expert systems developer. The five chapters in this part concentrate on several such issues. The specifics are:

Chapter 1: Selecting a Knowledge-based System Application

The development of an expert systems, especially of a large one, is viewed as a fairly complex process. This paper proposes a detailed process which was implemented in Boeing Military Airplane Company. The important steps of the process are:

- identify the necessary software that will match the problem (KEE, in this case),
- conduct the rapid prototyping properly
- prepare an implementation plan
- prepare a management plan for this large project

The chapter proposes a well-known multiple objective methodology (called TOPSIS) for the selection of appropriate project. This methodology ranks the candidates by their weighted importance.

Chapter 2: Expert System Prototyping as a Research Tool

Rapid prototyping, which is a dominating strategy in expert systems development, can be used also as a tool for both applied and theoretical research. The iterative nature of prototyping permits quick experimentations. Furthermore, because its ability to handle symbolic manipulations so nicely, expert systems prototyping may expand the boundaries of quantitative research by adding qualitative dimensions. Several methods of knowledge acquisition for prototyping are examined together with appropriate experimental controls. Expert systems prototyping is described next as being used as a database for researchers both for "theory generation" and for "theory testing."

The research issues a that are suitable for expert systems experimentation are: understanding the nature of problems, understanding he problem-solving process,developing a proof of concept that a particular idea can be implemented as a computer program, understanding human intelligence and expertise and analyzing the use of expert systems prototyping as a research tool.

The chapter ends with a discussion of the limitations of expert systems prototyping as a research tool and raising some methodological issues that need to be addressed.

Chapter 3: Multiple Criteria Decision Making and Expert Systems

This chapter attempts to interrelate and integrate the topics of multiple criteria decision making (MCDM) and expert systems. The authors point to several potential applications:

- knowledge acquisition from multiple experts (see Chapter 5)
- project selection (see Chapter 2)
- problem formulation
- model selection
- improvement of solutions

- user interface

The paper suggests the use of inference rules related to issues of multiple criteria.

A prototype program is described to execute the proposed methodology. It was constructed with Personal Consultant Plus (from Texas Instruments). This shell enables both rules and frames representation.

Chapter 4: The Integration of Multiple Knowledge Sources (Experts)

This chapter deals with the important situation of knowledge extracted from several experts. Three approaches are described: 1) Blending lines of reasoning using consensus methods, 2) use different lines of reasoning for different situations, and 3) decomposes the acquired knowledge into specialized knowledge sources. This topic is very difficult and very important. In many cases, companies use only one expert. This makes life easy, but you may sacrifice a considerable amount of knowledge and reduce the quality of your system.

Chapter 5: Management Use of Artificial Intelligence

The first part of the book ends with a comprehensive view regarding the relationship between expert systems and computerized decision making. The chapter brings forth the following points:

- The relationship between the complexity of decision making and computer based information systems were expert systems at the extreme.
- Heuristic problem solving as an opposing approach to algorithmic decision rules.
- The important role of information is decision making
- The importance of creative decision making.
- The identification of decision areas which are more relevant to expert systems.
- The relationship between decision styles and expert systems.

The chapter proposes two models. First, a causal integrative model is offered and then an Artificial Intelligence in managerial decision making is outlined.

Part II: Practical Applications

Part II deals with practical applications of expert systems in various functional areas and in different organizational structures. Most of these applications deviate from the usual diagnosis and repair type, for which expert systems are known. Furthermore, most of these examples included some interesting integration of decision making and management science methodologies with expert systems. The specific chapters in this part follow.

Chapter 6: A Simulation Expert System Framework for Flexible Manufacturing Systems

As simulation becomes commonplace and the underlying models become more complex, the need for a new generation of simulation systems which possess some degree of online intelligence becomes more desireable. This chapter presents a conceptual framework for the design of Expert System based simulation system for a Flexible Manufacturing System (FMS). FMS is chosen for illustration since simulation systems are an integral part of and are used routinely in this environment. A simulation based generator is developed to illustrate the feasibility and features of the proposed framework.

Chapter 7: Intelligent Production Planning System (IPPS)

The integration of an expert system and a decision support system (DSS) is demonstrated in this chapter in a production planning system. The model handles the qualitative factors in a rule based expert system while the quantitative analysis is executed in a standard optimization (linear programming) model. The IPPS permits not only the integration of the two subsystems but allows a tradeoff between a qualitative goal (such as employees' morale) and a quantitative goal (such as cost minimization). The problem treated by the system is the determination of production plan, inventory level and work force which are needed to accommodate fluctuating demand.

Chapter 8: An Expert System for R & D Projects

This chapter introduces the development and application of a rule-based expert system to the area of R&D project management. The issue tackled by the system is whether to continue or terminate an on-going R&D project. Such a decision is to be made periodically, during the life cycle of the project. The system makes interpretation of data collected during the monitoring process. Of special difficulty is the decision made during the development phase of the life cycle.

The methodology partitioned the tasks into four modules and uses the ID3 algorithm. The system runs on a micro computer with the commercially available shell 1st CLASS (from Programs in Motion, Inc.). Note: this shell can be used to build rules and to generate rules from examples.

Chapter 9: An Expert System for Promotion Marketing

This chapter presents a marketing expert system designed to investigate the planning of consumer sales promotion campaigns for mature consumer packaged goods. The system is micro-based, developed with a shell (Personal consultant from Texas Instrument). it works with backward chaining and it includes certainty factors. In addition to the specific case, the chapter deals with several methodological issues:

- Multiple knowledge sources which include nontraditional sources used in marketing (e.g., scanner and survey data)
- Measuring the systems' performance
- Representation of the information in the form of rules, analytical functions and declarative parameters with associated measures of uncertainty
- Codifying and representing knowledge acquired from survey data and scanner data

In addition, the chapter discusses some other expert systems under development as well as it points to several crucial expert systems issues.

Chapter 10: Developing Consolidated Financial Statements Using a Prototype Expert System

FINSTA is an expert system developed for the consolidation of financial statement data across accounts. The program determines which accounts should be aggregated, then it identifies the nets of accounts to be aggregated and then makes a final choice of which accounts to include in each set.

The knowledge is represented in both rules and frames; the prototype was developed by using Prolog as the development language.

Chapter 11: Expert Systems for Use in Finance

The area of finance is experiencing a rapid growth in the application of ES technology. This chapter discusses areas where ES technology is being applied in finance such as banking, insurance, securities trading and others and provides a framework which highlights areas which have promise for future benefit from ES applications.

Chapter 12: Expert Systems-Based Robot Technology

One of the most promising applications of expert systems is their integration with robotics. This chapter outlines a framework for such an integration. The framework is based on the life-cycle for robotics. While still in an experimental stage, such an integration exists in all phases of the life cycle. The objective is to make the robots intelligent so they can perform tasks which currently are performed only humans. Actual applications of such integrated systems are demonstrated in three areas: assembly lines, material handling and welding. Initial results are very encouraging.

Chapter 13: Expert Systems in Business Venturing

This chapter presents a unique application of a combination ES and Decision Support System (DSS) for the analysis of business ventures and for the matching of such ventures with potential investors. Each potential investor has certain requirements and constraints which must be considered for each business venture available. since there are thousands of business ventures in the data base, the matching is difficult and time consuming. The expert system eased this situation by finding the preferences and requirements of the investors and incorporating it into a decision model.

The expert system evaluates, like a human expert, the result of the data generated by the model for each business venture, that it attempts to find an appropriate match, based on the investors' profile and preference.

Chapter 14: An expert system for Operations Analysis (OASES)

This chapter presents an application of a complex expert system called OASES for conducting operations analysis in a fiberglass manufacturing process. The chapter makes use of the powerful diagnostic capabilities of expert systems.

The problem under investigation is downtime, which is very expensive in process industry (an hour can cost up to one hundred thousand dollars). The analysis of the causes of downtime is done in two phases: (1) finding the general principles of operations analysis; and (2) finding the specific problem.

The system was programmed from scratch, using Franz LISP as a programming language. It was implemented on a VAX 11/780. It used a forward chaining approach to the diagnosis.

Special methodologies which were used in conjunction with this project are:

1) The Dempster-Shafer formulas were incorporated in the inexact reasoning mechanism.

2) A partitioning of the knowledge base was used.

3) Whinston's Augmented Tree Transition methodology was used to allow a very unstructured dialog (such that would have conducted by a human expert).

Chapter 15: Expert Systems in Industry: Actual and Potential Applications

This chapter views expert systems as providing decision support to management. In addition to their advisory capabilities, expert systems are being viewed as providers of intelligent information management. Finally, expert systems can increase productivity and quality thus increasing corporate competitive edge.

Chapter 16: Knowledge-Based System for Academic Advising

This concluding chapter is provided as a case study in an academic environment which uses an expert systems shell (M1) to facilitate providing advice and aiding in the registration process for an industrial engineering program. Insights are provided into the structuring of the knowledge and in the dialog that takes place between users and the system. Also, some discussion is provided of integration issues with the appropriate university databases at some future point in time.

REFERENCES

[1]   Smart, G. and J. Langeland-Knudsen, *The CRI Directory of Expert Systems*. Oxford, N.J.: Learned Information Systems, 1987.

[2]   Walker, T.C. and R.K. Miller, *Expert Systems*. Madison, Georgia: SEAI Technology, 1986, 1987, 1988.

Efraim Turban
Paul R. Watkins

TABLE OF CONTENTS

Part 1

APPLIED METHODOLOGIES

Applied Expert Systems, E. Turban and P.R. Watkins (Editors)
© Elsevier Science Publishers B.V. (North-Holland), 1988

SELECTING A KNOWLEDGE-BASED SYSTEM APPLICATION: CONSIDERATIONS AND EXPERIENCES

Dr. Abu S. M. Masud * *and Dr. Don Hommertzheim*

Industrial Engineering Department
The Wichita State University
Box 35, Wichita, KS 67208, USA

The success of a knowledge-based system application, especially the first one in an organization, requires that the application be selected with care. Thus, a systematic generation and evaluation process for the potential applications will have to be adopted if knowledge-based systems are to be incorporated into a wide range of management decision situations within an organization. This chapter describes the use of a systems analysis approach for identifying potential knowledge-based applications in an organization. The considerations involved and the details of analysis required in each step of a multi-step procedure are explained with the help of an actual application case study.

1. INTRODUCTION

Two recent parallel developments have made the knowledge-based system (KBS) technology practical for application in solving complex decision making problems in management and engineering. One development is the commercialization of the KBS technology where it has been taken out of the rescarch lab environment to commercial product environment. The other development is in the area of computer technology by making computers affordable to a much wider range of organizations. As a result, many organizations are getting involved (or thinking of getting involved) with KBS as a decision support tool. Because of the hoopla created by popular press, one gets the impression that KBS is easily applicable for solving any decision problem. Thus, the stage may have been

---

* Current Address: Techno-Economics Division, Kuwait Institute for Scientific Research, P.O.Box 24885, 13109 Safat, Kuwait

set for disastrous consequences due to improper problem selection or implementation. This paper addresses the problem of how to properly select KBS applications, especially if it is the first one in an organization.

The literature of artificial intelligence (AI) and KBS is substantial. With few exceptions, they can be grouped under three categories: (1) very technical discussions assuming a high level of reader knowledge about AI and KBS -- these deal with issues of knowledge representation, inferencing mechanisms, etc.; (2) reviews and very general discussions assuming that reader has no technical/science background -- these deal with commercial/technical status, potential areas of applications, etc.; and, (3) application descriptions assuming varying degrees of reader knowledge -- these deal either with the technical issues of knowledge representation, control schemes, etc., of the specific application or with the capabilities of the developed system.

Selecting appropriate projects for funding is an important activity and has significant impact on organizations involved in research and service. A variety of tools have been developed over the years to aid in this process [1, 2, 3, 4, 5, 6]. Some of these techniques are very structured and utilize analytical methodologies, while others are less formal and focus on the more qualitative factors. In general, many of these tools progress through a series of phases that include screening, evaluation, prioritizing, and analysis. Those projects that support the operational objectives of the organization are usually ranked the highest. There are usually numerous factors that are considered in these exercises. Selection of factors for consideration is influenced by whether the organization is in the private, nonprofit, or government sector.

Only a notable few books and articles discuss issues related to how KBS application projects are selected, how to select a development tool, or how to go about implementing a KBS application [7, 8, 9, 10, 11]. In general, their advices boil down to : 'select an application for your first KBS project which appears to be too easy or too simple.' This is a valuable advice, but a team that is contemplating its first step in the KBS arena needs more guidance. We have, therefore, developed a more detailed and systematic approach for the initial KBS project selection.

During the course of a research project involving the selection and implementation of the first KBS application in the Operations Analysis (OA) unit of the Boeing Military Airplane Company (BMAC) in Wichita [12], we faced issues that we believe would be faced by other organizations when they consider whether or not KBS is an appropriate tool to be used in their organization. If appropriate, they must also select a particular decision problem for implementation. Another critical decision facing an organization that has selected the application problem is the determination of which development tool is appropriate under various criteria. What follows in the rest of this paper is our experience from the BMAC project and recommendations based on that experience. The paper is organized as follows: some background information about the project in section 2, a methodology for KBS application selection in section 3, a method for ranking potential applications in section 4, experience in applying the methodology at BMAC in section 5, and some concluding remarks in section 6.

2. PROJECT BACKGROUND

The OA unit of BMAC is involved in various kinds of mathematical and simulation studies conducted for the Boeing Company, the U.S. Air Force, and other defense organizations. There has been a growing realization within the OA unit that incorporation of KBS in many such studies would become inevitable and the unit wants to be ready for that eventuality. Therefore, a project was funded by Kansas Advanced Technology Commission and BMAC to identify possible areas where KBS could be used in the different activities of OA unit and to actually implement in one of the identified areas. It was anticipated that such an implementation would improve the flexibility, capability, and/or useability of an OA model or methodology. It would also, as a side benefit, provide general awareness and training in KBS development and use.

3. A METHODOLOGY FOR KBS APPLICATION SELECTION

The KBS application selection procedure we have developed consists of 8 steps. Other teams who want to implement a similar plan may skip or combine some steps depending on the background and requirements. The step details are as follows.

Step 1. Review KBS Technology. This is basically an educational and literature review process. The idea here is to gain as much information as possible on the various aspects of KBS terms, characteristics and requirements, and the development process. At the end of this step the team members should have a general familiarity with the: (i) characteristics of a KBS, (ii) difference between a conventional computer program and a KBS, (iii) components of a KBS and their requirements, (iv) various forms of knowledge representations and their advantages/disadvantages, (v) search mechanisms (forward and backward chaining, depth- and breadth- first, etc.), and (vi) search control schemes.

Step 2. Identify Potential Areas of Application. This step consists of studying reported applications in the literature, finding parallels with the activities in the organization, and developing a list of potential application areas. Specifically, the activities in this step will consist of: (i) review reported applications and their characteristics (classification into application areas, characteristics of problems in these areas, etc.), (ii) study details of specific applications (problem domains, specifics of knowledge representation and searching schemes, programming language or tool used, development process or steps, etc.), (iii) review of current and past projects/activities of the organization (characteristics of projects, manpower and resource requirements, type of information/experience used, frequency of use, etc.), (iv) review of study process and models used (how the projects/ activities are carried out, project/activity selection mechanism, what models or preestablished procedures are available, frequency of their use, maintenance of models/procedures, availability of manpower knowledgeable in the models and their application, etc.), and (v) develop a list of potential applications (ask: what are the possible areas of applications, which activities are similar to those of reported applications, which activities appear to possess characteristics of KBS, which activities appear to be knowledge intensive/cognitive/difficult to perform without experience, etc.).

Step 3. Develop/Select Applications Ranking Method. This is a crucial step. Care must be taken to consider all relevant factors into consideration while ranking the application projects developed in step 2. Unless the organization has a well developed methodology that it uses in all situations where alternate projects are ranked, the project team may consider reviewing the literature on ranking alternatives in order to get a general understanding of the process. Formal and informal methods can be used; we suggest that, if possible, a formal method be used. A formal method has several advantages: it is well understood by the team members and the management, all the team members contribute towards ranking and selection, it can be documented easily, and, most importantly, the management can be convinced easily to accept the team recommendation. We have used the Consensus Ranking Approach (CRA), which will be explained in the next section, to assist our project team in ranking a set of potential applications. For other methods, see [13].

Step 4. Review and Rank Application Projects. This step should be a straight forward application of the method developed/selected in step 3 to the set of application projects on hand.

Step 5. Recommend Prototype Application. Once the projects have been ranked, the management (i.e. appropriate decision makers with authority to commit monetary and other resources) action is necessary to proceed any further. The best approach is to arrange an oral presentation, along with the delivery of a written report, to the decision makers. It is a good idea not to present the management with just one application as the recommendation since it implicitly conveys a 'take it or leave it' impression. If possible, it is better to recommend the top two or three applications, especially if they are close to each other in terms of the weighing scheme. However, if the team feels strongly, it should also indicate its preference and the reasons for its preference.

Step 6. Review and Recommend KBS Tool/Language. Once an application has been identified, it is then important to select the most appropriate KBS tool or programming language that best matches the selected application's requirements. A mismatch between the type of application and the tool has the potential to be disastrous. Since the KBS tools provide a number of knowledge engineering aids that are normally not available in such high level languages as LISP and PROLOG or in an environment like OPS5, it may be worthwhile to limit the search to well developed tools for the development and implementation of the first prototype. Of course, if there are team members who are well versed in knowledge engineering and in the AI languages/ environments then languages/environments should also be considered. However, it is suggested that a review of what is available in terms of language/environment/tool and their characteristics, restrictions, requirements, etc. should be one of the activities in this step. The team should also develop a list of constraints (such as budget limit, hardware availability, etc.), selection factors (such as: has certain knowledge representation capability, can be interfaced with other programs and/or databases, etc.), and a method of ranking the alternatives. The number of available commercial tools is relatively small and, hence, a very formal method of ranking the tools may not be needed. If hardware decision is also needed, then selection decision about hardware and software should be combined because they are often interlinked.

Step 7. Develop Implementation Plan. A successful transition from the application selection to the KBS development requires a well thought out implementation plan. At the very least, it should identify the resource requirements and a detailed schedule for the development effort. The resource requirements plan should consider: (i) hardware requirements (what is available and what need to be procured, when they should be available, how much it will cost, and who are the vendors), (ii) personnel requirements (who are the available experts, who are the knowledge engineers and other team members, the availability/roles/responsibilities of each person), and (iii) software requirements (what additional software need to be procured, what databases/other programs to be interfaced with, characteristics/structures of these databases/other programs). The tentative schedule should identify the milestone dates and the planned accomplishments on those dates. In addition, it should develop a resource requirements schedule indicating which resources and in what amounts would be required at some specified times during the implementation phase.

Step 8. Implement Prototype Application. This step will require the most time and effort. Also, it requires the interest and commitment of an expert and one or more persons with skills in knowledge acquisition/representation and programming. Since the perceived success of the prototype will influence the approval of subsequent KBS applications, it is important that the implementation phase is given ample support and opportunity to succeed. Hopefully, the prototype will demonstrate the usefulness of KBS to the organization. Also, it should result in several persons in the organization becoming more knowledgeable about the application of the KBS and their implementation. It should be kept in mind during this step that the purpose of the first application is primarily to show proof of concept (as opposed to developing a fully operational system) and it is usually a learning experience.

4. THE CONSENSUS RANKING APPROACH

During the course of KBS application selection for the OA unit, we have developed a general procedure for all similar studies. As part of this procedure for selecting a KBS application, a ranking of all the potential applications is required. In this section we will describe a ranking method, to be called the Consensus Ranking Approach (CRA), that is a part of the developed applications selection process. The complete applications selection process has been described in section 3.

CRA consists of two major phases: a filtering phase and a ranking phase. *The filtering phase* has been devised to eliminate from further consideration any project that does not meet some minimal standards/conditions. For this, a set of filtering criteria has to be developed by the project team. The filtering criteria should be such that the projects satisfying them would be feasible within the imposed resource and other constraints. Care has to be taken so that the criteria are not too restrictive to filter out most of the potential application projects and, at the same time, they should not be so lax as to find almost all the potential projects to be satisfactory. For example, one of the filtering criteria could be: is there availability and commitment of expert/knowledge source? Obviously, this is an important consideration. If the team can not identify or get commitment from domain expert/knowledge source for a particular application project, then all the efforts in developing the KBS for that application would be futile. There will also be some factors which may have to be considered at a relatively broad level in the filtering phase but considered again at the ranking phase. For example, the dollar budget for KBS implementation could be one such factor. A particular team might wish to filter out all potential applications with budgets, say, above $1 million. All surviving applications with budgets below this amount would again be evaluated in the ranking phase based on, along with other factors, the budget because the general preference could be to select a project with a low budget.

The potential applications surviving the filtering phase are reevaluated in the ranking phase. *The ranking phase* consists of the following activities:

1. Develop a set of *ranking factors.* These factors should be based on the important attributes that the team members would like to evaluate the projects with. The factors could be quantitative and/or qualitative. While the factors should include all the important attributes, if the number of factors is too large the ranking process may become unwieldy. As a rule of thumb, try to limit the maximum number of factors to less than 10 or 12.

2. Develop a set of *factor weights* that indicate the relative importance of the individual factors compared to the other factors in the set. It is not necessary that the weights should add up to 1 or 10 or 100, etc. There are various methods for developing weights under the condition of group decision making with multiple attributes [13]. Any rational method, acceptable to all the team members, would suffice. One such method is: (i) each team member ranks all the factors (the most important factor is given the highest numerical ranking), (ii) sum the ranks given to each factor, and (iii) develop a set of weights that reflect the distribution of the rank sums. Another method is: (i) each team member divides a total of 100 points among each factor, (ii) find the average point received by each factor, and (iii) develop a set of weights reflecting the distribution of the average points. Let, W_k be the weight of the kth factor, developed by using any chosen method.

3. Determine *weighted rating* of the potential applications. Each team member evaluates the projects surviving the filtering phase on a scale of 1 to 5 (5 = very high and 1 = very low) for each ranking factor. Let, R_{ijk} be the rating given by the ith rater to the jth project for the kth ranking factor. Next compute R_j, the weighted rating for the jth project as follows:

$$R_j = W_k * R_{ijk}$$

4. *Rank order* the projects according to the weighted ratings, R_j's. Review and reassess the rank order, if necessary. Reassessing may be necessary if there is no truly dominating alternative and, instead, there is a small group of projects that are close to the top ranked project in terms of their R_j's. In such a case, it might be worthwhile to gather additional information and review the project rankings.

Note that the above developed approach implements a variation of the much used linear additive weighing model for multi-attribute decision making [14]. In the linear additive models, it is assumed that the combined value (or utility) of the multiple attributes can be separated into independent utilities for each individual attribute. If that is not the case or when the measurement units of the attributes are not comparable, then a nonlinear form should be considered. However, our use of a linear model is justified on two grounds. One, by using the same intra-attribute measuring scale for all attributes, we have eliminated the problem introduced by noncomparable measurement scales. Two, in most cases

Table 1. Project Ratings By "Rater A"

Criterion (Weight)	X_1	X_3	X_4	X_6	X_7	X_8	X_{10}
Problem Size (2)	3*	3	5	5	5	5	2
Nature of Knowledge (2)	4	4	5	5	5	5	5
Knowledge Accessibility (5)	3	3	5	5	4	4	3
Test Case Availability (3)	1	4	4	4	4	5	4
Importance/Relevance (5)	5	1	5	5	3	3	4
Others (1)	3	3	4	4	3	4	5
Weighted Rate ($\doteq W_k * R_{Ajk}$)	60	49	86	86	70	74	66

Rating scale: 1 (= very low) to 5 (= very high) in t erms of each criterion.

(when the dependency is not extreme) the linear model yields extremely close approximations to very much more complicated nonlinear forms while remaining far easier to use and understand [14].

5. EXPERIENCE IN USING THE METHODOLOGY

Table 2. Summary of Weighted Rates By All Raters

Rater	X_1	X_3	X_4	X_6	X_7	X_8	X_{10}
A	60*	49	86	86	70	74	66
B	62	46	79	80	65	74	44
C	54	43	61	77	60	82	58
D	60	49	66	63	51	62	52
E	27	70	62	90	70	70	56
F	48	37	56	68	64	70	51
G	47	47	54	71	66	83	47
Total Weighted Rate ($= Rj$)	358	341	464	535	446	515	374

Possible range of values is 18 to 90.

The methodology explained in section 3 has been developed as part of our KBS project with BMAC. The following step by step discussion of the methodology is limited to the experience from that project.

Step 1: The activities in this phase were aimed at bringing all the team members' understanding of KBS technology and operating terms to an acceptable minimum level. This was achieved through individual reading of books and articles , attending seminars and workshops(among these were the televised seminars sponsored by IEEE and Texas Instruments), and review of some training video tapes. In addition, group discussions were held to examine KBS terms (such as: knowledge engineering, knowledge-base, backward-chaining, etc.), characteristics of KBS requirements, and the KBS development process itself. We found that these activities were worthwhile because they provided the basis for a common understanding of key KBS concepts/terms for all the team members and helped in the identification step of potential applications.

Step 2: In addition to reviewing reported KBS applications, a significant amount of time was spent in reviewing the current activities and past projects of the OA unit itself. These reviews resulted in several interesting observations.

a) About Projects and Efforts: (i) general areas of effort were in methodology development/maintenance, strategic penetration studies, tactical mission analyses, intelligence analyses, and industrial modeling; (ii) significant amount of effort was used for methodology development and the use of models (optimization and simulation type); and, (iii) many projects required extensive flow time and resources.

b) About Model Usage in OA: (i) a large number of models were available; (ii) many of the models were very complex and may not be completely understood by all users; (iii) most models required a large quantity of input and, hence, it was very easy to use wrong or inconsistent data; (iv) there was a limited number of OA analysts that knew the full capability and application of any particular model; (v) there was a sufficient turnover in the OA group such that knowledge was being lost and required regular training efforts; (vi) updated documentation of models was not always available; (vii) many studies required the use of a series of models; and, (viii) analysts sometimes had difficulty in selecting the appropriate model(s), scenario(s), and interpreting the results.

These reviews and a series of brainstorming sessions lead to the identification of a total of 12 potential applications in six areas: (to maintain confidentiality, we will identify these applications by X_1 through X_{12} in the rest of the discussion)

Tactical/Battle Management - X_1, X_2, X_3
Modeling/Methodology - X_4, X_5, X_6
Planning - X_7, X_8, X_9
Data/Database - X_{10}
Training - X_{11}
Aircraft Operation - X_{12}

Step 3: A significant amount of effort was spent in this step to ensure that the identified projects were judged in a consistent and valid manner. After literature search and discussion, we developed CRA and the two-phase evaluation process. We also decided, for validating the CRA rankings, to use TOPSIS - a well documented multiattribute decision method [13].

Step 4: Much discussion went into the development of the filtering as well as ranking factors. The filtering factors used were: availability and commitment of expert/knowledge source, primarily cognitive nature of the problem, availability of required resources to ensure the completion within planned timeframe and budget, and other constraints (such as data needed is unclassified, project domain consistent with funding source, etc.). The following 7 candidate projects survived filtering: X_1, X_3, X_4, X_6, X_7, X_8, X_{10}. The surviving candidate projects were then rated with respect to the following factors (the developed factor weights are shown in parentheses): accessibility of knowledge (5), importance/relevance of the application (5), availability of test cases for system verification (3), overall problem size (2), nature of knowledge - symbolic vs data processing (2), and incremental nature of the problem (1). Notice that two factors, problem size and nature of knowledge, were also considered in the filtering process. In the application of these two factors during the ranking phase the emphasis was on the degree of differentiation between the projects, while in filtering the emphasis was on the primary nature. The projects were first rated independently by each of the seven raters. Table 1 shows the ratings of "Rater A" as an example of the individual ratings by the team members. These individual weighted ratings were then combined to derive the following initial rank order (see Table 2): X_6, X_8, X_4, X_7, X_{10}, X_1, X_3.

The top 4 projects appeared to form a fairly tight grouping and, hence, the raters decided to discuss these projects more and rerank them again, if necessary. Additional information concerning the projects were collected to discuss their applicability, relative levels of available expertise, and the degree of inherent modularity (or ease of starting small and growing in complexity). Based on these discussions, they were reranked by consensus agreement. The resulting final rank order by CRA was: X_8, X_4, X_6, X_7, X_{10}, X_1, X_3. Due primarily to a lower score (not weight) given to X_6 in the area of "importance/relevance" during the re-evaluation, X_6 was demoted, making X_8 the preferred first choice. Two other factors that indirectly affected the reranking were the presence of forceful advocates and articulate domain knowledge sources. Factors such as modularity were developed in earlier steps but were not considered at that time because they were not deemed to be very important at that stage. Other factors emerged only after the initial ranking. All the raters agreed after reranking that X_8 was significantly more attractive than the second or other lower ranked projects.

Step 5: A presentation of the team work was made to the senior management. While a summary of all 7 potential applications were presented, the top 4 ranked applications were emphasized and presented in more detail. The team's recommendation that X_8 be selected as the first project to implement received unanimous support from the senior management.

Step 6: Considering the available resources and other factors, the following constraints were developed for KBS tool selection:

a) The tool must run on Apollo computing workstations or on Symbolics machine if their Apollo version would become available by end of the project timeframe and the supplier would replace the Symbolics version of the software with the Apollo version at no additional cost.

b) Procurement and training cost must be within acceptable limit. This was not a hard constraint as we were never given an upper limit on the cost; but, we were told to keep it low. As it turned out, the cost of a software depended on such factors as: whether it was the first copy in the organization (in which case cost was usually very high; the cost dropped based on some sliding scale and the number of copies), amount of maintenance support provided, amount of training and/or consulting provided, and any additional software (such as LISP or C) needed to be procured.

c) Appropriate training must be available.

d) Must be able to embed in (or could be interfaced with) other software. This was an important requirement because the OA unit already had a number of other software and databases that it wanted to use in conjunction with any KBS developed.

In addition to these constraints, the following factors were developed for evaluating the candidate KBS tools: (i) language used in the tool (C, LISP, PROLOG, etc.), (ii) Knowledge representation schemes supported by the tool (production rules, frames, etc.), (iii) inferencing and control mechanisms supported by the tool (forward chaining, backward chaining, etc.), (iv) other features supported (for editing, debugging, graphics, etc.), and (v) whether the tool was well accepted in the KBS user/developer community. Another requirement of the project team at this point was that while the tool should be suitable for the selected first project, it must also be applicable to a broader range of projects of the OA unit. This concern arose because the primary purpose of the tool selection was not only to support the selected first application but also for future applications. Therefore, to give excessive weight to the characteristics of the first application in the tool selection may result in a suboptimal solution that is too narrow for future potential applications.

Seven KBS tools (ART, KEE, KES, Knowledge Craft, Rulemaster, S.1, and TIMM) were identified initially as possible candidates for selection. These tools were considered to be broad enough for a wide range of possible applications and still be suitable for the selected project. Considering the set of constraints and evaluating factors, KEE and S.1 were retained for final consideration. Both were almost equal in terms of capabilities, cost, and supplier support. The major differences were in: (i) the implementation language (KEE in Common LISP and S.1 in C), (ii) availability of the Apollo version (S.1 was immediately available while KEE would be in future but within the project timeframe), and (iii) availability of additional training/ consulting support from Boeing Computer Services, another unit within the Boeing organization (available for KEE only). After these considerations, the team recommended, and the management accepted, to select KEE as the development tool to be procured for the selected KBS application.

Step 7: An implementation plan detailing the training and the development activities, a schedule, costing, and software/ personnel requirements was prepared.

Step 8: The implementation took longer and was more difficult than expected. But, more was learned on the first application than was expected. Knowing that the prototype would later be expanded, additional effort was expended to establishing a structure that could accommodate future expansions. Also, there were features of the KBS shell that appeared useful for future applications. Therefore, tests were made of these features. The implementation has been completed and considered a success by senior management. Additional KBS applications are currently being considered for future prototyping.

6. CONCLUDING REMARKS

Our BMAC project dealing with KBS application selection and implementation was devided into four phases. Phase I consisted of the first 5 steps of the proposed methodology; 4 to 6 persons spent a total of approximately 2.5 man-months over a 3 calendar month period in this phase. Phase II consisted of steps 6 and 7 of the proposed method and 3 to 4 persons spent nearly 1.5 man-month over a period of 3 calendar months. Phase III consisted of the procurement and training activities and required about 1 man-month from 2 to 3 persons over a 3 calendar month period. The project has just completed Phase IV which consisted of development, testing, and validating a prototype of the selected application. This phase required about 9 man-months from 2 to 3 persons over a 12 calendar month period. The developed prototype has demonstrated that KBS helps improve the performance quality and productivity in the specific application; it will, however, require additional efforts to expand the knowledge-base to make the prototype into a routine decision support tool.

The proposed methodology for KBS applications development and selection is based on system analysis approach and it evolved from our experience in applying new techniques/methods in different industrial settings. We also benefited from reading KBS development efforts described in [15, 7 ,8, 9, 10, 11]. The proposed approach requires the involvement of all the team members in each step of the process and it is specially helpful in developing a KBS team in the organization to carry forward the activities after the first prototype has been successfully developed.

ACKNOWLEDGEMENT

The study reported here was supported in part by grants from Kansas Advanced Technology Commission and Boeing Military Airplane Company. Thanks are due to the other contributing members of the study team: S.Woodson, C.Mansfield, D.Hansza, and D.Burtner. We are also thankful to the anonymous reviewer who made invaluable suggestions for improving the paper. Any remaining errors and ommissions are, of course, the authors' fault.

REFERENCES

[1] Ahmed, N.U. and J.N.D. Gupta, "An Efficient Heuristic Algorithm for Selecting Projects," *Computer and Industrial Engineering,* 12(1987).

[2] Block, R., *The Politics of Projects.* New York:Yourdin Press, 1983.

[3] Gear, A.E., A.G. Lockett, and A.W. Pearson, "Analysis of Some Portfolio Selection Models for R&D," *IEEE Transactions on Engineering Management,* EM-18, November(1971).

[4] Roman, D.D., *Managing Projects: A Systems Approach.* New York:Elsevier Publishing Co., 1986.

[5] Souder, W.E., "Project Evaluation and Selection." In *Project Management Handbook,* edited by D.I.Cleland and W.R.King. New York:Van Nostrand Reinhold Company, 1983.

[6] Souder, W.E., *Project Selection and Economic Appraisal.* New York:Van Nostrand Reinhold Company, 1984.

[7] Gevarter, W.B., *Artificial Intelligence, Expert Systems, Computer Vision and Natural Language Processing.* Park Ridge, N.J.:Noyes Publications, 1984.

[8] Harmon, P. and D. King, *Expert Systems.* New York:John Wiley & Sons, 1985.

[9] Hayes-Roth, F., D.A. Waterman, and D.B. Lenat, *Building Expert Systems.* Reading, Mass.:Addison-Wesley Publishing Company, 1983.

[10] Hayes-Roth, F., "The Knowledge-Based Expert System: A Tutorial," *IEEE Computer,* September, 1984.

[11] Stefik, M., J. Aikens, R. Balzer, J. Benoit, L. Birnbaum, F. Hayes-Roth, and E. Sacerdoti, "The Organization of Expert Systems: A Tutorial," *Artificial Intelligence,* 18(1982).

[12] Hommertzheim, D., A. Masud, S. Woodson, C. Mansfield, D. Hansza, and D. Burtner, "Selection and Implementation of Knowledge-Based Technology for an Operations Analysis Evaluation Model Project - Phase I Report," College of Engineering, The Wichita State University, Wichita, Kansas, March, 1986.

[13] Hwang, C.L. and M.J. Lin, *Group Decision Making Under Multiple Criteria - Methods and Applications.* New York:Springer-Verlag, 1987.

[14] Hwang, C.L. and K. Yoon, *Multiple Attribute Decision Making - Methods and Applications.* New York:Springer-Verlag, 1981.

[15] Buchanon, B. and E. Shortliffe, *Rule Based Expert Systems: the MYCIN Experiments.* Reading, Mass.:Addison-Wesley Publishing Company, 1984.

SUMMARY

This paper presents a 8-step plan for knowledge-based system application selection. The proposed plan is especially helpful in the selection of the first KBS application in an organization and in developing a team to carry forward the KBS development activities after the first prototype has been successfully developed. Each step of the plan is explained through an application case study.

Applied Expert Systems, E. Turban and P.R. Watkins (Editors)
© Elsevier Science Publishers B.V. (North-Holland), 1988

EXPERT SYSTEM PROTOTYPING AS A RESEARCH TOOL

Daniel E. O'Leary

Graduate School of Business
University of Southern California
Los Angeles, California 90089-1421

Expert system prototyping is analyzed as a research tool. Because expert system prototypes allow for the storage and manipulation of symbolic information they can be used for research projects for which other tools are inappropriate. The experimental bases of expert system prototypes and experimental controls for expert system prototypes are analyzed. The use of expert system protoytpes as research databases also is discussed. Then the kinds of research issues that expert system prototypes can be used to examine and research issues in the use of prototypes as a research tool are analyzed.

1. INTRODUCTION

There is a well-established tradition of prototyping in engineering as a means of testing a product in order to determine if a product can be built and to ascertain if there are any operating anomalies in the design. Prototyping the system provides a "proof of concept."

However, prototyping is no longer the exclusive property of engineering. In recent years, prototyping has become accepted as a means of designing information systems (Earl [1]), decision support systems (Henderson and Ingraham [2]) and expert systems (Hayes-Roth et al. [3]). The extensive bibliography in Jenkins and Fellers [4] provides evidence of the growing use of prototyping as an application system design and development methodology.

Still *expert system* prototyping is relatively new. Its recent development is due, in part, to a number of changes in software and hardware. The development of artificial intelligence languages and expert systems shells and recent developments in hardware, e.g., personal computers and artificial intelligence work stations, have brought artificial intelligence-based computer power directly to the user. Its development also is due, in part, to the successful development of working expert systems (e.g., MYCIN).

However, the newness of expert system prototyping and the operational successes of building prototype expert systems may have camouflaged the value of prototype expert systems as a research tool. Accordingly, this paper is concerned with analyzing expert systems prototyping as a *research tool*, rather than as just an operational design and development tool. If expert system prototypes are to be regarded as a research tool, then there needs to be an understanding of

- the basic process and output of expert system prototyping (section 2),
- the unique advantages offered by expert system prototyping (section 3),
- the relationship of expert system prototyping to other forms of experimental analysis (section 4),
- some of the experimental controls useful in expert system prototyping (section 5),
- use of expert system prototypes as research databases (section 6),
- the kinds of issues that we can expect expert system prototypes to be useful in investigating (section 7),
- some of the limitations of expert systems prototypes (section 8), and
- some research questions into using expert systems prototypes as a research tool (section 9).

2. EXPERT SYSTEMS PROTOTYPES

An expert systems prototype is a small version of the expert system that is to be developed. Generally, such systems have few frills. The prototype provides a preliminary solution approach to the decision under consideration, without a substantial resource commitment.

In applications, the prototype is part of the process in the development of a larger expert system for a particular application. Expert systems prototypes provide an opportunity to test assumptions about the knowledge base, inference strategies of the expert and other characteristics of the system. In many cases the expert system prototype is thrown away, after these issues become better understood. Then, a new system is built using the knowledge garnered from the prototype development process.

Expert systems prototyping consists of designing and developing that computer program without an extensive preliminary examination of the problem area. This means iteratively discovering the expert's knowledge and developing the system's knowledge, i.e., knowledge acquisition. Prototyping is not mechanical, but generally is exploratory. Because of the iterative approach of knowledge acquisition, generally knowledge is discovered in layers.

Expert systems prototypes generally are designed for decision making situations requiring a certain amount of "intelligence." Typically, prototyping is done using an expert system shell to ease the development process, e.g., EXSYS, or an artificial intelligence language, e.g., LISP. Such artificial intelligence languages and expert system shells are designed to manipulate symbolic, rather than numeric variables.

3. PROTOTYPING AS A UNIQUE RESEARCH TOOL

Typically, statistical and mathematical representations are used to analyze research questions. Unfortunately, in some situations, mathematical or statistical representations of problems cannot be easily made. Generally, this is because the variables involved in the models do not take on numeric values or situations are not easily structured in a statistical or mathematical fashion. It may be that prototyping is the only type of tool that can be used to represent a problem because of the capabilities of representing symbolic information in expert systems.

3.1. Understanding and Learning from Expert Systems Prototypes

Piaget [5] noted that "All mathematical ideas begin by a qualitative construction before acquiring a metrical character." He also noted that by moving too rapidly from the qualitative structure to the quantitative or mathematical formulation often affects the ability to understand mathematics.

Since expert system prototypes allow the use of symbolic variables, the user does not have to quantify the knowledge and the decision making processes as part of the modeling process or move from the qualitative to the quantitative until the user is ready (Howe [6]). However, prototyping does allow the user to structure the problem in a manner that ultimately may lead to quantification.

An example of this learning process recently occurred in the development of an expert system prototype for an auditing problem. The firm trying to solve the problem developed and threw away two expert systems prototypes without finding a satisifactory solution. Then, based on the understanding gleaned from those prototypes, the developers realized that the problem could be solved as a linear program.

3.2. Resource Requirements to Employ Expert Systems Prototyping

Expert systems prototypes also provide the opportunity to analyze problems without a substantial resource commitment of the researcher. Watkins and O'Leary [7], in a field study, examined the ability of domain experts to develop expert system prototypes using an expert system shell. They found that domain experts, with little computer experience, were able to rapidly develop expert systems prototypes with little formal training. Thus, this would suggest that researchers, also experts in particular domains, would be able to rapidly develop expert systems prototypes.

3.3. Theory Biases of Expert Systems Prototypes

However, as with most research tools, researcher bias can be embedded into the expert system prototype. The bias can occur in at least three different ways. First, the researcher can bias the system based on the choice of "first principles" or theory on which the system is based. As noted by Davis [8, p. 403] in a discussion of electronic trouble shooting, first principles refer to "... an understanding of the structure and function of the devises they are examining." The use of an alternative theory could have a substantial impact on the knowledge used in the system.

Second, the knowledge representation scheme may affect the expert system prototype. Wilensky [9] reviews the importance of knowledge representation.

Third, the inference engine impacts the manner in which the knowledge base is analyzed by the system, in response to inquiries made to the system prototype. Many inference engines simply search through the knowledge base in a "top to bottom" or "side to side" manner (e.g., Hayes-Roth et al. [3]). Few would argue that humans process information in that manner.

In any case, the biases of the researcher can be controlled, in part, by implementing the appropriate research methodologies and controls. These are discussed in more detail in sections 4 and 5.

3.4. Theory Laden Tools

Since expert system prototypes can accommodate symbolic variables, they are a very flexible tool. As a result, prototyping can offer an alternative tool to investigate a number of research situations.

Often, it can be used as an alternative tool to investigate questions where the original tool(s) used in the research is "theory laden." For example, linear regression is used in conjunction with the Brunswik Lens model (Dudycha and Naylor [10]). Measurements of human performance are variables in a linear regression model. In this case linear regression is a theory laden tool in the study of human information processing. Expert systems prototyping offers an alternative tool that is not wed to that approach to understanding human information decision making.

4. EXPERIMENTAL BASIS FOR KNOWLEDGE ACQUISITION FOR EXPERT SYSTEM PROTOTYPES

The development of the expert system prototype requires the acquisition of the knowledge base for the system. The approach used to gather knowledge will impact the knowledge base of the expert system prototype that is developed (e.g., Burton et al. [11]). As a result, if expert system prototypes are to be used as a research tool then it is critical to ensure that the knowledge is gathered using a systematic and accepted research methodology.

Further, identifying expert systems prototyping as making use of particular experimental techniques is important. This allows the use of controls and established literature associated with each of these methodologies in knowledge acquisition for expert system prototypes.

The primary knowledge acquisition methods potentially include using any of a number of experimental techniques including (e.g., Simon [12]): Deductive Reasoning, Case Study, Participant Observer, Content Analysis, Simulation. Other experimentally accepted techniques, such as time series analysis or surveys are rarely used in expert systems analysis because these approaches do not generate enough detail or qualitative information for knowledge acquisition.

4.1. Deductive Reasoning

As noted by Simon [12, pp. 203-204], "The principle of deductive reasoning for obtaining knowledge is that, if A is true and if B is true then, under specified conditions one can safely say that C is true". Thus, deductive reasoning takes the form of "If ... Then ..." rules, which probably is the best understood form of knowledge representation. This suggests that expert systems prototypes are an ideal vehicle for encoding and analysis of deductive reasoning. Unfortunately, decision makers rarely think and reason using "If ... Then ..." rules (Biggs et al. [13]).

4.2. Case Study

At another level, knowledge acquisition for expert system prototypes is analogous to a case study. Oftentimes in the development of an expert system prototype a particular decision making situation is used to elicit the knowledge require to solve a problem. Clearly, "case study" could be replaced with "expert system prototype" in the following definition of a case study.

> The case study is ... the method of choice when you want to obtain a wealth of detail about your subject. You are likely to want such detail when you do not know exactly what you are looking for. The case study is therefore appropriate when you are trying to find clues and ideas for further research; in this respect, it serves a purpose similar to the clue-providing function of expert opinion. (Simon [12, p. 206])

Case study methodology can lack rigor without appropriate attention to its implementation. Case study methodology has been discussed by Yin [14] and others.

4.3 Participant Observer

In the development of some expert systems, developers have found the need to become "near experts" before they could develop an appropriate system (Lethan and Jacobsen [15]). Alternatively, experts may be trained to develop an expert system prototype (e.g., Watkins and O'Leary [7]). This is suggestive of the participant observer methodology. As noted by Simon [12, p. 207], "If you wish to understand the full complexity of a case situation in social science, you may have no alternative but to get yourself involved ...." Thus, the participant observer approach may be necessary both in order to understand the problem and to solicit the knowledge.

4.4. Content Analysis

Content analysis is aimed at objectively and systematically analyzing symbolic information ([Holsti [16]). As noted by Simon [12, p.212],

"The content analyst sets up various classification schemes, which he then applies to speeches or writings. These classifications either count particular kinds of words or ideas, or they measure the amount of words or time that is devoted to particular ideas."

A straight content analysis approach may not be appropriate. Since content analysis is limited to counting occurences, it may be limited in its ability to elicit key heuristic decision rules. As a result, other forms of content analysis have been developed.

One of the primary content analysis tools used in developing expert system prototypes is protocol analysis (e.g., Newell and Simon [17]). Protocols may derive from either audio or video tape. Protocol analysis has been used in the development of a number of expert system prototypes (e.g., Meservy [18]).

An alternative method of content analysis is the linguistic approach of Frederiksen [19]. That approach employs a grammatical structure that represents the logical and semantic structure of knowledge acquired from discourse.

4.5. Simulation

Simulation is a term that includes any laboratory experiment or game study (Simon [12, p. 215]). Games or experiments are used to simulate the way that the participants would behave in various aspects of real life competition (e.g., Rowe et al. [20]). The researcher can vary the simulation to ascertain what actions are taken under what circumstances. This knowledge can then be embedded in the context of the knowledge base of an expert system prototype. This technique has been used in a few situations to elicit knowledge for an expert system prototype (e.g., Bouwman [21]).

5. EXPERIMENTAL CONTROLS IN KNOWLEDGE ACQUISITION

If an expert system prototype is used as a research tool then in order to ensure that the system is developed in a rigorous manner, the developer must implement the system in an environment with the appropriate experimental controls. There are a number of controls that are associated with each of the above forms of knowledge acquisition. In addition, there are some other experimental controls that derive from the uniqueness of the need to gather knowledge, as opposed to numeric data.

First, whether unobtrusive or obtrusive means of knowledge acquisition is preferred likely is a function of the research project or the group of experts. Oftentimes, information should be gathered using unobtrusive means. The development of one expert system prototype used phone taps to gather the knowledge without altering the expert and question askers' behavior. Alternatively, sometimes obtrusive means may provide the best method of obtaining the necessary knowledge (e.g., Sphilberg et al. [22]).

Second, Kolodner and Reisbeck [23] note that memory organization is constantly changing to reflect new events. As a result, the expert may alter his approach to problem solving based on the analysis of problem by the researcher. To test this the researcher can perform both pretests and posttests. For example, the researcher can use a problem solved before developing the knowledge base and an analoguous problem solved after developing the the knowledge base. Then the researcher can compare the solution methodologies and knowledge to ascertain if the expert altered the initial approach. If the two approaches are not the same then the knowledge gathered prior to this latest knowledge acquisition may not reflect the expert's current approach to problem solving.

Third, the physical location of the expert during the knowledge acquisition may impact the system. If the system was not developed on site (e.g., at the laboratory) then some contingent knowledge that the expert associated with the site may not be placed in the knowledge base. Alternatively, if the knowledge is gathered on site then there is little control over the environment (e.g., interruptions and the amount of time that the expert can spend).

6. EXPERT SYSTEM PROTOTYPES AS RESEARCH DATABASES

Expert system prototypes can be used as databases for researchers in at least two different manners. Each system can be treated as an independent database or they can be aggregated with other prototypes. Then these databases can be used to test theories or generate theories.

6.1. Experimental Use of Single Expert System Prototype Knowledge Bases

Cook and Campbell [24] use the term "passive" observation to refer to studies where experiments are performed with existing data. Prototype expert systems knowledge bases form "databases" that can be analyzed. Researchers can investigate the knowledge base of an expert system prototype in the same sense that a user would consult the system for a solution. In this case, each use of the expert system prototype is used as a single data point. As noted in Winston [25, p. 2]:

> Computer programs exhibit unlimited patience, they require no feeding and they do not bite. Moreover, it is usually simple to deprive a computer program of some piece of knowledge in order to test how important that piece really is. It is impossible to work with animal brains with the same precision.

6.2. Experimental Use of Developed Prototypes

In a similar manner, if the researcher has access to information about a number of expert system prototypes then additional inferences can be made, based on commonalities between the systems. For example, this approach has been used by O'Leary [26] in the analysis of validation of expert systems. In this situation, each prototype becomes a single data point.

6.3 Theory Testing vs. Theory Generation

The use of expert system prototypes as a database can be used either for Theory Testing or Theory Generation. As noted in Winston [25, p. 2]:

> Computer models force precision. Implementing a theory uncovers conceptual mistakes and oversights that ordinarily escape even the most miticulous researchers. Major roadblocks often appear that were not recognized as problems even before beginning the cycle of thinking and experimenting.

Expert system prototypes can be used to *test theories* about the knowledge base. For example, given an expert system prototype, the user can test theories by inquiry into the knowledge base or experiments with the knowledge base. For example, Meservy [18] developed an expert system prototype, in part, to test some hypotheses of auditor behavior.

Alternatively, expert system prototypes can be used to *generate theories*. Some of the first expert system prototypes were developed to solve problems for which there was no established theory. In effect, the development of the knowledge base was an assemblage of knowledge not related by any theory (e.g.,

Davis [8]). Thus, interaction by the researcher with the knowledge base allows the possibility of the development of theory.

However, as noted by McDermott [27], it is more difficult to develop an expert system if there is no existing theory to guide the development efforts. Accordingly, it is likely to be more difficult to develop a system for theory generation.

7. WHAT KINDS OF RESEARCH ISSUES CAN AN EXPERT SYSTEM PROTOTYPE BE USED TO INVESTIGATE?

Expert system prototypes can be used as a tool or vehicle to understanding particular problems, understanding the process of solving a problem, developing a proof of concept that a particular idea can be implemented as a computer program or analyzing the use of expert systems prototyping as a research tool.

7.1. Understanding Particular Problems Using Prototype Expert Systems

Expert system prototypes may provide better methods of decision making than other tools. For example, if a prototype expert system could be developed to improve bankruptcy prediction, then that model would likely be of interest to those doing research in bankruptcy prediction.

In addition, expert system prototypes summarize some of the knowledge in a given area. This can lead to a structuring of previously unstructured knowledge. Thus, the development of a prototype may move unstructured or poorly structured problems into a more structured framework. In those situations where there is no central storage location of the knowledge or where there is no structure to the knowledge, simply the development of the prototype may provide a research opportunity.

Expert system prototypes also can be used to assess the "fineness" of the knowledge about the problem. Fineness is a characteristic of information structure. Marschak and Radner [28] say that

> ... given two information structures, n_1 and n_2, that n_1 is as fine as n_2 if n_1 is a subpartition of n_2; That is, if every subset in n_1 is in contained in some set in n_2. (Thus, n_1 tells us all that n_2 can tell, and possibly more besides.) If n_1 and n_2 are distinct, and n_1 is as fine as n_2, then we shall say that n_1 is finer than n_2.

Few other tools that the researcher can use would even contain or have the ability to capture differences in the fineness in the knowledge base. However, because the knowledge base captures symbolic information, it is likely to capture the fineness of the information. Accordingly, the knowledge base of an expert system prototype can be used to analyze the comparative fineness of information in the knowledge base.

Fineness may reflect the understanding of the information in the knowledge base. If the knowledge is not equally fine throughout the knowledge base, then this may lead to efforts to better "understand" the part that is not as fine. Alternatively, the existence of different levels of fineness in the knowledge base may reflect the state of nature of the knowledge. Some knowledge may come in "bigger chunks" (e.g., Newell and Simon [17]).

7.2 Understanding Human Intelligence and Expertise

Alternatively, developing a prototype can result in a better understanding of how humans make decisions in general or in particular types of situations. Further it may provide insight into the notion of expertise.

As noted by Winston [25, p. 1], "Making computers intelligent helps us understand intelligence." In particular, as noted by Winston [25, p. 2],

> Computer metaphors aid thinking. Work with computers has led to rich new language for talking about how to do things and how to describe things. Metaphorical and analogical use of concepts involved enables more powerful thinking about thinking.

Intelligence includes such issues as memory structures, causal relationships and problem formulation. Expert systems prototypes allow researching such issues (e.g., Biggs and Selfridge [29]).

In addition, part of the research on expertise lies in understanding the amount or kind of knowledge or processing of knowledge necessary to develop good decisions. As noted by Winston [25, p. 4]

> Computer implementations quantify task requirements. Once a program performs a task, upper bound statements can be made about how much information processing the task requires.

Since expert system prototypes summarize knowledge gathered from an expert and they are computer programs, they allow research into such evaluations of task quantification.

7.3 Proof of Concept

Alternatively, an expert system can be used to provide a proof of concept. That is, although it may be asserted that a particular technique can be used in an expert system, until it actually is programmed there is uncertainty as to feasibility.

Theoretical developments in artificial intelligence concepts require proof of concept in order to ensure that they can be adapted to particular domains.

This may include research in the areas of uncertainty representation and in automated knowledge acquisition by, e.g., reading text. For example, the expert system GC/X (Biggs and Selfridge [29]), tests the use of some concepts required to read and organize new knowledge in accounting systems.

7.4 Analyzing the Use of Expert System Prototypes as a Research Tool

Expert systems prototypes also can be used to examine various facets of using prototypes as a research tool. Although this section reviews two particular applications, other research questions are summarized in section 9.

In the case of information fineness, if the information is not equally fine throughout the model then this may affect the parameterization of the model, which also is likely to be a research issue. For example, in a rule-based system which employs weights on the rules to represent uncertainty or strength of belief, should two rules that reflect information that are not equally fine but have the same likelihood of occurring, have the same weight?

Alternatively, Langley, et al., [30, p. 44] argue that "In recent years there have been several challeges to the idea that the process of theory generation is mysterious and inexplicable." They argue that there are "rules" of discovery. This opens the process of discovery to, e.g, other expert systems. Langley et al. [30] present analysis of this issue and discussion of prototypes that can discover theory.

8. LIMITATIONS OF EXPERT SYSTEM PROTOTYPING

Although prototyping can be a useful research tool, there are some limitations of prototypes that should be recognized. This section discusses some of these limitations, in addition to those mentioned earlier.

First, *a working prototype is not prima facie evidence of a successful representation of the expert* (Winston [25]). Although the model "works" it may not be a very good representation of expertise and decision making capabilities that the expert used.

Second, *problems can be overlooked, buried or shirked* (Haugeland [31]). In order to get a working model certain simplifications must be made. If critical problems are avoided then the prototype may be representative of only a small portion of the decision making capabilities of the expert.

Third, *domains may be unrealistically or artificially restricted or unrealistically prestructured* (Haugeland [31]). If the domain or problem is too narrowly stated then the system may not be important or may not solve the problem of interest.

Fourth, *prototype solutions may be suboptimal* (Henderson and Ingraham [2]). The prototype may provide an inappropriate, incomplete or less than an optimal solution to the problem it was designed to solve. If the system is suboptimal then studying the system may not yield what the researcher is interested in.

Fifth, when developing a prototype *it may be very difficult to know when to stop building the prototype.* There are few or no stopping rules for the overall quality of the prototype.

Sixth, *there are few ways to determine if a model is parameterized correctly.* In least squares analysis, the parameterization that minimizes the sum of the squares of the errors is used as the basis to choose the coefficients on the variables. There is no such analogous method for use in expert systems prototypes.

Seventh, *expert system prototypes may include a researcher bias.* As noted earlier, the choice of first principles, or the choice of using an alternative approach when first principles exist, may reflect the researchers' bias. By employing research methods, and the appropriate controls, these biases can be mitigated to a certain extent.

9. SOME RESEARCH QUESTIONS INTO USING EXPERT SYSTEM PROTOTYPES AS A RESEARCH TOOL

This paper is only a first layer in the analysis of the use of expert system prototypes as research tools. Based on the analysis in this paper, a number of research issues about the use of expert system prototypes as research tools have been addressed. This section summarizes some of the questions elicited above.

First, what are the experimental controls that can be implemented in prototypes? Should we do a pre and a post test on the expert to see if the model development process has changed the expert's knowledge?

Second, what types of experimental controls are unique to expert systems prototyping?

Third, how do we measure the fineness of information in a knowledge base? What is the impact of different levels of fineness on the parameterization of an expert system's weights?

Fourth, what relationship is there between the use of knowledge in an expert system prototype and that of a human?

Fifth, in some research tools there are established measures of "goodness." What are some measures of goodness that can be used to evaluate the parameters in expert systems?

Sixth, what mechanisms are available to ascertain when an expert system prototype is "good enough" to stop building the model and use it to investigate the research question?

Seventh, to what extent is expert systems prototyping a cost beneficial research tool to employ? That is, how easy is it for researchers to learn expert systems prototyping as a research tool.

Eighth, which forms of knowledge acquisition are "preferred."

At this point, there has been little presented in the way of solving these issues, and many open questions remain. However, the purpose of this paper has been to elicit and summarize these issues.

10. SUMMARY

This paper has argued in favor of expert systems prototyping as a research tool. Prototyping can be used in those situations where the research question requires the investigation of nonnumeric, symbolic information. Expert systems prototyping can be an intermediate step in developing a more structured representation of the problem. Further, expert systems can be used in those situations where an alternative research tool is desired to those that may be theory laden.

The development of the knowledge for an expert system can be done in a number of established manners (e.g., case study) each of which has its own set of controls. In addition, there are other controls that may be somewhat unique to expert systems prototyping.

Once an expert system prototype has been established it can be used as a database for either Theory Generation or Theory Testing. Further, expert system prototypes can be used to develop alternative solution methodologies, study human intelligence and expertise and develop proof of concept.

Finally, the paper summarizes some of the limitations of expert system prototypes and develops some of the research questions associated with the use of expert system prototypes as research tools.

ACKNOWLEDGEMENT

The author would like to thank Alan Rowe and Efraim Turban for their comments on an earlier version of this paper. Of course, any limitations remain due to the author.

REFERENCES

[1] Earl, M., "Prototyping Systems for Accounting and Control," *Accounting, Organizations and Society,* Vol. 3, No. 2, pp. 161-170.

[2] Henderson, J. and R. Ingraham, "Prototyping for DSS: A Critical Appraisal," in Ginzberg, et al. [31], pp. 79-96 (1982).

[3] Hayes-Roth, F., D. Waterman, and D. Lenat, *Building Expert Systems*. Reading, Mass.:Addison-Wesley, 1983).

[4] Jenkins, A. and J. Fellers, "An Annotated Bibliography on Prototyping," Graduate School of Business, Indiana University, Institute for Research on the Management of Informations, Working Paper W613, (1986).

[5] Piaget, J., *To Understand is to Invent*. New York:Grossman, 1973.

[6] Howe, J., "Learning Through Model Building," in D. Michie, *Expert Systems in the Micro-electronic Age*. Edinburgh University Press, 1979.

[7] Watkins, P. and D. O'Leary, "Knowledge Acquisition for Small Scale Expert Systems from Consulting Experts: A Field Study Approach," in *Proceedings of the First European Workshop on Knowledge Acquisition*, September, 1987.

[8] Davis, R., "Reasoning From First Principles," *International Journal of Man-Machine Studies,* Vol 19, (1983), pp. 9-16.

[9] Wilensky, R., "Knowledge Representation -- A Critique and a Proposal," in Kolodner and Reisbeck [22] (1986).

[10] Dudycha, L. and J. Naylor, "Characteristics of the Human Inference Process in Complex Choice Behavior," *Organizational Behavior and Human Performance,* Vol. 1 (1966) pp. 110-128.

[11] Burton, A., N. Shadbolt, A. Hedgecock, and G. Rugg, "A Formal Evaluation of Knowledge Elicitation Techniques for Expert Systems," in *Proceedings of the First European Workshop on Knowledge Acquisition*, September, 1987.

[12] Simon, J. L., *Basic Research Methods in Social Science*. New York: Random House, 1978).

[13] Biggs, S., W. Messier, and J. Hansen, "A Descriptive Analysis of Computer Audit Specialists' Decision Making Behavior in Advanced Computer Environments,"*Auditing,* (Spring, 1987) Vol. 6, No. 2, pp. 1-21.

[14] Yin, R. K., "The Case Study Crisis: Some Answers,"*Administrative Science Quarterly* (March 1981) Vol 26, pp. 58-65.

[15] Lethan, H. and H. Jacobsen, "ESKORT -- An Expert System for Auditing VAT Accounts," *Proceedings of Expert Systems and Their Applications,* Avignon, France 1987.

[16] Holsti, O., *Content Analysis for the Social Sciences and Humanities*. Reading, Mass.:Addison-Wesley, 1969.

[17] Newell, A. and H. Simon, *Human Problem Solving*. Englewood Cliffs, N. J.:Prentice-Hall, 1972.

[18] Meservy, R., "Auditing Internal Controls: A Computational Model of the Review Process," Unpublished Ph. D. Dissertation, The University of Minnesota, 1985.

[19] Frederiksen, C. H., "Cognitive Models and Discourse Analysis," in Cooper, C. R. and Greenbaum, S. (Eds.), *Studying Writing Linguistic Approaches* Beverly Hills, Ca.:Sage Publications, 1986, pp. 227-267.

[20] Rowe, A., R. Mason, and K. Dickel. *Strategic Management and Business Policy*. Reading, Mass.:Addison-Wesley, 1985.

[21] Bouwman, M., "Human Diagnostic Reasoning by Computer," *Management Science* (June 1983) pp. 653-672.

[22] Shpilberg, D., L. Graham, and H. Schatz. "ExperTAX: An Expert System for Corporate Tax Planning," *Expert Systems*, (July, 1986).

[23] Kolodner, J. and C. Reisbeck, *Experience, Memory and Reasoning*. Hillsdale, N. J.:Lawerence Erlbaum Associates, 1986.

[24] Cook, T. and D. Campbell. *Quasi-Experimentation*. Skokie, Il.:Rand McNally, 1979.

[25] Winston, P., *Artificial Intelligence*. Reading, Mass.:Addison-Wesley, 1984.

[26] O'Leary, D., "Validating Expert Systems," *Decision Sciences* (Summer 1987) pp. 468-486.

[27] McDermott, J., "Comments in, Knowledge-Based Expert Systems," The Second Artificial Intelligence Satellite Symposium, Texas Instruments (1986).

[28] Marschak, and Radnor, *Economic Theory of Teams*. New Haven:Yale University, 1972.

[29] Biggs, S. and M. Selfridge, "GCX: An Expert System for the Auditor's Going-Concern Judgment," Unpublished Presentation, American Accounting Association, New York, (1986).

[30] Langley, P., H. Simon, G. Bradshaw, and J. Zytkow, *Scientific Discovery*. Cambridge, Mass:The MIT Press, 1987.

[31] Haugeland, J., Unpublished Presentation, Forum on Artificial Intelligence in Management, Virginia, (1986).

[32] Ginzberg, M., W. Reitman, and E. Stohr, *Decision Support Systems*. New York:North-Holland, 1982.

Applied Expert Systems, E. Turban and P.R. Watkins (Editors)
© Elsevier Science Publishers B.V. (North-Holland), 1988

MULTIPLE CRITERIA DECISION MAKING AND EXPERT SYSTEMS

Chen-En Ko and Thomas W. Lin

School of Accounting
University of Southern California
Los Angeles, CA 90089-1421

Multiple criteria decision making (MCDM) refers to making decisions in the presence of multiple criteria. Many decisions or judgments involve with MCDM such as medical diagnosis judgment, engineer design choice, business decision alternatives, public policy choices and others. Two general approaches may be used to assist MCDM problems, the model-based approach and the heuristic-based approach. Model-based approach relies on formal and structured models to find the optimal solution while heuristic-based approach uses the decision maker or expert's heuristics to search for satisfactory solution. Model-based approach is implemented in various mathematical models and heuristic-based approach is currently implemented in expert systems. As there are many intertwining relationships between these two approaches, it would be beneficial to cross-examine their implications to each other.

This paper provides a framework to study the related issues and implications for the development and integration of ES and MCDM. It investigates the nature and role of MCDM in the context of ES development as well as the potential use of ES in MCDM model building and selection.

1. INTRODUCTION

Multiple criteria decision making (MCDM) refers to making decisions in the presence of multiple criteria. Many decisions or judgments involve with MCDM such as medical diagnosis judgment, engineer design choice, business decision alternatives, public policy choices and others. Two general approaches may be taken to deal with MCDM problems: the model-based approach or the heuristic-based approach. By using the model-based approach, the decision maker explicitly structures his/her decision problem according to some formal models to evaluate the decision alternatives. There are several formal MCDM models developed to assist the decision maker ([1], [2], [3]). On the other hand, by using the heuristic-based approach, the decision maker applies some heuristics to generate and evaluate decision alternatives. It is recognized that heuristic approach could produce effective and efficient solutions for complex problems, especially with the advancement in the artificial intelligence and expert systems [4].

Expert systems (ES) are developed to provide expert decisions or judgments as advice for decision makers. The ES use domain-specific expert's knowledge and heuristics to search for solutions in specific problem area. Many ES deal with MCDM problems using heuristics rather than structured approach. Nonetheless, the incorporation of certain formal MCDM method in the ES may provide decision maker additional information and insight in forming his/her decisions or judgments. On the other hand, the ES developer also faces many MCDM tasks at various stages of ES development. These MCDM tasks pertain to, although not limited to, the choice of ES developing language or shell, the choice of knowledge representation or inference engine, and the evaluation of recommendation made by the ES.Therefore, an in-depth investigation of the intertwining relationship between ES development and MCDM approach will assist the ES developer to deal with MCDM issues more effectively in the developmental process and the ES design.

This paper aims at shedding lights on the interrelated area of the MCDM and ES. It examines the nature and role of MCDM in the context of ES development and discusses related issues in this area. The organization of this paper is as follows: The next section discusses the nature of MCDM problems and formal models for their solutions. Section III provides a general discussion of ES components, development stages, and applications. Section IV examines the MCDM issues and models in the ES development. Section V discusses the use of ES in the MCDM model building and selection. Last section concludes this paper with a summary and implication for further research and development of ES and MCDM.

2. NATURE OF MULTIPLE-CRITERIA DECISION MAKING

Multiple criteria decision making (MCDM) involves with making decision or judgments in the presence of multiple criteria. Three common characteristics pertain to most MCDM problems: (1) each problem has multiple objectives or attributes measured by different units or criteria, (2) these multiple objectives usually conflict with each other, and (3) there are many alternatives to accomplish these objectives and the decision maker has to evaluate or rank these alternatives according to these often conflicting objectives.

A major issue for MCDM is one of value tradeoffs. When conflicting objectives are faced by the decision maker, he/she will have to make tradeoffs in reaching a decision or a judgment. When the value of the criteria can be quantified, the decision maker can use the model-based approach to explicitly formalize and quantify his/her value structure and then evaluate the competing alternatives. There are several models developed by management scientists and psychologists to deal with value tradeoffs as reviewed in MacCrimmon [1], Hwang and Yoon [2] and Zeleny [5]. These models fall into the following categories: (1) observer-derived weighting or indirect elicitation models, (2) direct elicitation or self-explicated models, (3) mathematical programming models, and (4) geometric models.

Table 1
Major MCDM Models

MODELS	DESCRIPTIONS	LIMITATIONS
1. Observer-Derived WeightingModels 1. Regression Analysis 2. Analysis of Variance	Use of mathematical functions to derive attribute or criteria weights.	Relying on the input/output of the decision making without explicit consideration to decision maker's process.
II. Direct-Elicitation 3. Analytic Hierarchy Process 4. Multi-Attribute Utility Theory	Use of simplified comparisons or lottery questions to elicit decision maker's weights or utilities of decision alternatives based on relevant theories.	The process to elicit weights or utilities can be very time consuming especially when the decisions are complex.
III. Mathematical Programming 5. Goal Programming 6. Linear Programming	Use of modified linear programming techniques to obtain optimal solutions safisfying multiple objectives.	Decision maker may not be able to quantify the goal values and relevant weights, and the solutions may be too complicated to be comprehended.
IV. Geometric Models 7. Multidimensional Scaling 8. Conjoint Measurement	Use of multi-dimensional representation of data and fit model to actual data.	The process to collect and analyze data is very laborious and the decision maker may have difficulty in discriminating different criteria.

Observer-derived weighting models require the decision maker to use mathematical functions such as regression analysis or analysis of variance to derive attribute or criteria weights. Direct elicitation or self-explicated models use direct queries to obtain the decision maker's weights or utilities for the criteria and alternatives. The Analytic Hierarchy Process [6] and Multi-Attribute Utility Theory [7] are two commonly used models in this category. The Analytic Hierarchy Process uses pairwise comparisons to derive the weights for the multiple criteria under consideration. Multi-Attribute Utility Theory elicits the decision maker's preference and utility functions through simulated lottery questions. Mathematical programming models include goal programming and multiple objective linear programming, both of which rely on linear programming techniques to derive optimal decisions. Geometric models usually generate a multidimensional representation of data and apply a specific model to fit a model to the actual data. Two widely used geometric models are multidimensional scaling and conjoint measurement models. In using the multidimensional scaling, the decision maker is asked to respond to a decision problem in terms of similarities and differences among criteria. The ordering of the alternatives based on the responses can then be used to construct the multidimensional representation. Conjoint measurement assumes a simple additive model based on a factorial design to provide the weights reflecting the importance of the attributes of the decision. Table 1 summarizes these MCDM models together with their limitations. As can be seen in Table 1, each model has its own strengths and limitations and no model is universally optimal to different decision problems faced by the decision maker. Instead, a model may be optimal to a set of problems depending on the objectives and characteristics of the decision. Thus, the choice of the appropriate model to solve an MCDM problem becomes essentially an MCDM problem.

3. EXPERT SYSTEM DEVELOPMENT AND APPLICATIONS

Expert Systems (ES) are problem solving computer programs that built on expert's expertise and heuristics to solve problems in specific domains. ES can be built to solve problems in the areas of interpretation, prediction, diagnosis, design, planning, monitoring, debugging repairing, instruction or control [8]. In solving these problems, the human experts and the ES face many MCDM problems which will be discussed later. There are five major components of an ES: (1) the language interface for building and communicating with the ES, (2) the knowledge base consisting of domain-specific facts and problem-solving rules, (3) the inference engine containing general problem-solving knowledge that decide how and when to apply the domain-specific knowledge and make inferences, (4) the database recording the intermediate hypotheses and decisions made by the ES, and (5) the explanation module providing justifications for the decisions obtained by the ES.

In building an ES, the system builder (called knowledge engineer) has to work with the domain-specific expert to extract the expert's knowledge and encode it in a computer program. This process is called knowledge acquisition. The steps involved in building an ES include the following [9]: (1) identifying the problem, its scope, objectives and goals, as well as the available resources; (2) conceptualizing major elements, relations and information characteristics in describing the problem; (3) formalizing the essential concepts and relations in specific knowledge representation according to the system building language or tool; (4) implementing the formalized knowledge and together with other needed facilities in a prototype program; (5) testing, evaluating, and revising the prototype system to conform to the performance of human expert.

Many ES have been developed in different application areas. For example, in medical application, MYCIN [10] is developed to provide assistance for the physician in choosing appropriate antimicrobial therapy for patients with bacteremia, meningitis and cystitis infections. There are others, such as DIAG-NOSER [11] for identifying congenital heart disease, PUFF [12] is to assist the diagnosis of lung disease, NEUROLOGIST-I [13] advises the physician in diagnosis of neurological disorders. In legal application, LRS [14] assists the lawyer in retrieving legal information about negotiable instruments. TAXADVISOR [15] advises the attorney in tax and estate planning for large clients. In engineering application, CRITTER [16] assists engineers in VLSI circuit design. SACON [17] assists the engineer in structural analysis problem. There is also a growing list of application in manufacturing, financial, accounting and other industries.

4. MCDM ISSUES AND MODELS IN ES DEVELOPMENT

Although ES developmental stages can be described as identification, conceptualization, formalization, implementation, testing and evaluations, these steps may not be distinctively separable or proceeded in exact sequence. Rather, they characterize a complex process to build the ES. Several phases of this process involve with MCDM issues for the system builder, i.e., the knowledge engineer. This section discusses the major MCDM issues in the process of developing ES. Table 2 provides a summary for the following discussions.

4.1. Identification of Problem

In building an ES, the knowledge engineer and the domain expert first have to identify the problem, its scope and characteristics. At this identification stage, the knowledge engineer need to ask many questions to derive proper characterization of the problem. Among these questions, several relate to MCDM such as the determination of the objectives of the ES, the sub-problems, the key at-

Table 2
MCDM Issues and Models in ES Development

Stages of ES Development	Relevant Questions on MCDM Issues and Models
Identifying Problems	Are problems related to MCDM? What are the applicable MCDM models?
Conceptualizing Decision Knowledge	What are the objectives, major attributes, decision criteria for the decisions or judgments? What are the requirements to frame the decision problem in a specific MCDM model?
Formalizing Knowledge Representation	What types of knowledge representation and inference engine are appropriate? Which language or shell should be used? What are the criteria for their choice? What particular MCDM model should be used?
Implementing Prototype	Can MCDM models be implemented in the prototype ES? How to implement the MCDM models? How to interface between the MCDM module and other components in the ES?
Testing and Evaluating	What are the criteria to evaluate the recommendations made by the ES? Can such evaluations be performed with formal MCDM methods?

tributes that characterize the problems, and the rules that lead to the solutions. In the ES case used by Hayes-Roth et al. [9] about detecting oil or hazardous chemical spills, MCDM consideration is implied in the construction of rules. Following demonstrates the relationship of rules used in the ES and their transformation to MCDM structure:

There are two rules in the ES:

R1   If the spill is sulfuric acid, then use an anion-exchanger.
R2   If the spill is sulfuric acid, the use acetic acid.

When both rules are applicable, which one should be used? In the ES, metaknowledge is used, i.e., the knowledge about knowledge, to select a rule. The metaknowledge, in fact, contains the criteria for the choice of cleanup solutions. These metaknowledge rules are:

R3   Use rules that employ cheap materials before those that
                employ more expensive materials.
R4   Use less hazardous methods before more hazardous methods.
R5   Use rules entered by an expert before rules entered by a
                novice.

These metaknowledge rules consist of multiple criteria to evaluate the alternatives. Rule R3 refers to cost while rule R4 deals with potential danger. Rule R5 alludes to the criterion of authority. The problem can be restructured in an MCDM problem framework: The ES is to choose among two alternatives, i.e., use of anion-exchanger or use of acetic acid, based on three criteria, i.e., cost, danger, and authority. Note that in the above rules, no quantified values are explicitly used. It is possible that quantifiable measures of weights or utilities for the criteria and alternatives can be extracted from human experts as a basis for making decisions. Approaching the same problem from this perspective, human experts or ES can some formal MCDM models, such as the Analytic Hierarchy Process or Multi-Attribute Utility Theory to invoke rules R1 or R2.

Therefore, in the problem identification stage, some implicit MCDM elements can be recognized. These include potential alternatives to solve the intended problem and key attributes and criteria for their evaluation.

4.2. Conceptualization of Problem

At the problem identification stage, the knowledge engineer and the human expert identify the objectives, decision attributes, and criteria for the problem or sub-problems. They then have to conceptualize the key elements of the system, their relations and possible knowledge representations. In addition, they can examine the possibility of framing the decision problem in certain MCDM models and incorporate these models as a part of ES knowledge base. At this conceptualization stage, the knowledge engineer and domain expert have to take into consideration the structure of the sub-problem as exemplified in the previous chemical spill cleaning rules and the appropriate MCDM model for its solution. Generally, to use the MCDM model, the domain expert will need to provide quantified measures according to the model specification. Therefore, the structural relations of MCDM models and the expert's heuristic rules will need to be identified.

4.3. Formalization of Knowledge Representation

In the formalization stage, the knowledge engineer has to decide the ES tool or representational framework that can best match the problem or sub-problem as conceptualized by the knowledge engineer and domain expert in the previous stage. Generally, the expert's knowledge can be represented in rule-based or frame-based schemes. In rule-based scheme, the expertise is represented in a set of rules with the form of IF-THEN (condition-action relations). When the condition of IF part of the rule is satisfied, the action in THEN part will be executed. In a frame-based scheme, the expert's knowledge is represented by a network nodes representing concepts and connected by relations in to a hierarchy. A set of built-in procedures are used to monitor the assignments of information to the nodes and execute proper actions when values in the nodes change.

The decision on the knowledge representation depends not only on the conceptual characterization of the problem but also the ES building tools.

Primary ES building tools are the computer languages for constructing the ES, including programming languages and knowledge engineering languages. Programming languages like LISP and PROLOG are designed to manipulate symbols and offer the most flexibility in building the ES as they have the least design constraints in their construct. However, the use of LISP and PROLOG require sophisticated programming skills which may not be possessed by the knowledge engineer. On the other hand, knowledge engineering languages offer the ES shells that have already had built-in skeletal elements of ES and support facilities to assist the design of the ES with ease and speed. For the same reason, these ES shells have different constraints that affect their generality and flexibility in building the ES. For example, EMYCIN is a shell derived from MYCIN [18], KAS is derived from PROSPECTOR [19], and there are many other commercially available ES shells.

The problem of choosing an appropriate ES shell itself is an MCDM problem. Several criteria have to be used for making the decision, including: knowledge representation scheme, inference engine, capacity to handle the rules or frames, the cost, the speed, the sophistication of explanation facility, user interface, interface to other systems and languages [20]. A formal MCDM model such as Analytic Hierarchy Process can be chosen that will allow pairwise comparisons for the criteria and obtain a aggregate weighting for the alternative shells.

4.4. Implementation

At the implementation stage, the chosen ES tool or language is used to implement the formalized knowledge in a prototype. The MCDM model needs to be constructed along with other components of the ES to determine the adequacy of the system. The results would be tested and evaluated to revise the ES.

4.5. Testing and Evaluation

With the implementation of the ES prototype, the system has to be tested and evaluated. The evaluation can be done by human expert using heuristics or formal MCDM models. The test and evaluation involve with two areas: (1) the operation of the system, and (2) adequacy and quality of the recommendations made by the system. For the operation testing and evaluation, the knowledge engineer should debug the system errors and determine whether the system functions as intended. System errors should be verified and corrected. In addition, the quality of recommendations made by the system needs to be evaluated for further refinement. Such evaluation may require human expert or a built-in evaluation function to examine the performance of the ES based on multiple criteria [9]. The criteria may include consistency of the recommendations, the completeness, feasibility of the recommendations and other specific criteria deemed necessary for the evaluation.

5. THE USE OF ES IN MCDM MODEL BUILDING AND SELECTION

In addition to examine the MCDM issues and models in the ES development, the ES concepts and approaches can be used to aid the MCDM model building and model selection. Specifically, ES can help decision makers in formulating MCDM problems, improving MCDM solutions, providing better user interface and selecting the best MCDM model in a given problem situation. Table 3 presents a summary of the use of ES in MCDM model building and selection.

Table 3
Use of ES in MCDM Model Building and Selection

MCDM Model Building & Selection Issues	Potential ES Aids
MCDM Problem Formulation	Es formalism can be used to identify the rules applied by MCDM experts in formulating problems.
MCDM Solution Improvement	ES heuristic search concepts can be integrated with MCDM optimization concepts to improve MCDM solutions.
User Interface	ES user interface facilities can improve decision makers' understanding of MCDM problem and solution methods.
MCDM Model Selection	ES can be used as an advisory system for MCDM model selection.

5.1. MCDM Problem Formulation

Most of MCDM models deal with problem solutions rather than problem formulations. That is, these models assume that the decision makers can formulate a particular decision problem easily with the help of MCDM specialists. But MCDM specialists are costly and not readily available when a particular problem or issue occurred.

MCDM specialists use their expertise to help decision makers to simplify and formulate MCDM problems. Zahedi [3] indicated that expert systems formalism could be used to identify the rules applied by such MCDM experts in formulating problems by using backward chaining from the problem attributes to the problem formulation.

After the problem has been formulated by the aid of ES, a particular MCDM can be applied to arrive a solution. If the decision maker is not satisfied with this solution, the problem should be redefined with added constraints and heuristics. The process should be repeated until an acceptable solution is identified.

5.2. Improving MCDM Solution

MCDM models use mathematical methods and algorithms to derive optimal solutions. On the other hand ES uses heuristics rules to solve the problems. We can integrate ES heuristic search concepts with MCDM optimization concepts to improve MCDM solutions.

Sykes and White [21] discussed the use of heuristic search concepts to improve integer programming, dynamic programming, and the multiobjective and parametric cases by using controlled randomization, learning strategies, induced decomposition, and tableau search techniques. That is, the forward-reasoning or data-driving solution approach of expert systems could use the integration of MCDM techniques and heuristics to arrive at a better solution faster.

Lehner, Probus, and Donnell [22] also proposed to incorporate rule-based procedures for assessing scores and weights of attributes in multiple criteria decision problems.

5.3. User Interface

One major problem in implementing an MCDM model is the lack of understanding by decision makers on reasons to use a particular model and its solution procedures. The user interface is a component of the expert system which insures that dialogue facilities of the system match with the communication needs of the user and the constraints of the task environment.

We can use ES user interface component and explanation generator to improve decision makers' understanding of MCDM problem and solution methods. For example, Lehner et al. [22] proposed to use ES rule-based program architecture for developing a user friendly interface. Zahedi [3] also indicated that to formalize the explanation of operation research (OR) techniques and to incorporate the explanation into OR expert systems can increase the acceptability of OR methods for mass application.

5.4. MCDM Model Selection

As discussed previously, there are many different MCDM models. For example, Hwang and Yoon [2] followed MacCrimmon [1] to classify MCDM into two groups of Multiple Attribute Decision Making (MADM) and Multiple Objective Decision Making (MODM). MADM is usually applied for evaluation and selection from finite alternatives such as selecting cars, computers, different policy alternatives. MODM is used for design of the best alternative by considering the various interactions within the constraints such as resource allocation decisions in production, marketing, finance, and manpower planning. Hwang and Yoon [2] discussed seventeen major classes of MADM models while Hwang and Masud [23] examined nineteen major classes of MODM models. Table 1 summarizes eight major MCDM models under four categories of MCDM methods. The choice of appropriate MCDM model can be a difficult problem.

Barlow and Fassino [24] developed a prototype expert advisory system for selecting MCDM models using Personal Consultant Plus shell. Their ES uses a backward chaining interface strategy and has three frames: FORMULATE, MODEL, and ROOT.

FORMULATE is used to formulate the user's MCDM problem by asking questions such as defining the different evaluation criteria and decision alternatives, specifying goals and objectives, environmental constraints and other general problem information.

MODEL is used to identify which type(s) of MCDM might be appropriate for the problem. It consists of five sub-frames to represent each type of MCDM: multiple goal programming (GOALS), multi-attribute utility theory (MAUT), multiple objective linear programming (MOLP), compromise programming (COMPROMISE), and other hybrid MCDM methods (hybrids). It helps the user to refine the problem and select a specific MCDM algorithm, as well as instructions on how to implement the solution method and any appropriate software if available.

ROOT frame has a goal of putting FORMULATE and MODEL frames together to help the business managers to select an appropriate MCDM model.

Most of Barlow and Fassino [24] available models are in MODM group. In fact only the multi-attribute utility model belongs to MADM group. At the minimum, they should extend their expert advisory system to include other popular MADM models such as analytic hierarchy process, multidimensional scaling, and conjoint measurement models.

6. CONCLUSIONS

This paper investigates the issues related to multiple criteria decision making and expert systems. It discusses the nature of MCDM problem in the context of ES development and approaches to their solutions. It is clear that many decisions or judgments at various developmental stages of the ES are MCDM related. Although the ES uses primarily expert heuristics to search for solutions for MCDM problems, the use of model-based approach which relies on formal model to evaluate alternatives provides another set of information for the decision maker in reaching his/her decisions. Model-based approach is constrained by its inherent structure which requires quantified data as inputs and rigorous methodology. This constraint presents a difficulty to process qualitative and non-quantifiable data while heuristic-based approach does not have such a constraint. Nonetheless, the heuristic-based and model-based approaches are not mutually exclusive in the ES development. Instead, the formal MCDM models can be incorporated as an integral part of the ES. It will allow the domain expert to examine his/her decisions in rigorous models and quantifiable terms as further inputs for his/her heuristic search for solutions.

In addition, the MCDM models can be used to help decisions in the ES development itself. Due to many available ES building tools, the choice of appropriate one for specific domain problem becomes an MCDM problem. Formal MCDM models provide knowledge engineer a structured approach for the selection of the system language or shell.

In order to take the advantage of the MCDM models in the ES development, it is necessary to consider the structural relationship of these models in the ES. How would the inputs be provided to these models? How would the outputs be integrated with heuristic rules in the ES? If there are differences in the recommendations solutions between the formal models and the heuristics, how to resolve the conflicts? Would there be higher level heuristics (metaknowledge) to provide a solution? These and other related issues need to be addressed in order to operationalize the integration of MCDM and ES.

REFERENCES

[1] MacCrimmon, K. R., "An Overview of Multiple Objective Decision Making." In *Multiple Criteria Decision Making*, edited by J. Cochrane and M. Zeleny. University of South Carolina Press, 1973, pp. 18-44.

[2] Hwang, C. L. and Yoon, K., *Multiple Attribute Decision Making*. New York: Springer-Verlag, 1981.

[3] Zahedi, F., "Artificial Intelligence and the Management Science Practitioner: The Economics of Expert Systems and the Contribution of MS/OR," *Interfaces*, Vol. 17, No. 5 (September-October 1987), pp. 72-81.

[4] Simon, H. A., "Two Heads Are Better Than One: The Collaboration between AI and OR," *Interfaces*, Vol. 17, No. 4 (July-August, 1987), pp. 8-15.

[5] Zeleny, M., *Multiple Criteria Decision Making*. New York: McGraw-Hill, 1982.

[6] Saaty, T. L., *The Analytic Hierarchy Process*. New York: McGraw-Hill, 1980.

[7] Keeney, R. L. and H. Raiffa, *Decisions with Multiple Objectives: Preferences and Value Tradeoffs*. New York: John Wiley & Sons, 1976.

[8] Waterman, D. A., *A Guide to Expert Systems*. Reading, Mass.: Addison-Wesley, 1986.

[9] Hayes-Roth, F., D. A. Waterman, and D. B. Lenat (eds.), *Building Expert Systems*. Reading, Mass.: Addison-Wesley, 1983.

[10] Shortliffe, E. H., *Computer-based Medical Consultations: MYCIN*. New York: Elsevier, 1976.

[11] Johnson, P. E., A. S. Duran, F. Hassebrock, J. Moller, and M. Prietula, "Expertise and Error in Diagnostic Reasoning," *Cognitive Science*, Vol. 5, 1981, pp. 235-283.

[12] Aikins, J. S., J. C. Kunz, and E. H. Shortliffe, "PUFF: An Expert System for Interpretation of Pulmonary Function Data," Computers and Biomedical Research, Vol. 16, 1983, pp. 199-208.

[13] Xiang, Z., S. N. Srihari, S. C. Shapiro, and J. G. Chutkow, "Analogical and Propositional Representations of Structure in Neurological Diagnosis," Proceedings of the First Conference on Artificial Intelligence Applications, IEEE Computer Society, December 1984.

[14] Hafner, C. D., "Representation of Knowledge in a Legal Information Retrieval System." In *Information Retrieval Research*, edited by R. Oddy, S. Robertson, C. van Rijsbergen, and P. Williams. London: Butterworths & Co., 1981.

[15] Michaelsen, R., An Expert System for Federal Tax Planning, Report, University of Nebraska, 1984.

[16] Kelly, V. E., "The CRITTER System: Automated Critiquing of Digital Circuit Designs," Report LCSR-TR-55, Laboratory for Computer Science Research, Rutgers University, Many 1984.

[17] Bennett, J. S. and R. S. Engelmore, "Experience Using EMYCIN." In *Rule-Based Expert Systems*, edited by B. Buchanan and E. Shortliffe. Reading, Mass.: Addison-Wesley, 1984, pp. 314-328.

[18] van Melle, W., E. H. Shortliffe, and B. G. Buchanan, "EMYCIN: A Domain-Independent System That Aids in constructing Knowledge-based Consultation Programs," Machine Intelligence, Infotech State of the Art Report 9, No. 3, 1981.

[19] Duda, R. O., J. G. Gaschnig, and P. E. Hart, "Model Design in the PROSPECTOR Consultant system for Mineral Exploration." In *Expert Systems in the Micro-electronic Age*, edited by D. Michie. Edinburgh: Edinburgh University Press, 1979, pp. 153-167.

[20] Hommertzheim, D., and A. Masud, "Considerations in Selecting an Expert System Shell," Paper presented at TIMS/ORSA Joint National Meeting, St. Louis, November 25-28, 1987.

[21] Sykes, E. A. and White, C. C., "Multiobjective Intelligent Computer-Aided Design," Proceedings of the IEEE Systems, Man and Cybernatics Conference, Atlanta, GA, October 1986.

[22] Lehner, P. E., Probus, M. A. and Donnell, M. L., "Building Decision Aids: Exploring the Synergy Between Decision Analysis and Artificial Intelligence," *IEEE Transactions on Systems, Man & Cybernatics SMC-15*, 1985, pp. 469-474.

[23] Hwang, C. L. and Masud, A. S. M., *Multiple Objective Decision Making.* New York: Springer-Verlag, 1979.

[24] Barlow, Judith A. and Fassino, Michael J., "An Expert Advisory System For Selecting MCDM Models," Paper presented at ORSA/TIMS Joint National Meeting in St. Louis, October 26, 1987.

Applied Expert Systems, E. Turban and P.R. Watkins (Editors)
© Elsevier Science Publishers B.V. (North-Holland), 1988

THE INTEGRATION OF MULTIPLE EXPERTS: A REVIEW OF METHODOLOGIES

S. M. Alexander and G. W. Evans

Department of Industrial Engineering
University of Louisville

This paper reviews methods for integrating the knowledge from multiple experts in the development of expert systems. The methods are classified under three categories. A description of methods in these categories is provided. Suggestions on which approach to use, under different circumstances, are made.

1. INTRODUCTION

Expert systems using a single knowledge source are being developed in a variety of domains, covering a wide range of applications. However, there is relatively little progress in developing methodologies for using the knowledge of several experts for solving problems in a single domain. In real world applications, in domains ranging from medicine to manufacturing, multiple experts are needed to solve problems. Hence, there is a real need to investigate and develop suitable methodologies for integrating the knowledge of multiple experts. Mittal et. al.,[1] reiterate this fact when they state that, "much research needs to be done to resolve issues such as identifying different aspects of a problem and corresponding experts, integrating knowledge from various experts, resolving conflicts, assimilating competing strategies, personalizing community knowledge bases, and developing programming technologies for supporting these activities."

When multiple experts are used, there are often differences in opinion and conflicts that have to be resolved. This is especially true when developing expert systems with multiple knowledge sources, since these systems typically address problems which involve the use of subjective reasoning and heuristics. The conflicts can arise owing to a lack of knowledge of a certain aspect of the problem, or owing to statistical uncertainty [2]. The term statistical uncertainty relates to the fact that the different experts may assign different event outcome probabilities with the same evidence.

The experts may also follow different lines of reasoning derived from their background and experience, which could lead to conflicting solutions. Multiple lines of reasoning can sometimes be used to combine the strengths of models, as demonstrated in the SYN program for circuit synthesis [3]. The program is used for determining values of components in electrical circuits. In the SYN program different models based on a line of reasoning are used in developing a solution. The models are designed so that they can contribute information that can be used by the other models. Since the models are developed from a single line of reasoning, they are consistent and therefore there are no conflicts. Stefik, et. al., [3] state that the two major purposes for using multiple lines of reasoning are to broaden the coverage of an incomplete search and to combine the strengths of different models. EXPERT- EASE, an expert system development tool [4], also allows for the input of multiple lines of reasoning. Once the multiple lines of reasoning have been input the system determines the most efficient way (using the theory of entropy or uncertainty reduction, [5] for reaching the solution. However, it is difficult to discern what line of reasoning is followed, since, the system blends the multiple lines of reasoning together in attempting to find the most efficient route to a solution. Another negative aspect of EXPERT-EASE is that it does not accommodate conflicts in lines of reasoning. When a conflict does occur, it simply avoids the problem by selecting the first occurrence of the conflicting rule.

Most of the expert systems that have been developed attempt to eliminate conflicts in the knowledge acquisition stage, or enable conflicts to exist by allowing multiple conclusions. The latter is done by integrating the knowledge from multiple experts using 'certainty factors' to indicate the confidence an expert had in a particular line of reasoning or the truth value that he associated with his conclusion(s) given certain evidence, for example see MYCIN [6]. Reboh [7] states that the user should not have to determine which conclusion to select. He suggests that the expert system should be designed to give the user advise, based on the user's input regarding what criteria or line of reasoning he (the user) favors, on what conclusion to select. This is possible since the lines of reasoning of the different experts can be made explicit in expert systems.

Most experts systems designed to integrate the knowledge of multiple experts, use one of the following three approaches:

1. Blends lines of reasoning through consensus methods.
2. Keeps the lines of reasoning distinct and selects a specific line of reasoning based on the situation.
3. Decomposes the knowledge acquired into specialized knowledge sources (Blackboard Systems).

This paper reviews these approaches. The paper concludes with suggestions for knowledge integration in expert systems.

2. CONSENSUS METHODS

There are two approaches for developing consensus solutions from a group of experts. These can be classified as analytical and interactive [2]. For example, suppose each expert can classify the outcome space by a probability distribution. In an analytical procedure, a weight is given to the probability distribution provided by each expert. This weight could be assigned in a Bayesian fashion based on the likelihood function of the experts assessment for a given state of nature. The weights could also be assigned based on the confidence the user places on the experts' judgments. The confidence of the user can be based on quantitative factors, such as a statistical evaluation of an expert's judgment or on a subjective evaluation. The consensus or group probability distribution can be obtained by using an "additive model" [8], and developing a weighted average of the individual probability assessments. Madansky [9] concluded that an additive model, with the weights assigned to the experts updated with new information was the "best" probability model. Morris [10,11] and Mosleh and Apostolakis [12] derive the group probability as an aggregation of individual probability assessments by expressing each expert's opinion as a variable plus a random error term.

In an interactive method, each expert is provided information on the judgment of each individual within the group and is provided an opportunity to revise his judgment based on this information. The interaction could involve a direct meeting of the experts, or the experts' identities might be concealed from each other to avoid personality influences. This is the case in the Delphi approach. The objectives of project Delphi was to obtain a consensus of opinion of a group of experts. The opinions of the experts were derived through a series of intense questionnaires and the interaction facilitated through controlled feedback [13, 14].

Pate-Cornell [2] suggests that interactive methods are appropriate when professional experience is the key ingredient to quality judgments, however, if external factors influence outcomes to a large extent, then analytical methods for combining the various factors are more suitable. In other words interactive methods are useful in alleviating scientific uncertainty and analytical methods are sufficient for combining statistical assessments. Hence, Pate-Cornell [2] suggests that interactive methods be first used in an attempt to reach a consensus. If this is not possible then it is beneficial to determine the hypothesis of the individual experts and their probability distributions estimates of assumptions (underlying theories) and outcomes based on the assumptions. This could be refined or modified by further interaction and then analytically aggregated to derive a group probability function.

The theory of arriving at a consensus can contribute to the development of multiple-expert knowledge systems (as opposed to multi-expert knowledge systems, where the lines of reasoning are not blended together LeClair [15], where one strives for a consensus of opinion among experts. However, it would sometimes be desirable to select one opinion above others, based on the situation. In order to achieve this, however, the expert system must accommodate multiple lines of reasoning, LeClair [15] suggests such a procedure for doing this.

3. THE SELECTION OF A SPECIFIC LINE OF REASONING

Steven LeClair in his dissertation [15] demonstrates a method for accommodating multiple lines of reasoning and developing multi-expert knowledge systems. In LeClair's procedure, multiple lines of reasoning are allowed to coexist without unwanted interactions which could compromise an experts advise. Hence, a deduction obtained through one expert's line of reasoning would not be used in the reasoning process of another expert. The philosophy behind the procedure, therefore, is not one cooperation, but accommodation. LeClair achieves this by labelling each assertion uniquely to distinguish the different reasoning paths of the experts. Control through meta rules are applied to the lines of reasoning, to avoid confusing the user on the progression of a task. This is important, since without the meta rules, the system may jump from one line of reasoning to another.

Once multiple lines of reasoning are accommodated in the expert system then the system would attempt to select a line of reasoning. Hence, in this procedure the goal is not to achieve a consensus solution, but to select a solution. LeClair achieves this by introducing information specific to the decision situation, the expert system then automatically selects a line of reasoning utilizing this information. The basis for this approach is that each expert's line of reasoning is based on his unique experiences in the problem domain and therefore represent a distinct philosophy regarding the problem domain. Hence, when a conflict is encountered, it may be resolved based on which expert's philosophy matches that of the user. The expert system would therefore seek additional information regarding the user's philosophy or what characteristics he would consider to be important, when there is a conflict. This method of conflict resolution does not attempt to disprove an expert line of reasoning, but attempts to select a line of reasoning based on supplemental information added by the user.

4. BLACKBOARD SYSTEMS

In the previous two sections two distinct approaches for integrating multiple knowledge sources were considered. In the first approach knowledge sources were blended together using consensus methods. In the second approach the lines of reasoning are kept distinct and separated from unwanted interactions. The Blackboard systems approach of integrating multiple knowledge sources maximizes independence among knowledge sources, by appropriately dividing the problem domain. In this approach expertise is divided among subdomains within a domain and the experts cooperate to solve the problem, however the interaction is kept to a minimum. The medium of interaction is referred to as the blackboard, hence the term blackboard system. Many experts systems have been developed using the blackboard system architecture, these include Hearsay-II [19], SIAP [16], CRYSALIS [17], and TRICERO [18]. The application domains covered by these systems range from speech understanding to military signal understanding and information fusion.

In blackboard systems, conclusions of the different knowledge sources are posted on a blackboard and these are available to all knowledge sources. The knowledge sources have a condition and an action part. The condition component specifies the situations under which a particular knowledge source could contribute to an activity [19]. A scheduler or an event manager controls the progress towards a solution in blackboard systems, by determining which knowledge source to schedule next, or which problem sub-domain to focus on.

REFERENCES

[1] Mittal, S. and C.L. Dym, "Knowledge Acquisition from Multiple Experts," *AI Magazine,* Summer 1985.

[2] Pate' Cornell, E., "Aggregration of Opinions and Preferences in Decision Problem." In *Risk Analysis, Issues, Methods and Case Studies,* edited by V.T. Corello, and R.A. Waller. New York: Plenum Press, 1984.

[3] Stefik, M., J. Aikins, R. Balzar, J. Benoit, L. Birnbaum, F. Hayes-Roth, E. Sacerdotti, "The Organization of Expert Systems-A Tutorial", *Artificial Intelligence,* 1983, 21, 285-325.

[4] Michie, D., "Expert Systems: Past Problems and New Opportunities," *Proceedings, IBM Engineering/Scientific Conference,* Nov. 1982, pp. 19-45.

[5] Shannon, C. and W. Weaver, *The Mathematical Theory of Communication,* Illini Books, 1963.

[6] Shortliffe, E.H., "MYCIN: A Rule-Based Computer Program for Advisory Physicians Regarding Anti-microbial Therapy Selection," Ph.D. Dissertation, Stanford University, 1976.

[7] Reboh, R., "Extracting Useful Advice from Conflicting Expertise," *Proceedings, Eighth International Joint Conference on Artificial Intelligence,* Karlsruhe, West Germany, August 1983, pp. 145-150.

[8] Oller, I.E., " A Method of Pooling Forecasts," *Journal of Operations Research Safety,* Vol. 29, 1978 pp. 55-63.

[9] Madansky, A., "Externally Bayesian Groups," Rm-4141-PR, Rand Corporation, 1964.

[10] Morris, P.A., "Decision Analysis: Expert Use," *Management Science,* Vol. 20, No. 9, 1974, pp. 1233-1241.

[11] Morris P.A., "Combining Expert Judgments: A Bayesian Approach," *Management Science,* Vol. 23, No. 7, 1977, pp. 679-693.

[12] Mosleh, A. and G. Apostolakis, "Models for the Use of Expert Opinions." In *Risk Analysis, Issues, Methods and Case Studies,* edited by V.T. Corrello and R.A. Waller. New York: Plenum Press, 1984.

[13] Dalkey, N. and O. Helmes, "An Experimental Application of the Delphi Method to the Use of Experts," *Management Science,* Vol. 19, No. 3, 1963.

[14] Linstone, H. and M. Turoff, *The Delphi Method: Techniques and Applications.* Reading, Mass.: Addison-Wesley Publishing Co., 1975.

[15] LeClair, S.R., "A Multi-Expert Knowledge System Architecture for Manufacturing Decision Analysis." Unpublished Ph.D. Dissertation, Arizona State University, 1985.

[16] Nii, P.H., "Blackboard Systems", *A. I. Magazine,* Vol. 7, No. 3., 1986, pp. 82-106.

[17] Terry, A., "The CHRYSALIS Project. Hierarchial Control of Production Systems. Tech. Rep. HPP-83-19, Stanford University Heuristic Programming Project 1983.

[18] Williams, M.A., "Distributed, Cooperating Expert Systems for Signal Understanding," Proceedings, Seminar on A.I. Applications to Battlefield, 1985.

[19] Erman, L.D., F. Hayes-Roth, V.R. Lesser and D.R. Reddy, "The Hearsay - Speech Understanding System: Integrating Knowledge to Resolve Uncertainty." *ACM Computing Survey 12,* pp. 213-253.

[20] Michalski, R.S., J.G. Carbonell, and T.M. Mitchell, *Machine Learning,* Palo Alto, Ca.: Tioga Publishing Co., 1983.

SUMMARY

Three approaches to integrating the knowledge from different experts for the development of expert systems have been reviewed. The consensus approach, attempts to eliminate conflicts among lines of reasoning in the knowledge acquisition stage. The second approach keeps the lines of reasoning separate without any unwanted interaction and selects a line of reasoning based on the situation. The third approach divides the problem domain into manage-able sets and decomposes the knowledge source such that each knowledge source is a 'specialist' in a particular aspect of the problem. The philosophy of the first and the last approach is cooperation. The basis behind the second ap-proach is to maintain separate lines of reasoning. The blackboard system ap-proach is appropriate when the solution space is large, the other two approaches may be utilized for relatively smaller solution spaces. These approaches can be extended by incorporating the concept of learning [20], i.e., learning over time, which solution strategies are most effective and what the solutions are, for cer-tain inputs. The methodology of integrating the knowledge of multiple experts is useful for learning systems. As an example, successful solution strategies could be 'learned' by the system and can be treated as an additional expert knowledge source.

Applied Expert Systems, E. Turban and P.R. Watkins (Editors)
© Elsevier Science Publishers B.V. (North-Holland), 1988

MANAGEMENT USE OF ARTIFICIAL INTELLIGENCE

Alan J. Rowe, Ivan A. Somers, Hal Schutt

Department of Management and Organization
School of Business
University of Southern California
Los Angeles, California 90089-1421

Hughes Aircraft Company
P.O. Box 902
Building E-8, MS G187
El Segundo, California 90245

Defense Systems Management College
DRI - S
Fort Belvoir, Virginia 22060

The application of Artificial Intelligence (AI) for managerial decision making has far reaching implications. Expert systems can significantly improve access to knowledge data bases which utilize rules of inference. Ultimately, artificial intelligence will augment the reasoning power of executives by incorporating knowledge representation that considers explicitly the cognitive aspects of decision making.

Why all the excitement about artificial intelligence when it has been around for a number of years? Perhaps, it is because it is being used to tackle problems that were not readily solvable by inexperienced managers. For example, artificial intelligence has been successfully applied in areas such as medicine, production scheduling, insurance and banking. The extension to broader management problems are, in fact, beginning to appear.

1. DEFINING ARTIFICIAL INTELLIGENCE

At the outset, we will define what we mean by artificial intelligence. Turing [1] defined it as "imitating human thinking". Winston [2] considers artificial intelligence as "ideas which enable computers to do the things that make people appear intelligent". We consider artificial intelligence as " the set of computer based systems that enhance the decision maker's ability to arrive at a better solution than what could be done without such systems".

The question one might ask is, how are such systems different from what has been used in the past? The answer is, that while we have had very useful computer based systems in the past, they have not been structured in a way to assure the inclusion of the knowledge of experts. Rather, most systems used by management were designed by system analysts.

1.1. Augmenting Human Reasoning

There is little doubt that computers can be made to behave in increasingly "intelligent" ways. Managerial problem solving is often poorly structured and relies on the intuition of the decision maker. The use of Expert Systems has improved the way problems are formulated. Furthermore, because we are able to incorporate "expertise" into programs, these systems can specify decision alternatives in a way that is generally superior to that of individuals with little expertise.

Artificial intelligence, in reality, is an umbrella that includes many topics to some people, AI is a totally misunderstood term and like the fear of the unknown, management has tended to avoid dealing with it. In part, suspicion is aroused when terms such as "AI imitates human thinking" or "AI systems are smarter than humans" or "AI systems will replace human beings" are heard. While there is some truth to these statements, the issue at hand is not whether computers are smarter than humans, but rather, how can they be employed to assist managers to make better decisions.

Although artificial intelligence is becoming increasingly useful, its ultimate potential is the ability to augment the decision maker's reasoning power. In order to explore how to augment reasoning power, we will examine cognition, knowledge representation, information usage and effective decision making. Another consideration is how to apply intuition and creativity so that it is integrated with optimization, simulation and heuristic reasoning in the solution of complex problems. Finally, we will examine the role of natural language, and machine learning in decision making.

1.2. An Overview of Artificial Intelligence

In order to explore the domain of artificial intelligence, we will present a classification scheme for examining its various elements.

The classification shown in Figure 1, differentiates structured and unstructured problem solving from the approaches used to solve these problems. We have chosen Artificial Intelligence as the horizontal axis. Computer systems are considered the simplest form of AI, and Expert Systems represent the extension of computer systems to deal with more complex problems by incorporating explicit heuristic rules to solve problems.

	UNSTRUCTURED	EXPERT SUPPORT SYSTEMS Interactive Networks Teleconferencing	AUGMENTED REASONING Creative Problem-Solving Non-Programmed Decisions Heuristic Logic Pattern Recognition Voice Recognition
		PROGRAMMED APPROACH MIS DBMS Computer Applications	EXPERT SYSTEMS/ MANAGEMENT SCIENCE Programmed Decisions Models Simulation Optimization Algorithmic Logic Inference Rules Knowledge Representation
	STRUCTURED	DATA PROCESSING	EXPERT SYSTEMS

D E C I S I O N — C O M P L E X I T Y (left axis)

CONTINUUM OF ARTIFICIAL INTELLIGENCE

Figure 1
Classification of Artificial Intelligence

Using this classification scheme, we represent the way in which artificial intelligence can be used to solve managerial problems. In the lower left hand quadrant is shown the applications of computers for management information systems used to provide managers with information needed to solve on-going problems. These systems seldom propose a specific solution, except for very straight forward applications such as reordering of inventory.

The upper left hand quadrant covers decision support systems that are used with less structured problems confronting managers. These problems require more information and better estimates of the implications of current data. Current efforts are directed at incorporating advances made in expert systems into decision support systems.

The lower right hand corner addresses those systems which use well defined data, available data bases, and knowledge of experts as inputs for problem solving and decision making. A review of many of the current applications indicate the progress that has been made in utilizing such systems. While the list of applications is extensive and growing, a reasonably well defined domain and a set of heuristic algorithms is required.

The final quadrant in the upper right deals with unstructured problems and with more sophisticated problems than currently are being addressed by expert systems. This area offers the potential for extending the application of Artificial Intelligence to the domain of complex, interdependent, stochastic categories of managerial decision problems. This quadrant requires a better understanding of decision making and an extension of knowledge representation to encompass the more complex problems. However, the payoff from such systems is bound to be significant.

1.3. Applications of Artificial Intelligence

One of the more successful applications of AI has been in robotics used in manufacturing processes. Robotics has helped to increase productivity and quality many fold over. However, they are not considered management decision systems but they do provide concrete evidence of success in AI

Pattern recognition has also been successfully implemented in a number of applications, such as electronic surveillance, and will become more important in systems of the future. Although it might seem strange to consider pattern recognition as important in decision making, nonetheless, it plays a role in the complex problems confronting decision makers. Most managerial problems have many interacting variables that, in essence, require the decision maker to utilize a form of pattern recognition. This involves perceiving combinations of observed events in order to arrive at meaningful conclusions. The extension to knowledge representation offers an interesting challenge.

2. PROBLEM SOLVING

Implicit in Expert Systems is the ability to use Knowledge Engineering to capture the "expertise" of persons who have the experience or know-how to perform a complex, ill-defined task. This knowledge is represented in terms of rules, states and events. One approach to view the relationships between computer based Expert Systems and Decision based systems is shown in Figure 2.

As can be seen in Figure 2, Expert Systems require interfaces with the computer systems and the decision maker. At the left hand side of the diagram is shown the computer or machine requirements while on the right hand side are shown the decision requirements. When viewed from this perspective, it is even more evident that there is a dual requirement that has to be met in order to make such systems operational.

The interface between the Expert System and Decision System poses a number of problems that extend beyond the technical issues of how to create an expert system. For example, the Knowledge Engineer must be able to extract the knowledge of the expert in order to formulate the algorithms needed for the ex-

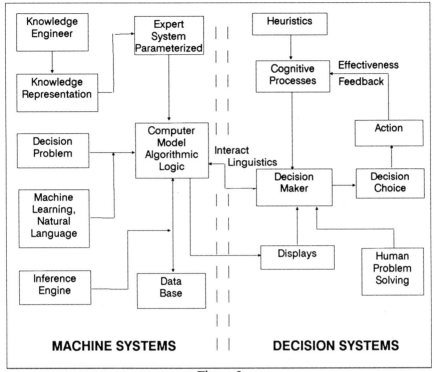

Figure 2
Machine/Decision Systems

pert system design and programming. This need presents two basic issues that need resolution. First, are experts the best source of knowledge and second, if they are, can Knowledge Engineers correctly represent a given situation.

For example, in a study of characteristics of experts, Shanteau [3] found that they have highly developed perceptual/attention abilities, and an ability to simplify complex problems. He claims they know when to avoid pursuing inappropriate strategies. They have a strong sense of responsibility and a strong sense of outward confidence in their decision making ability. Interestingly, they reveal an unexpected degree of adaptability and responsiveness, and seem to have a high tolerance to stress. The implication of these findings, according to Shanteau [3], is that preserving the role of the decision maker in Expert Systems is as important as developing such systems.

When dealing with knowledge representation, we need to address the issue of how to avoid errors that are introduced by experts. The following considerations are illustrative of areas that experts may overlook or misunderstand:

1.   Dealing with trade-offs among variables.
2.   Understanding suboptimization.
3.   Knowing when to decouple elements of a system.
4.   Taking time lags and variability into account.
5.   Correlating changes in one variable with another.
6.   Making allowances for changes in sequence.
7.   Dealing with transients or shock effects.
8.   Resolving conflicting goals.
9.   Estimating the accuracy of inputs.

This list illustrates the need to be aware of potential errors that enter into the formulation of problems and the representation of expert's knowledge. At present, there is an implicit assumption that the input from experts will lead to the development of realistic models of phenomena that are amenable to solution by computers using appropriate algorithms. While this assumption might be correct for many cases, there is the need for a broader look at the question of how best to formulate problems and to represent the knowledge used to solve managerial problems.

2.1. Heuristics and Problem Solving

There are many definitions of heuristics, including rules of thumb, intuition, educated guesses, application of experience or prior knowledge. For our purpose we will consider heuristics as the use of any cue, rule or technique that reduces the need for extensive search for the solution to a problem. Simon [4] has used the term heuristic programming as developing a detailed prescription or strategy that controls the sequence of response to a complex task. Because heuristic reasoning requires intuition, judgment, and ability to evaluate and integrate information, it can be used for extremely complex problems. However, solutions tend only to approximate the real problem. For example, the Pareto Law helps to identify which elements of a given problem contribute the maximum payoff to a solution. Using this approach, very good solutions have been found by Rowe and Bahr [5] for the assignment and traveling salesman problem.

In addition, priority rules for job shop scheduling were developed based on the fact that the sequence in a queue did not affect the expected delay [5]. This, in turn, lead to developing an heuristic algorithm that would simultaneously reduce lateness in jobs and the cost of inventory.

We can use generalized heuristic rules for managerial decision making. For example, if the problem is too difficult to solve, then solve half of the problem, or solve the inverse of the problem to reach a solution to the original problem. Heuristics are often associated with such rules. However, that is a limited view of the potential use of heuristic approaches. For example Polya [6] described heuristics as provisional reasoning that should not be regarded as final or strict. Pearl [7] has described heuristics as intelligent search strategies for computer problem solving based on compromises between the need to make search criteria simple and at the same time to correctly discriminate between good and bad choices.

Our use of heuristics includes "intelligent search of a complex situation using intuitive logic". This approach may seem like a contradiction in that it suggests combining logic with intuition. However, based on cognitive psychology, heuristics can be considered the ability to use both left and right brain capability. This approach to heuristics implies that a better understanding of the cognitive processes would facilitate appropriate knowledge representation and formulation of solutions for decision problems.

In a study by Davis and Patterson [8], they compared heuristic decision rules with optimal solutions for resource constrained project schedules. The problem involved scheduling activities in a project network in order to minimize project duration under conditions of multiple limited resource requirements and availabilities. The experiment consisted of comparing eight heuristic sequencing rules for eighty three different problems using a bounded enumeration procedure to determine optimum schedule duration. The results showed that the minimum slack rule produced the optimum in 24 out of the 83 problems and on the average was only 5.6% higher than the optimum solutions.

Again one might argue, if we know what the optimum solution is why do we need heuristics? Or, can we embed the expertise of the decision maker into the problem solution so that we can solve these problems without having to resort to finding good heuristics rules? These are important questions because they are at the heart of the question, when should Expert Systems rely on the intuition of the decision maker?

As mentioned earlier, experts have biases and are prone to a number of possible errors. Expert Systems, on the other hand may be too constrained in their approach to the solution of a problem. Even with interactive systems, they can not include all the factors that a human decision maker might want to consider. For example, D'Agapayeff [9], in his survey of the use of expert systems in the U.K. found that systems will have to be designed to interface with popular database languages and with other systems. He indicates that managers who are responsible for computers require relevant technical advances to avoid the temptation to rely on familiar methods or approaches.

2.2. Information and Decision Making

If we recognize that one of the basic functions of an organization is the use and transmittal of information, it is readily understood why computers have had such a significant impact on the functions of management decision making. Traditionally, there are three levels of decision making: Executive or top management, Middle Management, and Operating Management. Normally, the executive level receives the least information while the operating level is inundated with details. On the other hand external information is most complete at the executive levels with the least amount at the operating level. This dichotomy in information content and usage helps to explain some of the differences and why executives rely less on detail information and more on aggregate information and external information.

In the research done by Jones and McLeod [10], they examined the relationship between information and decision making and concluded that information systems embedded within an organization will tend to integrate both the formal system and the informal unstructured sources of information needed by the decision maker to do their job. In a study of what specific aspects of information contribute to information quality and usefulness, it was concluded that the use of formal information systems depends on whether the decision maker perceives relevance, accuracy, reliability, timeliness, completeness and readability. Further that the "perceived" quality of information depended on the decision maker's cognitive complexity, response to uncertainty, risk taking propensity, prior experience with the problem at hand, norms or constraints of the organization, and the ability to tolerate considerable variety.

For example, in highly uncertain situations decision makers will rely on verbal information which is discussed with individuals who are knowledgeable. This is in contrast to the use of written reports, especially where these reports do not reflect the current situation.

2.3. Managerial Decision Making

If we relate these and similar findings to the requirements for effective decision making, we find that there are basically four categories of decisions that have to be dealt with:

- Deterministic problems: These generally are well structured and are more operational in nature.
- Stochastic problems: These involve considerable uncertainty and require dealing with many unknowns.
- Complex problems: Ones which involve many interacting variables that are highly interdependent and that change over time or are combinatorial in nature.
- Organizational problems: These are ones which require an understanding of behavior, interpersonal interaction, conflict resolution, negotiation, leadership, etc.

Obviously, any classification scheme can be challenged by yet another taxonomy. It is not our intention here to resolve the question of what is an adequate classification of decisions confronting management, rather it is to highlight the requirements confronting the Knowledge Engineer when dealing with experts in attempting to find appropriate solutions to complex problems. Perhaps, the most critical elements of problem solving are believability and acceptability. For, if a decision maker does not believe or accept the answers provided by an expert system, then the likelihood of successful implementation is seriously diminished. Thus, it is not sufficient to have systems which provide answers. The solutions have to be meaningful, operational and usable. Without these requirements, we will be limiting the use of Artificial Intelligence and Expert Systems.

3. UNDERSTANDING THE HUMAN MIND

Fundamental to the field of Artificial Intelligence is "real intelligence". More recently articles have appeared with titles, such as: "Computers Simulate Human Reasoning by Utilizing Problem Solving Methods". The question that needs to be answered is : can human thought processes be reduced to If-Then, or Test-Operate-Test-Exit rules? Our position is that this approach is perfectly satisfactory for many problems confronting decision makers, but that it does not incorporate explicitly the intuitive, creative or heuristic processes that often are utilized by decision makers. Then, how does the human mind "reason" about information that is received? Are facts always considered facts? Or, is interpretation, judgment, preference and bias the real basis on which decisions are made?

When treating deterministic problems (category 1), a rigorous, structured approach is appropriate. However, for the remaining three categories, there are many instances where the outcome depends on the acceptability of the solution, not its correctness nor its optimality. It is in the latter three categories that reasoning may be the critical determinant and be even more important than the precision of the solution. However, it is precisely these categories of decisions that can greatly benefit from Artificial Intelligence and Expert Systems. Why? Because Artificial Intelligence can help to reduce conflict because it helps make alternatives clear so that spurious arguments are avoided.

There is general agreement that the creative process is not well understood even though there are some 2000 books with creativity in their titles. Creativity is complex because it requires an integrative personality which can blend knowledge, experience, imagination, and diverse and seemingly unrelated information. The question one might ask is, do you need creative problem solving for all situations? The answer is that successful managers learn how to adapt to unknown situations by "creating" meaningful solutions to complex problems. How then can AI and Expert Systems contribute to this mental process? Perhaps, by recognizing that there are differences in cognitive complexity among decision makers and by matching machine intelligence to that complexity using machine learning, we can achieve the best of both worlds - the power and structure imposed by the computer and the intuitive, creative and heuristic capability of the human mind.

3.1. The Cognitive Process

If we look at the way in which decision makers use information to make choices, we would observe the process shown in Figure 3 below:

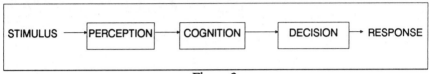

Figure 3
Cognitive Process

A stimulus represents the input information such as a periodic report, an exception report or a critical event requiring attention. In the case of Expert Systems, it could be the response to a specific inquiry for action to be taken. Perception deals with the way in which we take in information. Some individuals prefer simple, bottom line inputs while others, who are more cognitively complex, demand complete information before taking any action. Cognition represents the way in which we process information mentally that leads to understanding, evaluation and preferred actions. Decision making is the voluntary act by which we use cognition to arrive at solutions and choice. Finally, what we actually do is reflected by the response.

3.2. Decision Styles

To take cognitive complexity into account, we can use the model shown in Figure 4.

This model also shows hemispheric preference, that is whether the individual is right or left brain. As is shown in Figure 4, left brain individuals prefer structured and logical information whereas right brain individuals prefer less structure information and want to see relationships or implications.

Referring back to Figure 3, in the cognition phase, the cognitively complex individuals are able to integrate diverse bits of information to produce a meaningful representation of reality. The less cognitively complex individuals process the information differently and reach different conclusions about what has been perceived. In addition, left brain people look at inputs in a deductive, serial manner to reach conclusions while right brain people consider the broader aspects of the inputs including the perceived outcomes.

Having reached conclusions regarding the information received, the decision maker is able to make choices about the alternative outcomes. Here again cognitive complexity and brain sidedness influence the manner in which choices are made. The more focused individuals prefer direct simple action.

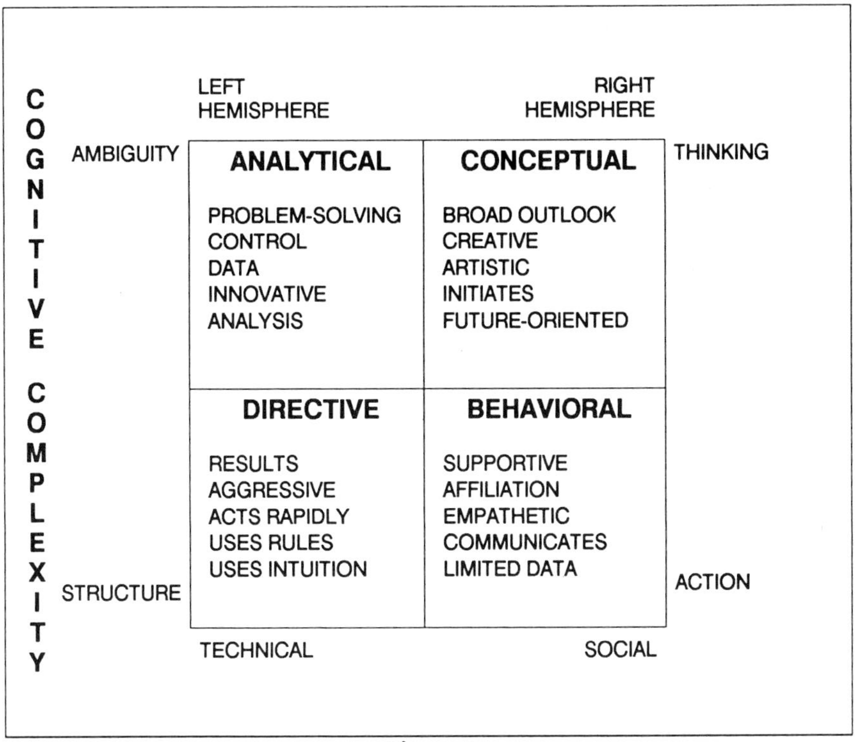

Figure 4
Decision Styles

The more cognitively complex individuals want to examine many alternatives and understand the consequences before taking action. Thus, choice, or the decision that is made depends not only on the information received and understood but also on the preferences for action versus deliberate review and the willingness to take risks.

Choices that are made often are negotiated, modified, compromised, delayed, etc. depending both on the cognitive complexity of the individual and the environment factors that impinge on the decision maker. Even after a decision has been made about which choice or alternative to pursue, action has to be taken to execute the decision. This phase of the decision process is sometimes as difficult as making the choice because others have to implement the decision. This then requires another series of decisions involving resource allocation, timing, personnel, etc. Although, strictly speaking, this phase can be separated from the choice or decision itself, a decision that is not implemented becomes wishful thinking.

What this implies for the integration of Expert Systems with managerial decision making is that decision categories 2, 3, and 4 (as previously discussed) may be more relevant and important than the deterministic decisions of category one. The implications are rather austere to contemplate, nonetheless, without considering the greater complexity of the other three decision categories Expert Systems will not achieve their full potential. This means that there will have to be a closer integration of the decision maker's decision style and specific decision requirements with the development and use of Expert Systems.

For problems that are extremely complex and subtle, Martins [11] maintains that the acquisition and exchange of knowledge and the use of problem solving methodology is deeply bound up with the pragmatic issues and the semantics that inevitably creep into real problems. "Successful computation in semantically complex domains requires insight, imagination, and a deep understanding of both computers and the application domain". These considerations and the need to better understand the cognitive process help point the way for the development of large scale, complex Expert Systems to tackle major decision problems.

4. THE CAUSAL INTEGRATIVE MODEL

As an illustration of a model which has highly interactive elements embedded that have causal relationships with high levels of uncertainty, we will briefly describe a computer program used to manage the uncertainty in the acquisition of major programs. The computer model was developed by Somers [12] and field tested in a major program office to determine the effectiveness of a program acquisition. The outcome demonstrated clearly the ability of a large scale model to assist in the evaluation of a system which involved many complex interactions. The model included the following major components:
- **Environmental Uncertainty:** This module dealt with the variables exogenous to the program which could cause delay or disruption.
- **Technological Uncertainty:** This module was used to determine the state of the art in technology and the interdependencies among the components of the program.
- **Customer Urgency:** This module covered such variables as time compression, stretch-out, concurrency, and change in scope of the program.
- **Organizational Slack:** This module dealt with the measure of organization's ability to perform the required tasks and the level of resources available to complete the project, including the required manpower.

Although the model was extremely complex, it proved to be a useful means for evaluating the most likely causes of cost over runs and program delays. It was initially tested on a program that involved an advanced state of the art hardware development. Data from the program was used to determine the impact of direct effects, as well as, second and third order effects on cost, technical performance and scheduled delivery. Prior to using the model, estimates by the program manager were over 40% in error in the estimation of labor costs. The program manager was unable to comprehend the interaction of the many delay and disruption factors involved or their causal relationships. The model was able to predict accurately the impact of changes in labor content and availability on all three measures of program performances: cost, schedule and technical quality. The model has since been applied by the program manager using the computer program as a knowledge base to comprehend the complex interactions that otherwise were not tractable. Although this program was not designed as an Expert System in the conventional sense, it nonetheless operated in the same mode as one would expect from an Expert System.

5. FUTURE EXPERT SYSTEMS

Future Expert Systems are predicted to include the capability as shown in Figure 5.

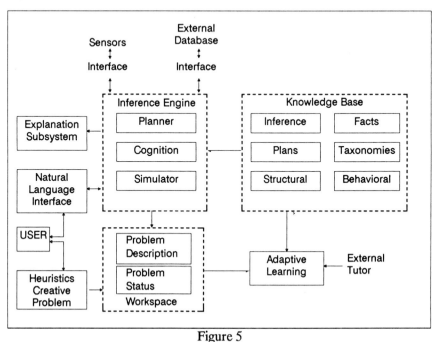

Figure 5
Expert System of the Future (Adapted from HIGH TECHNOLOGY)

As Figure 5 shows, the cognitive aspects of the decision maker and behavioral models are explicitly considered for such systems. In addition, adaptive learning, that is responsive to continuously changing environments,
parameters and relationships, will become an integral part of future systems.

6. CONCLUSION

How does one tackle problems as difficult as those addressed here? The
magnitude of the disciplines touched are so vast that even the treatment in this
paper, at best, is an overview. The message that we have tried to convey is that
there is little doubt that Artificial Intelligence is making a contribution to important managerial problem solving, but that its potential can be extended if we
recognize that the recipients of such systems are intelligent decision makers who
are acting in a rational manner and are concerned with achieving improved
answers to difficult problems that need to be solved.

The interface problem is perhaps the most challenging one facing system
designers. Some of the areas such as improving the formulation of problems in
terms that are closer to the actual problems confronting many managers, or a
better understanding of the cognitive process so as to know how to provide for
adaptive learning or information processing, will require further research and
experimentation. Our objective here has been to identify some of the critical issues that need to be considered and to provide a perspective from which they
can be viewed.

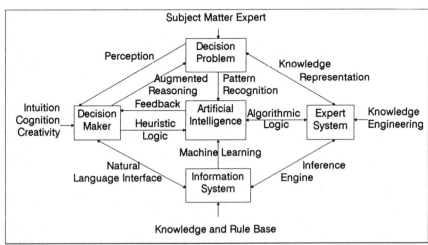

Figure 6
Artificial Intelligence in Management Model

The final diagram, Figure 6, is an attempt to illustrate how the field of Artificial Intelligence links the decision maker with decision problems, expert systems and the information knowledge base. As a holistic representation, it is intended to illustrate that an effective system will have to integrate all the factors shown so as to achieve the potential that is possible when applying such systems to complex decision problems.

Finally, how can we tie the elements of AI, augmented reasoning, and human decision-making together? Augmented reasoning comes from the synergistic integration of the parts of AI related to management. These parts are related to management's need for better "tools". All indications are that they will be developed in the future and they will become an integral part of a management expertise. We can anticipate Expert Systems that have a natural language interface, incorporate adaptive learning, that have complete and correct knowledge representation, and that build on the natural relationship between the decision maker and the computer. These systems will support unstructured decision making and this will lead to Executive Support Systems. This is what we envision as the future of Artificial Intelligence in Management.

REFERENCES

[1]   Turing, A. M., et al., "Digital Computers Applied to Games." In *Faster Than Thought,* by B.V. Bouden. London: Pitman, pp. 286 - 310, 1957.

[2]   Winston, P.H., *Artificial Intelligence.* Reading, Mass.: Addison-Wesley, 1984.

[3]   Shanteau, James, "Psychological Characteristics of Expert Decision Makers", U.S.C. Symposium on Audit Judgement and Expert Systems, Los Angeles, February, 1986.

[4]   Simon, Herbert, *The Science of the Artificial.* Cambridge, Mass.: M.I.T. Press, 1969.

[5]   Rowe, A.J., and F.R. Bahr, "A Heuristic Approach to Managerial Problem Solving", *Journal of Economics and Business*, p. 153-163, 1969.

[6]   Polya, G., *How To Solve It.* Garden City, N.Y.: Doubleday & Co. Inc., 1957.

[7]   Pearl, Judea, *Heuristics: Intelligent Search Strategies for Computer Problem Solving.* Reading, Mass.: Addison-Wesley, 1984.

[8]   Davis, Edward W. and Patterson, James H., "A Comparison of Heuristic and Optimum Solutions in Resource-Constrained Project Scheduling", *Management Science,* Vol. 21, No. 8, April, 1975.

[9]   D'Agapayeff, A., "A Short Survey of Expert Systems in U.K. Business", *R&D Management,* Vol. 15.2, 1985.

[10] Jones, J.W., and R. McLeod, Jr., "The Structure of Executive Information Systems", *Decision Sciences,* Vol. 17, 1986, pp. 220-262.

[11] Martins, G.R., "The Overselling of Expert Systems", *Datamation*, Vol. 29, No.11 pp. 68-80, November, 1983.

[12] Somers, I.A., "Causal Integrative Model - A Management Tool for the Analysis of Cost Overrun on Major Acquisitions", Ph.D. Dissertation, University of Southern California, 1982.

Part 2

PRACTICAL APPLICATIONS

Applied Expert Systems, E. Turban and P.R. Watkins (Editors)
© Elsevier Science Publishers B.V. (North-Holland), 1988

A SIMULATION EXPERT SYSTEM FRAMEWORK FOR FLEXIBLE MANUFACTURING SYSTEMS

Jorge Haddock and Cheng Hsu

Department of Decision Sciences
and Engineering Systems
Rensselaer Polytechnic Institute
Troy, New York 12180-3590

As the use of simulation is becoming increasingly commonplace and the models increasingly complex, the need for a new generation of simulation systems which possess certain online intelligence to assist both the developers and the users becomes more imperative. An approach to developing intelligent simulation systems is to incorporate expert system (ES) capabilities into the design.

The ES approach is significantly beneficial to flexible applications of simulation, such as decision support systems. The benefits are even greater for enterprises where simulation systems are an integral part of their operating mechanism and will be used routinely for various tasks. A Flexible Manufacturing System (FMS) is such an enterprise.

This paper presents a conceptual framework for the design of ES-based simulation systems for FMS. The development of the simulation expert system and its components is discussed. A simulation based generator for SIMAN is developed to illustrate the feasibility and features of the proposed framework.

1. INTRODUCTION

The development of simulation models requires more than just computer programming skills and business knowledge about the target systems. The modeler/analyst (developer) also has to understand the analytical nature of the problems under investigation, including the technical goals of the simulation, the statistical requirements for the interpretation of the results, and the computing and information needs of the models. This analytical knowledge determines the structure (the components and their inter-relationships), parameters, and input-output design of the models, and ultimately determines the models' performance. It is not unusual for the modeling tasks to overwhelm even veteran developers in dynamic settings.

Furthermore, the use of simulation models may also require the same kind of knowledge, especially when the models are to be executed adaptively or interactively. In these cases, the users are also developers in the sense that they may have to fine-tune the models, specify the goals or parameters for the models, or provide run-time directives. They, however, will likely lack the necessary analytic knowledge. Thus, as the use of simulation is becoming increasingly commonplace and the models increasingly complex, the need for a new generation of simulation systems which possess certain online intelligence to assist both the developers and the users becomes more imperative.

The so-called fifth generation systems [1] underlines the progress in the state-of-the-art of simulation technology toward meeting with this need. These systems invariably call for the incorporation of certain analytical capabilities into the traditional simulator, either in a hard-coded manner or employing the knowledge-based approach of applied Artificial Intelligence to facilitate convoluted reasoning as well as to afford flexibility.

To shed light on the cost-effective side of the new approach, it might be mentioned that it may not be desirable in certain classes of simulation systems. For instance, when the underlying processes and problems of a simulation system are highly structured and constant, the users may prefer the model to be designed as an isomorphism throughout -- fixed input (requirements), fixed parameters, fixed simulation program and modules, fixed output (information contents), and ultimately a structured procedure for using the system as a black box. In fact, most early-developed systems fall into this category and many systems at the present still do.

However, the new approach is entirely relevant and is significantly beneficial to flexible applications of simulation, such as decision support systems (i.e., use of the simulator as a tool for ad-hoc tasks). The benefits are even greater for enterprises where simulation systems are an integral part of their operating mechanism and will be used routinely for various tasks. A Flexible Manufacturing System (FMS) is such an enterprise.

Many of the components of an FMS -- such as workstation control, shop floor configuration, materials routing, production schedule and information handling -- are designed to be capable of responding efficiently to dynamic product demand, particularly small-batch orders. Therefore, adaptive planning and control is vital for FMS operations. The information needed to control the FMS, to a great extent, will be generated online relying on knowledge-based decision systems [2] including information handling and simulation. As such, a responsive simulation system, coupled with an information system, will be an integral part of the FMS's adaptive planning and control mechanism.

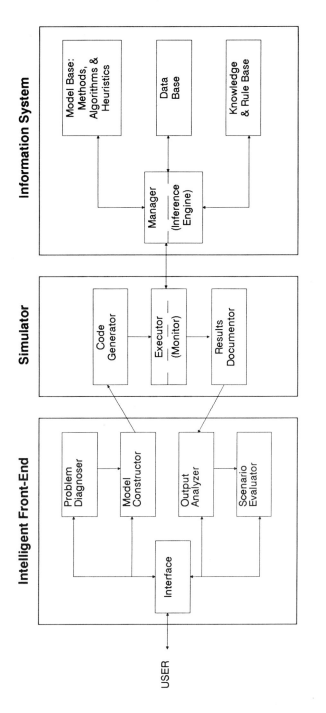

Figure 1
ES Framework

The system will participate in the scheduling (and rescheduling), routing (and rerouting) and other decision processes, continuously responding to the dynamic operating conditions. These tasks require fast execution because this environment is highly dynamic. Moreover, the simulation models required by these tasks are typically inter-dependent. For instance, to reschedule certain products or workstations will require real-time inventory, routing and configuration information in addition to other current scheduling information.

This class of simulation systems, in sum, is characterized by three major execution properties. First, the simulation model is comprised of a series of models representing a sequence of intertwined problems in which the order of execution is relevant. Second, the entire simulation process has to be conducted concurrently with the FMS's real-time operation. Finally, the simulation runs themselves may be open systems in that they may interact with the FMS's information system during the course of modeling or execution. For instance, they may recourse or preempt certain tasks based on the results of other simulation runs (which may be conducted in parallel for other FMS components). Evidently, these properties indicate that the simulation systems must be adaptive and intelligent.

This paper presents a conceptual framework for the design of intelligent simulation systems for FMS. The development of the system and its components is discussed. A simulation based generator for SIMAN [3] is developed to illustrate the feasibility and some of the features of the proposed framework, which is formulated in the next section.

2. THE DESIGN

An approach to developing intelligent simulation systems is to incorporate expert system (ES) capabilities into the design. Although the relationship between ES and simulation varies in the literature [4], this approach will entail a synergy of them and call for ES components to be included in the execution of simulation programs, as well as in the modeling and the analysis of the results. The execution of simulation programs in a complex system typically involves interfacing with other modules. These modules can either be simulation models created for generic problems or other simulation systems; they can be analytical models such as optimization algorithms for scheduling and Monte-Carlo procedures for generating convolution probability distributions. The correct use of these procedures typically requires problem formulation and results interpretation. While these tasks are traditionally performed in advance by developers, the new ES components can conduct them online and adaptively incorporate the modules into the overall simulation program according to the developer's or user's input.

Figure 1 depicts three general components of a simulation expert system. The Intelligent Front End (IFE) performs two major tasks. First, the IFE assists the user in the (interactive) data entry and, second, it generates the simulation model. The simulation program generators perform its functions based on information formulated by the IFEs, and execute the simulation. The simulation generators usually provide a summary of the simulation results. The information system may either be stand-alone -- a designated subsystem as a component of the framework -- or be a part of the overall FMS information system. It is this latter property which allows the framework to be integrated into the decision and operating system on a online basis.

The organization of the framework is presented next, specifying the objectives and requirements of each of the components.

3. FUNCTIONALITY

3.1. The Intelligent Front-End (IFE)

As will become apparent, each component of the IFE entails online intelligence for certain tasks and is actually an expert system in its own right. As expert systems, IFEs interface the user with the simulation system, generate the simulation code (i.e., model) following a dialogue with the user, and interprets the results of the simulation.

Interface The interface program can be a natural language dialogue or query language. Graphics capabilities are also needed to display the output and assist the user in inputting the data in iconic form. Using graphical displays, the user has a visual representation of the simulated system, thereby better comprehending the problem. For instance, the graphical representation of an FMS can be created by choosing from a menu of the available components of the real system. The layout can be complemented with information about the behavior of the system such as arrival rates of assemblies into the virtual cells of the shop floor, machine break-down rates, and other pertinent parameters. These system parameters may be available via the information system as well as being furnished by the users.

Problem Diagnoser The problem diagnoser assists the user in identifying the nature of the problem and identifies the goals of the simulation (e.g., a location problem, scheduling problem, or configuration problem) and other plausible objectives based on the technical idiosyncrasy of the user's problem. Depending on the goals of the study, the diagnoser assists the user in identifying, among other things, the performance measures of the model. The performance measure(s) can be statistics based on observation (e.g., average time in the system for a part), time-persistent statistics (e.g., machine utilization) and/or a function of the state variables (e.g., average inventory cost).

Model Constructor The simulation model constructor formulates the simulation model, specifies the performance measure(s) and selects the appropriate solution methods and models. In other words, this subsystem is responsible for the specification and integration of appropriate modules from the model base for the simulation. The input to the model constructor is generated from the user's input and the results of the problem diagnoser. The simulation model can be combined with other modules which provide input to the simulation model, analyze the output and/or interact with the simulation model. For instance, an optimization module can determine the optimal scheduling policy that can serve as input to the simulation model. Another example would be for the simulation solution to provide the input to an optimization module which determines the production schedule. A third illustration would be a simulation program that heuristically determines the loading policy in the simulation of the real-time operation. The integration of modules or models may either be based on problem-specific strategies [5] or utilize knowledge-based inference [6], or both.

Output Analyzer The output analyzer interprets the significance of the results in light of the problem diagnosis or formulation. As will be discussed in Section 4 (An Illustrative Case), the experimental conditions of the simulation runs can be prespecified or can be controlled by the simulator (see Figure 1). In the case where the conditions are prespecified, the statistical accuracy of the performance measure(s) is computed after the simulation run is finished. In this case, the output analyzer is responsible for interactively assisting the user in evaluating the results and deciding how to change the experimental conditions before rerunning the simulation. With the available information, the output analyzer is able to determine, for both terminating and non-terminating systems, the necessary experimental conditions to achieve a desired level of confidence. However, a more efficient method consists of incorporating output analysis techniques in the simulator module to assist the user in determining the experimental conditions before the end of the simulation.

Scenario Evaluator The scenario evaluator performs sensitivity analysis as implied by the problem. Its major objective is to recommend alternative strategies to the user for subsequent simulation runs, if needed, according to the overall objective. These strategies include experimental design and optimization procedures, as well as the usual system parameters. These procedures may be recommended in the form of suggestive queries or other input to the system.

3.2. THE SIMULATOR

The simulation generator as proposed here will convert the user's description of the target system (in symbolic form) and the problem formulation by the

IFE into a machine-executable simulation code. Once the model is generated, the simulation is automatically executed. The notion of a simulation generator is well established in the literature. It is defined by Mathewson [7] as: "an interactive software tool that translates the logic of a model described in a relatively general symbolism into the code of a simulation language and so enables a computer to mimic model behavior". Compared to Figure 1, the existing simulation generators perform some of the functions of IFEs, although they do not actually execute and interpret the results [4].

Code Generator There are three basic approaches for the development of the model. The simulation model can be a combination of discrete-event modules or subroutines usually programmed in a language such as FORTRAN and PASCAL. The discrete-event subroutines can also be part of the software structure of commercially available simulation languages such as SIMAN and SLAM. This approach takes advantage of some of the simulation language functions available such as random variable and variate generation, as well as the calendar of events. The third approach is to generate the model in block-diagram form for a process oriented simulation language such as SIMAN, SLAM and GPSS ([8], [7]). A variation of this application is viable because some simulation languages allow the incorporation of user-written subroutines within the software structure (or simulation program) in the execution of the process-oriented models. This paper addresses the latter approach.

Executor/Monitor Based on the information provided by the user, the simulation model and modules are generated (coded). The generated code usually consists of alphanumeric characters stored in a file. The file represents an executable set of statements that can be used by a process-oriented simulation language or can be interpreted/compiled by a programming language such as FORTRAN or PASCAL. The generated code for process-oriented simulation languages is converted into a file that will serve as input to the simulation language. In some cases the subroutines can be incorporated within the software structure of the simulation language. The simulation executor/monitor is responsible for physically, as well as logically, combining the pertinent modules or subroutines, executing the simulation program and monitoring its execution in case of early terminations. Three possible situations that will result in early terminations are: abnormal intermediate results, preemptive (termination) due to adaptive control, and preemptive (termination) due to changes in experimental conditions triggered by other systems. The adaptive control -- e.g., on early satisfaction or recourse in a sequential simulation mode -- can be based on a systems reliability framework ([9] and [10]).

Results Documenter The statistics to be collected can be chosen by the user. Some of the programming languages allow the creation of user-written modules for the output of simulation results. An ES module can interact with the user in explaining the results and the confidence level at which the statistical inferences are drawn. Moreover, the module should be able to report the experimental conditions in which a higher confidence level can be obtained (e.g., number of replications, number of batches, etc.).

3.3. The Information System

As noted in the introduction, the information system may either be a designated system developed for the simulation per se, or an interface to the universal system employed by the FMS. We generally assume the second notion in our discussion below.

Manager The manager is an operating system for the information system; it is similar to the usual software management systems that are commonly employed in database systems [11], knowledge-based systems [12] and decision support systems [13]. An inference engine is also included for knowledge processing. A flexible manufacturing system requires vast amounts of data (typically in the range of millions of transactions of all kinds) for its operation, especially the materials flow. Specifically, in an FMS, the workstations are grouped in cells, each performing similar operations. The product is routed to particular cells, however, the sequence of operations is usually different for each product. All of these operations involve large-volume information handling, thus necessitating the use of modern information system technology. Such information systems, in turn, can provide the simulation with the real-time data it requires.

Model Base The model base includes simulation modules, statistical methods, Operations Research models and stand-alone expert systems (e.g., an expert forecasting system [6] to effect real-time, mass forecasting for system parameters) for performing specific functions. It will contain both generic and problem specific procedures for FMS operations, as well as for specific simulation tasks. These methods, especially search procedures, will not only participate in the classified tasks of simulation (e.g., output analysis and experiment design), but also facilitate the adaptive control of simulation. For instance, a search procedure is combined with the simulation model in order to find the "optimal" value of the decision variable(s) in a sequential fashion [5]. The resulting simulation-optimization module can then be employed by the simulator for monitoring the value of the decision variable(s) and trigger a preemptive termination when the "optimal" solution is obtained.

Data Base The data base contains both the results of simulations that need to be reposited (either for future/further simulations or as a part of the global information base) and the data that the simulation models need (e.g., Industrial Engineering standards, sales records, demand forecasts, productivity, machine break-down rates and other pertinent "real" data). As stated above, this data base may either be stand-alone or be a part of the global operational database system.

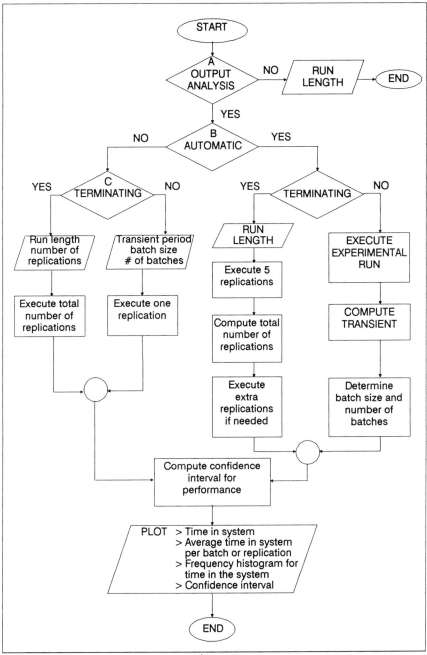

Figure 2
Output Analysis Rules

Knowledge and Rule Base The knowledge and rule base comprises FMS operating rules and knowledge pertaining to the enterprise, as well as the rules and specifications governing the simulator under different combinations of parameters or requirements (e.g.,the minimum number of runs needed, abnormal termination handling, code diagnosis, etc.). In addition, generic simulation information, along with model specific knowledge, will also be contained in this repository. It includes, for instance, the analytical models' characteristics and their match to certain problems, the heuristics and decision rules for integrating models for specific objectives or problems, and the properties of statistical analysis. This knowledge and rule base will serve as a global resource for every ES component to draw from and it may retain specialized knowledge for particular applications. The size and organization of this knowledge and rule base are basically functions of both the scope and strategy of system implementation.

In the next section the development of some components in the above-described design is discussed.

4. AN ILLUSTRATIVE CASE

The feasibility of the proposed framework is illustrated by means of a simulation model generator for FMSs. The illustration represents a first phase functionality of the framework that can evolve from a hard-coded implementation into a knowledge-based system. The code generator component of the ES is based on a previous design due to Haddock [8](also see [14]). This component is coupled with a user interface, simulation executor and results interpreter. The system uses an existing simulation language, SIMAN, for the execution of the simulation. The generator converts the user's description of the FMS to be studied (in data form) into a simulation model, automatically runs the simulation program and interprets the simulation results.

The FMS simulation generator encompasses some of the components in Figure 1, namely, the interface, model constructor, output analyzer, code generator, executor/monitor, results documenter, and knowledge and rule base.

FMS Simulation Generator

The information/description of FMSs is classified in three major elements: arrival pattern, machine centers and material handling device. The characteristics associated with these three components that the simulation generator is able to capture and model are arrival distribution and its parameters, number and proportion of part types, batch size, number of machine centers, number of machines at each center, part sequence, setup and processing times, transportation device (i.e., carousel or transporter), distance between stations, and others. The interface consists of a series of user-oriented screens.

In terms of the model constructor, SIMAN models consist of two frameworks, the model and the experiment. The model constructor creates a pure, network-oriented SIMAN model -- a process oriented model or entity flow model -- and experimental frameworks, rather than executing discrete-event subroutines programmed in FORTRAN. Numerous FMSs configurations and scenarios can be created and analyzed. However, the modeling of these alternatives is possible with minimum variation on the structure of the model and/or experimental framework. Although the selection of the material handling device and the buffer (storage) capacity impose differences in the structure of the model and experimental frameworks, most scenarios differ by the value of the parameters. The powerful modeling capabilities of SIMAN (and other recent languages) enable the modeling of complex and realistic situations.

The code generator creates two external simulation files, the model and experimental frameworks in addition to a file containing the FMS description data. (For a complete description of the screens and the models see Haddock [8]).

Although a global data base is not available at present, some editing capabilities are provided. The data inputted by the user to describe the system is stored in an external file. This file can be edited if input errors are detected or if a different scenario is to be created. Two components will serve to illustrate the executor/ monitor. First, the executor is a DOS batch file that integrates the IFE with SIMAN and the output processor (i.e., SIMAN's output processor is used to graphically present the output and it is an independent, post processor). The output analyzer also monitors the simulation as it is executing.

The knowledge and rule base include procedures to determine the conditions under which the simulation results -- for both terminating and non-terminating systems -- are statistically valid. The knowledge and rule base in this case is limited to statistical output analysis and is incorporated within the output analyzer in this illustration. Figure 2 (reproduced from Haddock [15]) shows the rules incorporated within the illustrated ES. The rule base interacts with the simulation through FORTRAN written subroutines. These subroutines, which are incorporated within the software structure of SIMAN, have the capabilities to interpret (automatically) the results of experimental runs and make statistical inferences about the performance measure.

As seen above, the results documenter is a combination of the FORTRAN-written subroutines for the statistical analysis of the results and standard SIMAN statistics collection and report. In this illustration the statistics collected are automatic and fixed.

5. CONCLUSION

A simulation expert system as proposed paper would facilitate the design and control of FMSs by making it more convenient to analyze a wide spectrum of scenarios. These scenarios (i.e., the model and its associated experimental conditions) incorporate a high degree of details, as well as time-dynamic characteristics, about the real system. Systems modeling and analysis, which requires expertise and is usually tedious and time consuming, is automatically executed.

Using simulation in a realistic environment, would require the expeditious development of the models due to the dynamic nature of FMSs. This requirement, in turn, demands online intelligence, as well as automatic coding and debugging. Also, complex and adaptive models would be required to realistically model an FMS. Therefore, a significant improvement on the utilization of simulation as a control tool for both performance modeling and optimal design is achieved using simulation expert systems.

In addition, some of the well-known issues critical to model implementation can be facilitated by this framework (e.g., model verification and validation, the performance of output analysis procedures and the software suitability of existing simulation languages). Models that are generated using ES components are verified in the development of the system (i.e., the code is represents the model accurately). However, model validation -- the comparison of the model with the real system - is the responsibility of the analyst. ES components can assist the user in using systematic and analytical techniques for the validation of the model. Moreover, components such as simulation animation and graphical output can assist in model validation.

The relative performance of different output analysis procedures is generally sensitive to the experimental parameters (e.g., batch size and the number of observations) which are chosen by the users. This sensitivity creates problems in the development of automatic procedures. Therefore, with proper knowledge engineering, the ES can alleviate this problem by assisting the non-simulationist in the statistical analysis of the simulation results. The IFE of simulation expert systems can assist the user in selecting the appropriate techniques, determine the parameters, and assemble the model base according to the problem formulation.

The software structure of the existing simulation languages is not suitable for the development of simulation ES. Difficulties are usually encountered in the interfacing of interactive and/or iterative ES components with the simulation language. This is expected as knowledge engineering and processing pose a whole set of requirements fundamentally different from simulation per se. Knowledge engineering and processing explicitly separate the knowledge, the model, and the data from the simulation program implemented in a rigorously designed information system. The intelligence part of the system will be handled by the inference engine and information manager. The simulation language can then perform the job that it was designed to do best.

A new expert system framework has been proposed in this paper. It differs in a fundamental way from previous efforts, which are basically simulation generators enhanced with ad hoc procedures to handle certain well-structured tasks. To move fully into the realm of ES the new framework proposes to draw strengths from the established literature of knowledge engineering and processing, as well as information handling. As such, a rigorous information system featuring a knowledge and rule base, database, and model base is included. The classical simulation program and online intelligence are thereby separated. This way, system intelligence will be handled in a unified and problem-independent (although still domain-specific) fashion, truly enjoying the efficiency and power of ES.

The basic functionality of most of the ES components pertaining to the IFE and simulation generator of this framework have been successfully implemented in an illustrative system. However, most of the effort has been focused on the interface, with more effort needed in the monitor and results interpreter components. Further, the information system is not yet available for the framework.

Major investigations are needed before a comprehensive system can be implemented. One task is the development of the monitor and results interpreter components, which are vital in the FMS environment. The actual development of procedures, the acquisition of pertinent knowledge, and the integration between ES processing and simulation programs are other major tasks of further research in the domain of FMS planning and control.

REFERENCES

[1] Shannon, R.E., R. Mayer and H.H. Adelsberger, "Expert Systems and Simulation", *SIMULATION*, Vol. 44, No. 6, June, 1985.

[2] Hsu, C., "A Metadatabase Approach to Information Management in Computer-Integrated Manufacturing", 1987 Working Paper, School of Management, Rensselaer Polytechnic Institute, Troy, New York (submitted)

[3] Pegden, C.D., *Introduction to SIMAN*, Systems Modeling Corporation, 1982.

[4] O'Keefe, R., "Simulation and Expert Systems -- A Taxonomy and Some Examples", *SIMULATION*, Vol. 46, No. 1, January, 1986.

[5] Bengu, G. and J. Haddock, "A Generative Simulation- Optimization System", *Computers and Industrial Engineering*, Vol. 10, No. 4, 1986.

[6] Kumar, S. and C. Hsu, "An Expert System Framework for Forecasting Method Selection", 1987 Working Paper, School of Management, Rensselaer Polytechnic Institute, Troy, New York (submitted).

[7] Mathewson, S.C., "The Application of Program Generator Software and Its Extensions to Discrete Event Simulation Modeling", *IIE Transactions,* Vol. 16, No. 1, March, 1984.

[8] Haddock, J., "Simulation Generator for Flexible Manufacturing Systems Design and Control", *IIE Transactions,* forthcoming in 1987.

[9] Hsu, C., "A Decision Support System for Database Evolution Using Data Model Independent Architecture", *Computers and Operations Research,* Vol. 13, No. 4, 1986.

[10] Charnes, A., W.W. Cooper, W.L. Gorr, C. Hsu, B. Von Rabenau, "Emergency Government Interventions: Case Study of Natural Gas Shortages", *Management Science,* Vol. 32, No. 10, October, 1986.

[11] Date, C.J., *An Introduction to Database Systems, Vol. I.* Reading, Mass.: Addison-Wesley, 1986.

[12] Waterman, D.A., *A Guide to Expert Systems.* Reading, Mass.: Addison-Wesley, 1986.

[13] Bonczek, R.H., C.W. Holsapple and A.B. Whinston, *Foundations of Decision Support Systems.* New York: Academic Press, 1981.

[14] Haddock, J. and R. P. Davis, "Building a Simulation Generator for Manufacturing Cell Design and Control", Proceedings 1985 IIE Spring Conference, Los Angeles, May, 1985.

[15] Haddock, J., "An Expert System Framework Based on a Simulation Generator", *SIMULATION,* Vol. 48, No. 2, February, 1987.

Applied Expert Systems, E. Turban and P.R. Watkins (Editors)
© Elsevier Science Publishers B.V. (North-Holland), 1988

INTELLIGENT PRODUCTION PLANNING SYSTEM USING THE POST-MODEL ANALYSIS APPROACH

Jae Kyu Lee and Byung Sun Kang

Department of Management Science
Korea Advanced Institute of Science and Technology
P.O. Box 150, Cheongryang, Seoul, Korea

Department of Planning
Korea Mining Promotion Corporation
686-48 Shindaebang-Dong, Dongjak-Ku, Seoul, Korea

This paper proposes the use of the Post-Model Analysis(PMA) approach to handle qualitative factors in aggregate production planning problems. The PMA approach excludes qualitative factors such as employee's morale and customer's goodwill from the optimization model. Instead, these factors are represented in a rule-type knowledge base. This approach automatically evaluates the optimal feasible solution that minimizes the cost function in terms of employee's morale and customer's goodwill. If any of the currently achieved goals are unsatisfactory, the tradeoffs may be invoked under the support of the non-dominated opportunity costs that are generated.

The formulation and solution process of the aggregate production planning problem by the PMA approach and its decision support system named IPPS(Intelligent Production Planning System) is described. The IPPS consists of a model management system, a knowledge management system, a PMA controller, and a data management system. The paper also demonstrates an illustrated dialogue using IPPS.

1. INTRODUCTION

Aggregate Production Planning(APP) problems are concerned with the determination of production, inventory, and work force levels to accomodate demand fluctuations. There have been numerous quantitative models for APP [1], [2], [3], [4], [5], [6]. In these models, the parameters are quantified whether the quantification is reasonable or not. This research adopts the Post-Model Analysis(PMA) approach to segregate the qualitative factors from the quantitative model in the formulation process by placing the qualitative factors in the knowledge base [7], [8], [9], [10]. The PMA approach supports the tradeoffs between the quantified objective function in the optimization model and the qualitative factors in the knowledge-based system via a unified framework.

This paper describes the formulation and solution procedure of APP by the PMA approach, and it also proposes an architecture of a decision support system - named IPPS(Intelligent Production Planning System) - that uses the PMA approach for APP. The prototype of IPPS implemented on the microcomputer has a model management system, a knowledge management system, a PMA controller, and a data management system.

2. FORMULATION OF THE AGGREGATE PRODUCTION PLANNING PROBLEM BY THE PMA APPROACH

To illustrate the formulation of APP by the PMA approach, we select a typical linear programming model as in (1)-(7) [3].

Decision Variables:

X_{it} = units of product i to be produced in period t

I^{+}_{it} = units of ending inventory of product i in period t

I^{-}_{it} = units of product i backordered at the end of period t

H_t = manhours of regular work force hired in period t

F_t = manhours of regular work force laid off in period t

W_t = manhours of regular labor used during period t

O_t = manhours of overtime labor used during period t

Parameters:

v_{it} = unit production cost for product i in period t

c_{it} = inventory carrying cost per unit of product i held in stock from period t to t + 1

b_{it} = cost per unit of backorder of product i carried from period t to t + 1

r_t = cost per manhour of regular labor in period t

o_t = cost per manhour of overtime labor in period t

h_t = cost of hiring one manhour in period t

f_t = cost of laying off one manhour in period t

d_{it} = forecast demand for product i in period t

k_{it} = manhour required to produce one unit of product i p   = overtime allowed as a fraction of the regular hours

T   = time horizon, in periods

N   = total number of products.

The model is:

$$\text{Minimize } Z = \sum_{i=1}^{N} \sum_{t=1}^{T} (v_{it}X_{it} + c_{it}I^{+}_{it} + b_{it}\Gamma_{it})$$

$$\sum_{t=1}^{T} + (r_tW_t + o_tO_t + h_tH_t + f_tF_t) \qquad (1)$$

subject to:

$$X_{it} + I^{+}_{i,t-1} - \Gamma_{i,t-1} - I^{+}_{it} + \Gamma_{it} = d_{it} \qquad (2)$$

$$\sum_{i=1}^{N} k_iX_{it} - W_t - O <= 0 \qquad (3)$$

$$W_t - W_{t-1} - H_t + F_t = 0 \qquad (4)$$

$$-pW_t + O <= 0 \qquad (5)$$

$$X_{it}, I^{+}_{it}, \Gamma_{it} >= 0 \qquad (6)$$

$$W_t, O_t, P_t, H_t, F_t >= 0 \qquad (7)$$

$$i = 1, \ldots N, \quad t = 1, \ldots T$$

In this model, the cost coefficients for hiring(h_t), firing(f_t), and backordering should be quantified. In most cases, however, it is extremely difficult to quantify them completely, i.e. the impact of firing and hiring on the employee's morale and the impact of backordering on the customer's goodwill.

Furthermore, the decision variables in the optimization model(hiring, firing, backordering) are not the only factors that influence the qualitative objectives (employee's morale, customer's goodwill). For example, the employee's morale is also affected by work conditions, the average rate of labor turnover, economic conditions, supply and demand in the labor market, and so on. In the same manner, the customer's goodwill is influenced by factors such as monopoly, quality of the product, competitors' delay in delivery and so on. Therefore, these factors are organized together into an independent knowledge base. The linkage between the optimization model and the knowledge base is the common decision variables such as hiring, firing, and backordering.

To formulate the APP by the PMA approach, h_t, f_t and b_{it} are re-defined. The h_t and f_t represent the hiring and firing costs respectively; however, they no longer include qualitative factors such as lost customer's goodwill. Instead, the qualitative goals are included in the two additional judgment functions as in (8) and (9):

$$J_G(\Gamma_{it}, i = 1,...,N, t = 1,...,T \mid E_G) \supseteq q_G \tag{8}$$

$$J_M(O_t, F_t, t = 1,....,T \mid E_M) \supseteq q_M \tag{9}$$

The symbol q_G denotes customer's goodwill, and q_M denotes the employee's morale. E_G and E_M in (8) and (9) denote the external factors relevant to q_G and q_M respectively. As mentioned earlier, in this case the structure of judgment functions is organized in the form of rules that are incorporated into the knowledge base independent of the optimization model. Therefore, the optimization model and the knowledge base can be maintained separately.

3. SOLUTION PROCEDURE OF APP BY THE PMA APPROACH

Using the formulation established in the previous section, the APP can be solved by the following procedure:

1. Prepare knowledge bases to include employee's morale and customer's goodwill.

2. Formulate the linear programming model manually or automatically. The IPPS supports the automatic formulation. If the model has been formulated previously,retrieve it.

3. Solve the linear programming model in (1) - (7) with the purely quantitative parameters.

4. Evaluate the optimal feasible solution of (1) - (7) using the knowledge base to account for the customer's goodwill and the employee's morale.

5. If the optimal feasible solution is satisfactory in terms of the customer's goodwill and the employee's morale, stop.

6. If the current solution is not satisfactory, then select the unsatisfactory qualitative goal(s) and set their target(s).

7. Identify the objectives that may be downgraded in return for the enhancement of unsatisfactory goals.

8. Compute the non-dominated opportunity cost which has the meaning of the best marginal rate of substitution. (This paper demonstrates a special type of tradeoff between a qualitative goal and a quantitative goal one at a time. In this case, the minimum opportunity cost is the non-dominated

opportunity cost. For a comprehensive review on the computation of non-dominated opportunity costs encompassing the objective function in the optimization model and qualitative objectives in the rule based system, see [10].)

9. Let the decision maker decide whether the opportunity cost is acceptable for the enhancement of unsatisfactory goals. If acceptable, the best solution is found, therefore stop; otherwise, modify the level of upgrade based on the advice from the knowledge-based system and repeat the step 8. In this process, support automatic modification of model to a maximum extent.

4. INTELLIGENT PRODUCTION PLANNING SYSTEM (IPPS)

The IPPS is an intelligent DSS designed to support the PMA approach for APP implemented on a microcomputer. Fig 1 depicts the overall architecture of IPPS. There are four subsystems in IPPS:

1) Model Management System

2) Knowledge Management System

3) PMA Controller

4) Data Management System

The following subsections describe each of the subsystems.

4.1. Model Management System

The role of the Model Management System(MMS) includes automatic formulation, optimization, storage and retrieval of optimization models.

(1) **Automatic Formulation**   The automatic formulator [11], [12], [13] accepts distinguishing factors for production planning such as starting time, ending time, time interval, and policies such as whether overtime, firing, hiring, backordering and safety stock are allowed or not. Once all of the factors are entered, the automatic formulator identifies decision variables, objective function and constraints. The Matrix Generator then generates the coefficient values from the database. The formulation process is depicted in Fig 2.

For example, suppose the decision maker wants to plan for T periods of time with N products, and allows for inventory, overtime, firing, hiring and safety stock without backlog. Then the generated formulation is the model (1) - (7) excluding all Γ_{it} terms, but including (10):

$$I^+_{it} \; > = \; ss_{it} \tag{10}$$

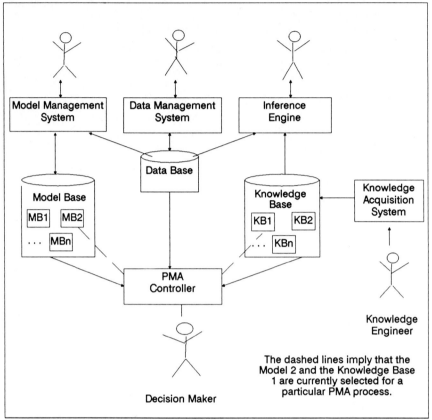

Figure 1

Overall Architecture of the Intelligent Production Planning System

where ss_{it} = safety stock of product i in period t.

(2) Find Optimal Feasible Solution Once the model is formulated completely, whether it is done automatically or manually, an algorithm such as the simplex method can find the optimal feasible solution, if it exists.

(3) Storage and Retrieval The formulated model can be saved for later use, or it can be retrieved if it already exists.

4.2. Knowledge Management System

Both the inference engine and the PMA controller use the knowledge base.

(1) Syntax of Knowledge Representation The knowledge is represented by rules using reserved words such as IF, THEN, ELSE, AND, OR, IS, NOT, , =, and . Each statement is expressed in fact type(true or false), numeric type, or OAV(Object-Attribute-Value) type. A typical rule looks like the following:

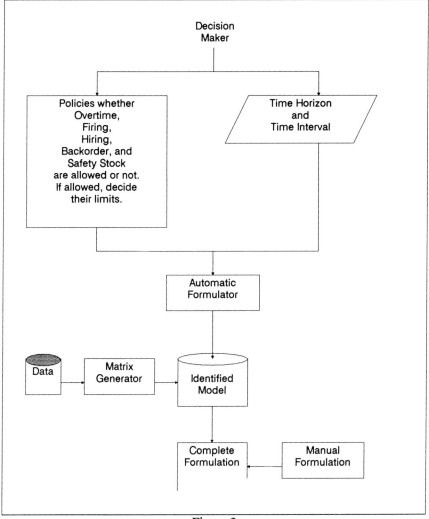

Figure 2
Automatic formulation process

RULE Goodwill 42

IF   the product IS a staple item

AND   status of competition IS almost perfect competition

AND   after-sales-service IS very good

AND   AVERAGE BACKLOG 700

THEN GOODWILL IS VERY GOOD

(2) Primitive Functions To represent the knowledge more compactly, TOTAL, ALL and AVERAGE are used in conjunction with the words FIRING, OVERTIME, HIRING, MORALE, GOODWILL and BACKLOG. To represent qualitative goals, the system uses 5 levels of marks : VERY BAD, BAD, UNDETERMINED, GOOD, and VERY GOOD.

For example,

TOTAL HIRING = sum of hiring over the all planning horizon

$$= \sum_{t=1}^{N} H_t$$

TOTAL BACKLOG = sum of backlog of all items over the all planning horizon

$$= \sum_{i=1}^{N} \sum_{t=1}^{T} \Gamma_{it}$$

AVERAGE BACKLOG of product i = TOTAL BACKLOG of product i / time horizon.

$$= \sum_{t=1}^{T} \Gamma_{it} / T$$

(3) Inference Inference is performed using backward chaining. For example, suppose the system reaches the conclusion "MORALE IS VERY GOOD", as depicted in the inference net in Fig 3. At the beginning, two facts about AVERAGE OVERTIME and AVERAGE FIRING should have been transferred from the solution of optimization model. However, the other statements in the leaf nodes about payment level and work environment should be asked unless they are already known. Fig 4 lists five rules that correspond to the inference net.

The conclusion about goodwill can also be obtained by using rules like the following ones :

RULE goodwill 5

IF   quality IS good

AND   AVERAGE BACKLOG competitor's average backlog

THEN   GOODWILL IS VERY GOOD

4.3. PMA Controller

The PMA Controller performs the following two functions.

1. Qualitative Evaluation : automatically evaluates current solution (such as quantitatively optimal solution) in terms of related qualitative objectives described in the knowledge base.

2. Marginal Rate of Substitutions(MRS) : generates the marginal rate of substitutions caused by the upgrade of certain quantitative or qualitative goals.

(1) **Qualitative Evaluation** The process of qualitative evaluation is the same as the process of inference explained in section 4.2. In this example, by selecting the appropriate knowledge base, the solution from the linear program-

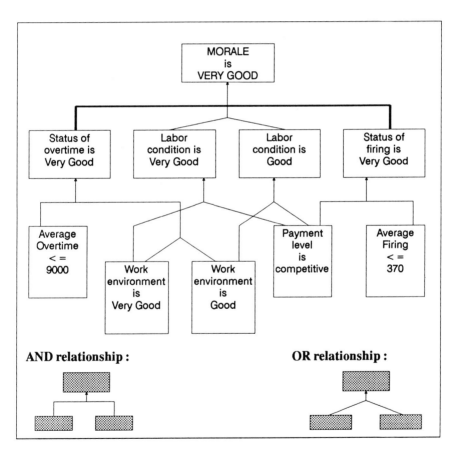

Figure 3
Inference Net

```
RULEmorale 1
IFwork environment IS GOOD
ORwork environment IS VERY GOOD
ANDAVERAGE OVERTIME = 9000
THENstatus of overtime IS VERY GOOD
RULEmorale 3
IFAVERAGE FIRING = 370
ANDpayment level IS competitive
THEN status of firing IS VERY GOOD
RULEmorale 15
IFpayment level IS competitive
ORwork environment IS GOOD
THENlabor condition IS GOOD
RULEmorale 20
IFpayment level IS competitive
ORwork environment IS VERY GOOD
THENlabor condition IS VERY GOOD
RULEmorale 32
IFstatus of overtime IS VERY GOOD
ANDstatus of firing IS VERY GOOD
ANDlabor condition IS GOOD
ORlabor condition IS VERY GOOD
THENMORALE IS VERY GOOD
```

Figure 4
Selected Rules about Employee's Morale

ming model can be evaluated from the perspective of customer's goodwill, corporate strategy, employee's morale, the purchase plan, and so on.

(2) Marginal Rate of Substitutions

Suppose the solution that minimizes the costs is "BAD" in terms of employee's morale and customer's goodwill. In this case, the decision maker wants to improve employee's morale and customer's goodwill, which may increase the cost in return. In this process, the decision maker needs to know the minimum impact of qualitative upgrades on the cost which can be obtained by computing the minimum MRS (or non- dominated MRSs if multiple impacted goals exist). For a comprehensive review on the computation of MRS, see [10].

In this paper, the special cases of tradeoffs will be described for illustrative purpose.

Notation

ΔC : changes in cost function in the optimization model

Δq_M : changes in employee's morale

Δq_G : changes in customer's goodwill

q^* : fixed level of a qualitative goal

The right hand side of the vertical bar in (13) - (16) is the fixed condition to be satisfied. The types of tradeoffs used in IPPS are (11) - (16) :

$$\Delta C(\Delta q_M) \tag{11}$$

$$\Delta C(\Delta q_G) \tag{12}$$

$$\Delta C(\Delta q_M \mid q_G = q_G^*) \tag{13}$$

$$\Delta C(\Delta q_G \mid q_M = q_M^*) \tag{14}$$

$$\Delta q_M(\Delta C \mid q_G = q_G^*) \tag{15}$$

$$\Delta q_G(\Delta C \mid q_M = q_M^*) \tag{16}$$

For example, the notation (17) means that improving the goodwill from "BAD" to "VERY GOOD" while maintaining the morale at the "GOOD" level will cost $80,000.

$$\Delta C(\Delta q_G = \text{VERY GOOD} - \text{BAD} \mid q_M = \text{GOOD}) = \$80,000 \tag{17}$$

The $\Delta C(.)$ in (17) will be computed by the post-optimality analysis with the additional constraints generated from the knowledge base. If $\Delta C(.)$ is acceptable to the decision maker for the upgrade of qualitative goals by Δq_M and Δq_G, the best solution has been found. If, however, $\Delta C(.)$ is too big to accept, the decision maker may set a limit on ΔC (for instance, $50,000) and may want to see how much Δq can be upgraded within that limit. For example, the MRS like (18) can be asked.

$$\Delta q_M(\Delta C = 50,000 \mid q_G = \text{GOOD}) \tag{18}$$

To compute $\Delta q_M(.)$ in (18), the goal programming model can be used as illustrated in the model (53)-(57). Once the solution is found, the qualitative objectives are evaluated with the solution. Since the $\Delta C = 50,000$ may be reduced to some extent while maintaining the currently obtained qualitative goals, the mininum ΔC will be pursued as the next step. This step is called the Upward Adjustment Process [8]. An example of Upward Adjustment can be found in the step 10 of next section. By providing the types of MRSs in (11) - (16), the decision making via tradeoffs can be supported effectively.

4.4. Data Management System

The data base includes two groups of data: one necessary for the formulation of a linear programming model, the other for the knowledge-based system.

Data for the Formulation of Linear Programming Model The necessary data includes product titles, processing time per unit, demand forecast, inventory carrying cost, hiring cost, and so on. To generate the relevant data for the planning period, the data should have been identified by the time. For example, suppose the first model is formulated for the year 1986. To use the same model for the year 1987, the data set of the first model should be updated, though the structure of model is sustained.

Data for Knowledge-based System To provide the data for the knowledge-based system, three types of data should be maintained: fact, numeric, and OAV type. The OAV type is well matched with the structure of a relational data base. "Object" corresponds to the tuple, "Attribute" to attribute, and "Value" to one of predefined candidate values as shown in Fig 5(a). The fact type and numeric type data, however, may be stored in a record form as illustrated in Fig 5 (b)-(c).

5. ILLUSTRATIVE DIALOGUE

This section illustrates the IPPS with a numeric example.

type attribute		Work Environment	Payment Level
Gold Star Co.	. . .	GOOD	Competitive

(a) OAV Type Data in Relational Form

Overall economy is good	True
Labor turnover is serious	False

(b) Fact Type Data

Average backlog	< =	800
Average salary	=	25,000
Competitive average salary	=	23,000

(c) Numeric Type Data

Figure 5
Three Types of Data for Knowledge-base System

(1) Preparation of Knowledge Base

The prototypical knowledge base consists of 33 rules for employee's morale and 54 rules for customer's goodwill. One should refer to the judgment functions in (8)-(9) in order not to miss relevant rules.

(2) Automatic Formulation

The Aggregate Production Planning model is generated via the following dialogs. The user's responses are in italic, and comments follow semicolons.

(3) Obtain the optimal feasible solution of (19)-(46).

Cost = \$259,537.2

```
* Title of items
    refrigerator
    heater
* Starting time (mon/year)
    Jan/1987
* Interval (months)
    3
* Ending time (mon/year)
    Dec/1987
* Modeling Policy
    Inventory allowed ? (Y or N)
    Y
    Limit                              ; Example of Limit
    refrigerator : 100
    heater : 100
    Overtime allowed ? (Y or N)
    Y
    Firing allowed ? (Y or N)
    Y
    Hiring allowed ? (Y or N)
    Y
    Backlog allowed ? (Y or N) Y
    Safety stock cannot be arranged.    ; Deduced statement
* AUTOMATIC FORMULATION in PROCESS!
    Data Base does not have the following data.
    Enter the ending inventory in Dec 1987
    0
```

* FORMULATION GENERATED

LOOK ? (Y or N)

   Y

$$X_{1j} = \text{refrigerator}$$

X_{2j} = heater

Minimize Z =

$8X_{11} + 8X_{12} + 8X_{13} + 8X_{14}$
$+ .5X_{21} + .5X_{22} + .5X_{23} + .5X_{24}$
$+ .7I^{+}_{11} + .7I^{+}_{12} + .7I^{+}_{13}$
$+ .2I^{+}_{21} + .2I^{+}_{21} + .2I^{+}_{23}$
$+ .5\Gamma_{11} + .5\Gamma_{12} + .5\Gamma_{13}$
$+ .1\Gamma_{21} + .1\Gamma_{22} + .1\Gamma_{23}$
$+ 1.0W_{1} + 1.0W_{2} + 1.0W_{3} + 1.0W_{4}$
$+ 1.5O_{1} + 1.5O_{2} + 1.5O_{3} + 1.5O_{4}$
$+ 7.0H_{1} + 5.0H_{2} + 5.0H_{3} + 5.5H_{4}$
$+ .5F_{1} + .5F_{2} + .5F_{3} + .5F_{4}$;(19)

subject to

$X_{11} - I^{+}_{11} + \Gamma_{11} = 2799$;(20)
$X_{12} + I^{+}_{11} - \Gamma_{11} - I^{+}_{12} + \Gamma_{12} = 4000$;(21)
$X_{13} + I^{+}_{12} - \Gamma_{12} - I^{+}_{13} + \Gamma_{13} = 4500$;(22)
$X_{14} + I^{+}_{13} - \Gamma_{13} = 1000$;(23)
$X_{21} - I^{+}_{21} + \Gamma_{21} = 7000$;(24)
$X_{22} + I^{+}_{21} - \Gamma_{21} - I^{+}_{22} + \Gamma_{22} = 100$;(25)
$X_{23} + I^{+}_{22} - \Gamma_{22} - I^{+}_{23} + \Gamma_{23} = 1000$;(26)
$X_{24} + I^{+}_{23} - \Gamma_{23} = 7000$;(27)
$5X_{11} + .5X_{21} - W_{1} - O_{1} 0$;(28)
$5X_{12} + .5X_{22} - W_{2} - O_{2} 0$;(29)
$5X_{13} + .5X_{23} - W_{3} - O_{3} 0$;(30)
$5X_{14} + .5X_{24} - W_{3} - O_{3} 0$;(31)
$W_{1} - H_{1} + F_{1} = 1000$;(32)
$-W_{1} + W_{2} - H_{2} + F_{2} = 0$;(33)
$-W_{2} + W_{3} - H_{3} + F_{3} = 0$;(34)
$-W_{3} + W_{4} - H_{4} + F_{4} = 0$;(35)
$-.2W_{1} + O_{1} 0$;(36)
$-.2W_{2} + O_{2} 0$;(37)
$-.2W_{3} + O_{3} 0$;(38)
$-.2W_{4} + O_{4} 0$;(39)
$I^{+}_{11} 100$;(40)
$I^{+}_{12} 100$;(41)
$I^{+}_{13} 100$;(42)
$I^{+}_{21} 100$;(43)

$$
\begin{aligned}
&I^+_{22}\ 100 &&;(44)\\
&I^+_{23}\ 100 &&;(45)\\
&X_{it},\ I^+_{it},\ \Gamma_{it},\ W_t,\ O_t\ 0\ i=1,2 &&;(46)\\
&\qquad\qquad\qquad t=1,2,3,4
\end{aligned}
$$

(3) Obtain the optimal feasible solution of (19)-(46).
Cost = \$259,537.2

Variables	Values	Variables	Values
X_{12}	4053.0	W_1	1000.0
X_{13}	4423.0	W_2	18845.8
X_{14}	3823.0	W_3	18845.8
X_{21}	2400.0	O_1	200.0
X_{22}	4700.0	O_2	3769.2
X_{23}	1000.0	O_3	3769.2
X_{24}	7000.0		
		H_2	17845.8
Γ_{11}	2799.0		
Γ_{12}	2746.0	F_4	18845.8
Γ_{13}	2823.0		
Γ_{21}	4600.0		

(4) Evaluate the current solution using the knowledge base.
The result with the current solution is :

Goodwill on refrigerator is BAD.
Goodwill on heater is BAD.
Morale is BAD.

(5) The current qualitative goals are unsatisfactory.

Suppose the decision maker wants to improve employee's morale to "VERY GOOD" level by the following dialog:

Do you want to improve ?
    Goodwill on refrigerator BAD
    Goodwill on heater   BAD
    | Employee's morale   BAD | ; Statement in the
                                      ; box is selected
    Target of improvement
    VERY GOOD
    GOOD
    UNDETERMINED
    BAD
    VERY BAD

Then the PMA Controller generates additional constraints in (47)- (48) by interpreting the condition of employee's morale to be "VERY GOOD".

$$\sum_{t=1}^{4} O_t <= 5{,}000 \qquad (47)$$

$$\sum_{t=1}^{4} F_t <= 3{,}000 \qquad (48)$$

(6) The opportunity cost is computed.

$$\Delta C(\ \Delta q_M = \text{VERY GOOD - BAD}\ ) = \$10{,}969.4 \qquad (49)$$

Suppose this opportunity cost is acceptable.

(7) Repeat the same procedure for goodwill.

The opportunity cost of goodwill on refrigerator is

$$\Delta C(\Delta q_{Gr} = \text{VERY GOOD - BAD} \mid q_M = \text{VERY GOOD})$$
$$= \$5{,}693.7$$

because of the additional constraint in (50):

$$\sum_{t=1}^{4} \Gamma_{1t} <= 1{,}500.0 \qquad (50)$$

(8) In the same way, the opportunity cost of goodwill on heater is

$$\Delta C(\, \Delta q_{Gh} = \text{VERY GOOD - BAD} \,|$$
$$q_{Gr} = \text{VERY GOOD, } q_M = \text{VERY GOOD} \,)$$
$$= \$6{,}137.8$$

because of the additional constraint in (51):

$$\sum_{t=1}^{4} \Gamma^{-}_{2t} \,< \,= 700 \tag{51}$$

(9) If the decision maker cannot accept the opportunity cost, he may ask "WHY".

Then the knowledge-based system can show the rules used to infer q_{Gh} = VERY GOOD. Suppose the decision maker would like to set the bound on $\Delta C(.)$ and wants to see the $\Delta q_{Gh}(.)$ in (52):

$$\Delta q_{Gh}\, (\, \Delta C = 6{,}000 \,|\, q_{Gr} = \text{VERY GOOD,}$$
$$q_M\; = \text{VERY GOOD}) \tag{52}$$

The $\Delta q_{Gh}(.)$ can be computed by the following goal programming model in (20) - (48), (50) and (53) - (57).

$$\text{Minimize } Z = d^{-}_2 \tag{53}$$

subject to

$$8X_{11} + 8X_{12} + 8X_{13} + 8X_{14}$$
$$+ .5X_{21} + .5X_{22} + .5X_{23} + .5X_{24}$$
$$+ .7I^{+}_{11} + .7I^{+}_{12} + .7I^{+}_{13}$$
$$+ .2I^{+}_{21} + .2I^{+}_{21} + .2I^{+}_{23}$$
$$+ .5\Gamma_{11} + .5\Gamma_{12} + .5\Gamma_{13}$$
$$+ .1\Gamma_{21} + .1\Gamma_{22} + .1\Gamma_{23}$$
$$+ 1.0W_1 + 1.0W_2 + 1.0W_3 + 1.0W_4$$
$$+ 1.5O_1 + 1.5O_2 + 1.5O_3 + 1.5O_4$$
$$+ 7.0H_1 + 5.0H_2 + 5.0H_3 + 5.5H_4$$
$$+ .5F_1 + .5F_2 + .5F_3 + .5F_4\; 282{,}200.3 \tag{54}$$
$$\Gamma_{21} + \Gamma_{22} + \Gamma_{23} + \Gamma_{24} + d^{+}_2 - d^{-}_2 = 700 \tag{55}$$

$$X_{it}, I^+_{it}, \Gamma_{it}, W_t, O_t \; 0 \; i = 1,2 \tag{56}$$
$$d^+_2, d^-_2 \; 0 \; t = 1,2,3,4 \tag{57}$$
and (20)-(48) and (50).

The right hand side (RHS) value 282,200.3 in (54) is the sum of the mini-mized cost in Step 3 and the accumulated opportunity costs. Interestingly, at the optimal feasible solution of the above goal programming model, d^-_2 is 136.2. This implies that $\sum^4_{t=1} \Gamma_{2t} = 836.2$, so q_{Gh} is GOOD according to the evaluation by the rules in knowledge base. Therefore the qualitative evaluation of the solution is as follows.

> Goodwill on refrigerator is VERY GOOD
> Goodwill on heater is GOOD
> Morale is VERY GOOD

(10) The next step is the Upward Adjustment Process
[8], [10] which obtains the minimum C without deteriorating the current level of qualitative goals. According to the rules, the upper bound of stockouts for q_{Gh} = GOOD is 2,500. To find the minimum ΔC which maintains q_{Gh} = GOOD, the model (19) - (48), (50) and (58) can be used.

$$\sum^4_{t=1} \Gamma_{2t} <= 2,500 \tag{58}$$

In this case,
$$\Delta C(\Delta q_{Gh} = GOOD - BAD \mid q_{Gr} = VERY\ GOOD, q_M = VERY\ GOOD)$$
$$= \$5,291.8.$$
Therefore the Full Opportunity Cost, which is the sum of three Incremen-tal Opportunity Costs [8], is

$$\Delta C(q_M = VERY\ GOOD, q_{Gh} = GOOD,$$
$$q_{Gr} = VERY\ GOOD)$$
$$= 10,969.4 + 5,693.7 + 5,291.7 = \$21,954.8.$$

(11) Assume that the current solution is acceptable from the point of both qualitative goals and the opportunity cost.
Then the best solution is found. The current solution and goals achieved can be summarized as follows:

Cost = $281,492
Goodwill on refrigerator is VERY GOOD
Goodwill on heater is GOOD
Morale is VERY GOOD
Full Opportuunity Cost = $21,954.8

Variables	Value	Variables	Value
X_{11}	2851.8	W_1	15955.7
X_{12}	3829.4	W_2	15955.7
X_{13}	3235.6	W_3	15955.7
X_{14}	2382.2	W_4	12955.7
X_{21}	6566.7		
X_{24}	8533.3	O_1	1586.8
		O_2	3191.1
I^+_{11}	52.8	O_3	222.0
I^-_{12}	117.8	H_1	14955.7
I^-_{13}	1382.2		
I^-_{21}	433.3	F_4	3000.0
I^-_{22}	533.3		
I^-_{23}	1533.3		

6. CONCLUSION

Using the optimization model and rules in the knowledge base, the Post-Model Analysis Approach solved the Aggregate Production Planning problem. Though the knowledge in the prototypical IPPS is not complete at this moment, more realistic knowledge can be organized for a specific company. The Aggregate Production Planning is not the only problem that can use the PMA approach. The PMA approach has a great deal of application potential, because the PMA can be used as a framework of integrating quantitative factors with qualitative factors by combining the optimization models with knowledge-based system.

REFERENCES

[1] Bhatnagar, S. C., "Implementing Linear Programming in a Textile Unit : Some Problems and a Solution", *Interfaces*, Vol. 11, No. 2, April, 1981, pp. 87 - 91.

[2] Boskma, K., "Aggregation and the Design of Models for Medium-term Planning of Production", *European Journal of Operational Research*, Vol. 10, 1982, pp. 244 - 249.

[3] Hax, Arnoldo C. and Dan Candea, *Production and Inventory Management*, Englewood Cliffs, Prentice-Hall, Inc., 1984.

[4] Oliff, Michanel D. and G. Keong Leong, "A Discrete Production Switching Rule for Aggregate Planning", forthcoming in *Decision Sciences*

[5] Rakes, Terry R., Lori S. Franz and A. James Wynne, "Aggreagate Production Using Chance-Constrained Goal Programming", *International Journal of Production Research*, Vol. 22, No. 4, 1984. pp. 673 - 684.

[6] Verhoeven, Kees J., "Corporate Manpower Planning", *European Journal of Operational Research*, Vol. 7., No. 4, 1981, pp. 341 - 344.

[7] Lee, Jae K., "Solving Semi-Structured Problem and the Design of Decision Supporting Systems : Post-Model Analysis Approach", Ph. D. Dissertation, Department of Decision Sciences, The Wharton School, University of Pennsylvania, 1985.

[8] Lee, Jae K. and E. Gerald Hurst, Jr., "Multiple Criteria Decision Making Including Qualitative Factors : The Post-Model Analysis Approach", forthcoming in *Decision Sciences*, 1987.

[9] Lee, Jae K. and Ho G. Lee, "Integration of Strategic Planning and Short-term Planning : An Intelligent DSS Approach by the Post- Model Analysis Approach", forthcoming in *Decision Support Systems*, 1987.

[10] Lee, Jae K. and Min S. Shin, Woong K. Lee, "The Integration of Optimization with Rule-based System by the Post-Model Analysis Approach", Working Paper, Department of Management Science, Korea Advanced Institute of Science and Technology, 1986.

[11] Orlikowski, Wanda and Vasant Dhar ," Imposing Structure on Linear Programming Problems", An Empirical Analysis of Expert and Novice Models, Graduate School of Business Administration, New York University, 1986.

[12] Binbasioglu M. and Jarke M., "Domain Specific DSS Tools for Knowledge Based Model Building", *Decision Support Systems*, 1986, pp. 213 - 223.

[13] Murphy, Frederic H. and Edward A. Stohr, " An Intelligent System for Formulating Linear Programming", *Decision Support Systems*, Vol. 2, No. 1, 1986, pp. 39-47.

Applied Expert Systems, E. Turban and P.R. Watkins (Editors)
© Elsevier Science Publishers B.V. (North-Holland), 1988

AN EXPERT SYSTEM FOR R&D PROJECTS

R. Balachandra

Associate Professor
College of Business Administration
Northeastern University
Boston, MA 02115

This paper describes the development and application of a rule based expert system in the area of R&D project management. The system looks at the specific decision of whether to continue or terminate an on-going R&D project, particularly during the development stage. The rules were developed from a data base of over 100 R&D projects from a wide variety of firms using the ID3 algorithm. The procedure was applied through a commercially microbased software expert system shell called 1stCLASS.

1. INTRODUCTION

Managing R&D projects is complex as it involves decisions based on subjective evaluations of a large number of variables. It involves getting new projects started, evaluating them to determine the fit with the firm's goals, monitoring their progress to decide whether to continue or terminate them, and finally to transfer the results of the projects to the manufacturing or other groups to introduce into the market.

One of the most critical phases in this sequence is the development stage, where the project has been approved by the top management, and resources have been allocated for the development. There are still many uncertainties in accomplishing this - either from a technological, marketing or environmental perspective. An important decision during this stage is whether to continue funding the project or to terminate it, thereby releasing resources for other more promising projects. This paper focuses on the issues of monitoring an ongoing R&D project during the development stage to arrive at the termination decision. It further describes the development and implementation of an expert system to aid in the monitoring process.

The application of artificial intelligence techniques to many management problems is growing rapidly with the increasing sophistication of computer programs, higher power of desk top computers, and the pervasive presence of

PCs in many managers' offices. Artificial intelligence techniques range from simple rule based systems to more complex learning systems which improve their performance with more experience. Monitoring R&D projects is a situation requiring a high degree of expertise, and therefore an ideal candidate for the application of expert system techniques.

2. R&D PROJECTS

There is no unique process for the start and completion of commercial R&D projects. However, some common stages have been observed in their starting and completion. The following brief description is a generalized sequence of stages.

Commercial R&D Projects usually start as an idea. The idea could be from any number of sources - marketing, engineering, R&D itself, or from the chief executive. The idea is explored initially for its economic feasibility and market attractiveness on an informal basis. If it is found to be reasonably attractive and if it is in the general line of business that the firm is interested in, a more systematic study may be attempted to evaluate the market potential, technological feasibility and economic aspects.

If the results of this more formal study are consistent with the business objectives of the firm, and if the projected returns from the successful commercialization of the project exceed the investment hurdle rates for the organization, appropriate budget will be allocated. Time schedules will be set and benchmarks will be developed. A project team will be assembled and a project leader appointed. At the time of approval of the project for development the assessments of the probability of success (both technical and commercial) for the project tend to be generally optimistic. Otherwise, the project may not be funded. As the project progresses, the assessments may be revised. Such revisions may be due to changes in a number of factors - in the market, in the technology, and even in the organization itself. In view of such changes, the project may sometimes have to be terminated, even though it was started with a great deal of optimism. For a more complete description of the various stages refer to any standard books on R&D management (Blake [1], Gibson [2]).

The problem of project termination is critical. By unnecessarily prolonging a project doomed to failure the organization wastes valuable resources, and deprive itself of opportunities in other promising areas. On the other hand, terminating a project which could have succeeded may result in the loss of a significant market opportunity.

Very few systematic studies have been made to establish the critical elements for monitoring the progress of a project. However, Balachandra [3] reported on a number of GO/NOGO signals for the success of a new product innovation.

Balachandra and Raelin [4] suggested a set of variables for monitoring the progress of an R&D project during the development phase.

Both studies relied on a limited number of factors which were derived through a discriminant analysis of a large number of variables from a sufficiently large sample. About 14 variables were found to be critical in these studies. A simple rating method for these variables was suggested to minimize the problems of scaling subjective variables. A scheme was developed using these variables to form a decision rule for the terminate/continue decision of an R&D project in its development stage.

Although the procedure produces good results it is not easily implemented. Since only 14 factors are used in the monitoring system, some factors which did not appear to be important, may play a significant role, but may not be captured by the system. Additionally, even though there may be a significant change in a key variable, the system will require that all variables be evaluated to reach a conclusion.

An expert system provides a viable alternative for monitoring R&D projects. If a key variable changes significantly, the system is more likely to capture this information to provide the appropriate decision. The next section describes the main features of an expert system.

3. EXPERT SYSTEMS

Expert Systems are one facet of Artificial Intelligence techniques, consisting of a set of rules to be applied to a given decision situation to arrive at a decision similar to one made by an expert in the field. Some well known examples are MYCIN for medical diagnosis, and XCON for designing configuration of computer systems based on a customer's specific needs (Harmon [5]).

The development of expert systems for a given situation usually follows one of two methods. The first method consists of intensive discussions with experts in the area to derive implicit rules the experts use in arriving at conclusions. So called Knowledge Engineers work with the experts in defining the problem and developing the rules. Consistency checks are applied to remove ambiguities and internal contradictions. The resulting set of rules are then coded using one of the AI languages, such as LISP, PROLOG or one of the expert system shells which allow one to write the rules in everyday English. The examples cited in the preceding paragraph were developed using this procedure. As can be deduced, such a process of developing an expert system is very time consuming and expensive.

The second method is to study a large number of cases where the expert or the decision maker has drawn specific conclusions. The underlying rules used by the expert can be inferred by applying some learning procedures. These procedures start with some initial assumptions about how the variables are combined to yield the result. With the addition of new examples, the procedure modifies the assumptions to fit the new examples. Finally, the procedure derives a set of rules to explain the expert's conclusions.

This method assumes that the expert has applied the rules consistently, and that there are sufficient number of examples to cover all possible combinations of conditions. A number of algorithms have been developed for deriving expert systems using the learning procedures. ID3 algorithm, developed by Quinlan [6] is widely used. Gallant [7] has developed another procedure called MACIE, which starts with equal weights for the variables, and updates them with the results from new examples.

In this paper, we use the second method of deriving rules from examples. The algorithm used is the ID3 algorithm as implemented by a commercial program called 1stCLASS [8].

4. EXPERT SYSTEM FOR R&D PROJECT MONITORING

As discussed above, one of the critical phases in the life of an R&D project is the development stage. During this stage large amounts of money would have been committed for the successful development of the project's idea, which has been technically proved to be feasible. There usually are a number of technical details that have to be worked out to make it a commercial success. Management has to constantly monitor the project during this period, especially when there are market imposed deadlines.

The earlier study [4] looked at over 100 projects during their development stage. These projects were all commercial projects, initiated by the firms with a view to add the outcomes to their product/process portfolio. None of these were sponsored projects, where the decision to continue or terminate is not usually in the hands of the firm.

The sample projects were studied in detail and information about more than 70 variables were collected for each. Some of the variables were evaluated at two points in time - one at the time of the latest review, where a decision was made to terminate or continue, and the second at the time of the previous review. Such information helped in highlighting the changes that took place in the interval. It was hypothesized, and later confirmed, that the changes in some variables are more important in the decision to terminate or continue, than their absolute values.

There are a number of Expert System shells available in the market, which can take information of the type described above, and deduce the underlying rules. However, there is a serious problem in converting the data to the form needed by these systems. We considered two systems for this application   -

EXPERTEASE and 1stCLASS. (For a description of these two and other systems please see Harmon [5]). Both use the ID3 algorithm, and operate somewhat similarly. Both have some limitations about the number of variables to be used and the number of cases.

The ID3 algorithm breaks the examples into groups such that each case is at the end of one branch of a decision tree, where the branches are the relevant factors. The factors are selected to achieve the most progress towards completing the decision tree. If the variables are categorical, the algorithm will try to find examples to fit each of the categories. Since it is not possible to have examples to fit each category of all variables, it is not uncommon to find a number of end points in the decision tree with no actual examples. In such a decision tree each branch (starting from the root and ending at a node) represents a rule. A decision tree, therefore, is a comprehensive representation of a whole series of rules.

The ID3 algorithm selects the most important or discriminating factors in its choice for incorporating into the decision tree. It also ignores factors that are not necessary to reach a decision. In this characteristic it is similar to the classical discriminant analysis. But unlike the discriminant analysis, the ID3 algorithm will fit all the examples provided into the decision tree. Thus, the classification rate for the examples with the ID3 algorithm is always 100 % of the cases, whereas discriminant analysis can produce classification rates of much less than 100 %.

4.1. Developing the Decision Tree

The decision tree for a specific situation is developed using the cases in the sample, and the appropriate variables and their data. The 1stCLASS system accepts these data, and a decision rule is derived. A number of alternative methods are available for generating the decision rule.

In the most general case, one could specify that an optimum rule be generated. In this method, the variables are chosen according to their power of classification, irrespective of their order in the variable list. This is the preferred method where one is not sure about the relative importance of the variables, and one does not want to prejudge their importance. One could also specify that the variables be chosen in a particular order. This is called the left-to-right rule, where the variables are listed left-to-right in order of decreasing importance. This implies that the analyst has a prior understanding of the importance of the variables. A third method, called the customizing method, allows one to build a rule from scratch, without deriving it from the data. This method is preferred when the data is limited in size, and the variables are too many.

For this study, we decided to use the optimizing method as there was a sufficiently large number of examples, and the number of variables was not too large. Even with the optimizing or the left-to-right rule, one can always customize and make some changes if the rule does not seem right or if there are too many end points without actual examples. This step may be necessary in situations where there are not enough cases. Some nodes in such situations will have a 'no data' outcome. This means that there were no examples corresponding to that branch in the sample. In such cases, the analyst can use judgment to provide an outcome for such a branch. Customizing the tree this way will help in providing a specific conclusion (including undecidable) for any given set of variables. Of course, great care and judgment should be exercised in providing these outcomes.

To increase the accuracy of the rules and their predictability, it is preferable to split the sample into two halves, develop the rules using one half of the sample, and test them against the remaining half. If the rules perform well with the second half of the sample, then the derived rules can be accepted as reliable. We tried this approach in this study. Out of the total of 114 cases, only 57 were used to develop the rules. The rules were then tested on the remaining 57. The results of these tests are reported later in this paper. Other fractions could be used to derive the rules and to test them. The efficacy and the reliability of a rule generally increases with the number of unused cases tested by the rule.

The size of the problem can be a serious limitation. The 1stCLASS program can handle a maximum of 256 examples. The number of variables is also limited to 32. The limitation on variables can be overcome by a simple strategy of developing a series of chained modules.

Since the number of variables in the study exceeded 70, which is far beyond the capability of either of the expert system development tools (EXPERTISE and 1STCLASS), the tools could not be applied directly. It was therefore decided to apply a chaining procedure.

4.2. Chaining of Modules

In the chaining procedure, the model is broken into smaller problems. Each sub problem has a final outcome. The outcome for the subproblem is decided on the basis of the variables relevant to that subproblem and its decision tree. The outcomes from many subproblems could then be entered as variables for a higher level problem. Thus, if the main problem had 100 variables, this can be broken into ten subproblems, each with 10 variables. The resulting outcomes or decisions from these ten subproblems will be the inputs for the final problem. The sub problems themselves can have lower level sub-sub problems. In the two expert system tools mentioned earlier, there is no practical limit to the number of levels of chaining for any problem, as long as each level conforms to the variable and case limits. Since the final system basically uses the same information, albeit in a hierarchical manner, the relationships and the interactions between the factors are maintained.

If the breakdown of the main problem could be accomplished in a logical manner, it will contribute towards making the system more powerful and understandable. The subproblems themselves could be used to draw some useful conclusions.

In the current study, the 70 variables encompassed a number of distinct aspects of the R&D project in different areas. After detailed study of these variables, and with an understanding of the development stage of R&D projects, four major groups of variables were identified. These groups of variables reflect the characteristics of the R&D project in different dimensions.

The four groups of variables are as follows:

1. Technological Strength of project

2. Market Strength of project and firm

3. R&D Environment of the firm

4. Characteristics of project staff

Previous studies ([3],[4]) have shown that the success of an R&D project essentially depends upon the above four aspects. A project should have a strong and realizable technology; the market should be ready to absorb the outcome of the project, and the firm should have the marketing capability to exploit the market; the R&D environment in the firm or division should be capable of providing the appropriate support for successfully completing the project; and finally, the project staff should be motivated and committed to the project to complete it in time.

The remaining variables which did not fit into one of these categories were kept separate. The final model included these variables, as well as the outcome from the four groups above.

The model would therefore work as follows. First the project will be evaluated for the four groups listed above (Technological Strength, Market Strength, R&D Environment and Project Staff characteristics). The results of these evaluations would be in the form of a rating on a nominal scale. These results and the remaining variables will then be chained into the final module for the evaluation of the project. Figure 1 shows the schematic of this process.

In the following paragraphs each of the individual modules, as well as the final module will be described.

4.3. The Four Sub Modules

Technological Strength of Project (TST1). This module evaluates the technological strength of the project. Technological strength pertains to the relative merits of the technological component of the project. It will indicate how current the technology is, and whether the technology is attainable in the given time frame.

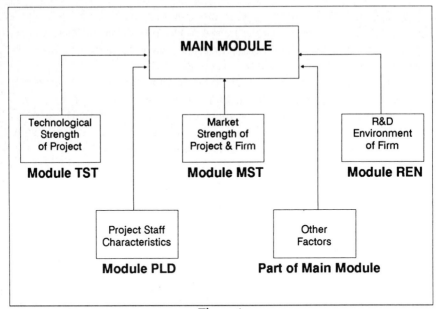

Figure 1
Schematic of Expert System for R&D Projects

The variables included for this evaluation have been carefully chosen to be representative tivetivetivetivetiveof the technological strength. Some examples of these variables include - Probability of achieving commercial success, Probability of achieving technical success, smoothness of the technological route being followed, lifecycle stage of the product/process under development and other similar variables. Some of the variables are evaluated on a nominal scale of 1 to 5, while some others as a number. Some are subjectively estimated. For example, the expected time for competition to come up with a similar product is entered as the number of months, while the smoothness of the technological route being followed is expressed on a scale of 1 to 5, where 1 represents a route that is highly uncertain with many complications in pursuing the technology, and 5 represents a relatively smooth technological route.

The final evaluation is on a scale of 1 to 5, where 5 represents excellent technological strength. The decision tree resulting from this module is shown in Figure 2. The decision tree has 41 branches. An example of one rule derived from the decision tree (shown in dark line in Figure 2) is as follows:

If Technological route (TECHROUTE) is smooth (4 or more)

- Time for competition to enter market (COMPTIME) is less than 27 months

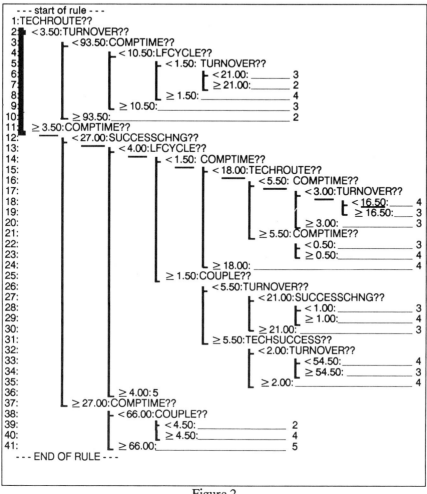

Figure 2

Decision Tree for Technological Strength

- Change in Probability of Technical Success (SUC-CESSCHNG) is less than 4
- Life cycle stage (LFCYCLE) is less than 1.5 (infancy)
- Time for competition to enter market (COMPTIME) is less than 18 months
- Technological route (TECHROUTE) is very smooth (5 or more)

- Time for competition to enter market (COMPTIME) is less than 3 months
- New products are entering the market (TURNOVER) at an interval of 16 months or less

Then the Technological Strength of the project (TST1) is 4.

The rule demonstrates that the ID3 algorithm can derive fairly complex rules. It should also be noticed that a variable (COMPTIME) can appear more than once in a decision rule.

Market Strength of project and firm (MST1). This module evaluates the market strength of the project, and the relative market strength of the firm. Market strength pertains to the relative strength of the outcome of the project to successfully enter and capture the planned market share, and the firm's ability to accomplish such market penetration within the planned time frame. It takes into account factors such as the size of the firm (both sales and number of employees), the profitability, strength of external competition, anticipated market share for the outcome of the project and other similar variables. As in the technological strength module, some of the variables require actual numbers to be entered. The result of the decision tree is in the form of a rating on a scale of 0 to 5. The decision tree for the market strength module has 61 branches.

R&D Environment of the Firm (REN1). This module evaluates the R&D environment within the firm. It attempts to capture how supportive the R&D department is towards new projects in general, and this project in particular. Stronger R&D environment leads to a greater probability of successful completion of the project. This module considers such aspects as Top Management support for the project, size of the R&D department (budget and personnel), number of projects in the portfolio, availability of expertise, availability of capital for the new project, presence of a project champion and other similar variables. The result of this module is also expressed as a rating between 0 and 5. The decision tree for this module has 45 branches.

Project Staff Characteristics (PLD1). This module considers the project staff and its leader. It evaluates the effectiveness of the project team in terms of motivation and commitment of the members of the team as well as the project leader. Some of the variables considered by this module are the influence of the project leader, his adaptability, the project staff commitment towards the project, and the pressure experienced by the project leader. This decision tree has a 33 branches and the outcome reflecting the effectiveness of the project staff is rated on a scale of 0 to 5.

4.4. The Main Module:

The remaining variables, and the results of the four sub modules are incorporated into the main module. The decision tree for the main module is shown in Figure 3. It has over 100 branches. It includes a number of variables such as alliance with corporate goals, the budget allocated to the project, meeting of cost and time schedules, number of end uses planned for the project, and the outcomes from the four sub modules (shown in the decision tree as TST1, MST1, REN1, and PLD1).

The outcomes of this module take on only two values, Continue or Stop (2 or 1 in the decision tree). Although the number of steps to reach the outcome in the decision tree appear to be small, it must be remembered that each of the outcomes of the sub modules is itself the end of a fairly long branch.

This decision tree was tested on the remaining unused examples to determine the accuracy of the expert system. It was found that the rules from the

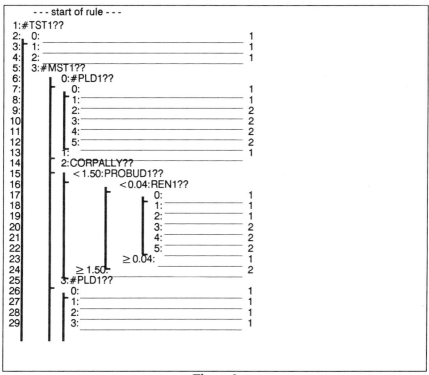

Figure 3
Partial Decision Tree for R&D Project Monitoring

decision tree were able to correctly classify 40 out of 57 cases not used in developing the decision tree (70 %). As a comparison, a discriminant analysis using all 114 cases classified 92% of the cases correctly. When a split sample approach was used the classification rate fell to less than 70%. This shows that the decision rule developed here is reasonably accurate, but needs to be examined carefully.

An issue that can be raised here is whether 70% classification rate is acceptable? It would appear that this classification rate is low. But on careful consideration of the decision situation in R&D projects, this is not unreasonable. With many subjective factors playing a major role, and with rapid changes in many of the important variables, it is a difficult area. There are innumerable examples of firms making expensive mistakes in this area, not because of lack of trying, but the information available is quite vague and highly subjective. Take for example, the case of Polaroid's Polavision - the instant movie system - which was given the go ahead and was developed at a cost of millions of dollars. It flopped as the technological strength of the project was very weak. (The video cassette recorders were just appearing on the scene).

After building the decision rules for the situation, we can now proceed to build the expert system advisor. With the decision trees at our disposal, it is a fairly simple matter to evaluate the variables in the branches of the tree and follow the branches depending on the values until a conclusion is reached. It is also simple to build a procedure, which asks the questions in a sequential manner as determined by the decision tree, and reach the conclusion. Detailed explanations can be provided for the variables and their values to enable an average user to respond to the questions. Such a system can be easily built in both 1stCLASS and EXPERTISE.

5. FURTHER RESEARCH

The system described in the foregoing paragraphs is a prototype. It has to be field tested to determine whether it has captured most of the nuances of an actual R&D project in the development stage.

A second study will be to compare the decision tree of the expert system with the results of a multivariate discriminant analysis. To a certain extent, the discriminant analysis identifies the significant variables and the weights assigned to them for effective discrimination. An expert system in the case described above does precisely the same thing. But depending on the values of the initial responses, the decision tree can be very short. In other words, one may reach a conclusion fairly rapidly if some of the key variables take on extreme values.

Discriminant analysis is typically a single step approach. When used as a classifying procedure, one has to supply values for all variables in the discriminant function to compute the discriminant value, on which to base the classification. On the other hand the expert system is a multi step approach. Some branches of the decision tree can be very short leading to a classification with very few responses. This happens usually when some of the key variables take on extreme values. An issue to be examined is whether the variables at the beginning of short branches in the expert system decision tree are the same with high discriminant function coefficients.

6. CONCLUSION

Expert systems for business applications is an emerging area. A number of such systems have been developed for fields where the cost of using a human expert can be very high. In areas where there is no expertise, systems can be developed which use actual data to derive the rules for making decisions. These decisions will correspond to what the firms had made in similar situations earlier, as they are based on previous experience. Looking at the rules derived from such systems, the analyst can modify them to reflect changes that will lead to better decisions.

The application described in this paper is an example of such a system. The system examines a number of actual cases and the corresponding decisions; a set of rules are derived from the data to best explain the decisions. Some of the rules are modified to account for changed circumstances or newer knowledge. The rules are then incorporated into an advisor system to take the user through a sequence of questions. The responses of the user can lead along different branches of a decision tree. Questions are asked until a final conclusion about the outcome is reached.

This paper describes the development of such an expert system for monitoring R&D projects. It uses one of the commercially available expert system development tools. Since the situation is more complex than what the tool can handle in a straight forward manner, the model was broken down into sub problems or sub modules. These sub modules were then integrated into a large comprehensive module. The actual variables used and the decision trees developed for each of the modules are described.

The advisor system using the expert system is also described and a sample session with the advisor system is illustrated. Some ideas for further research are identified and discussed.

REFERENCES

[1] Blake, Stewart P., *Managing for Responsive Research and Development.* San Francisco, CA: W.H. Freeman and Co., 1978.

[2]   Gibson, John E., *Managing Research and Development*, New York: John Wiley and Sons, 1981.

[3]   Balachandra, R., "Critical Signals for Making GO/NOGO Decisions in New Product Development," *Journal of Product Innovation Management*, (2) 92-100, 1984.

[4]   Balachandra R. and Joseph A. Raelin, " Should You Kill That High Tech R&D Project," *Research Management*, June 1984.

[5]   Harmon, Paul and David King, *Expert Systems*, New York: John Wiley and Sons, 1985.

[6]   Quinlan, J.R., "Learning Efficient Classification Procedures and their Application to Chess End Games." In *Machine Learning, An Artificial Intelligence Approach*, edited by R.S. Michalski, et al, pp. 461-482, Palo Alto: Tioga Publishing Co., 1983.

[7]   Gallant, S.I., "Automatic Generation of Expert Systems From Examples," *Proceedings of Second International Conference on Artificial Intelligence Applications*, IEEE Computer Society, Miami Beach, Florida, December 11-13, 1985.

[8]   Hapgood, William, *1stCLASS - It makes you an Expert Systems Expert*, Natick, Mass.: Programs In Motion, Inc., 1986.

Applied Expert Systems, E. Turban and P.R. Watkins (Editors)
© Elsevier Science Publishers B.V. (North-Holland), 1988

PEP: AN EXPERT SYSTEM
FOR PROMOTION MARKETING

Judy Bayer, Stephen Lawrence, and John W. Keon

Assistant Professor, Marketing & Industrial Administration
Graduate School of Industrial Administration
Carnegie-Mellon University
5000 Forbes Avenue
Pittsburgh, PA 15213

Assistant Professor,
Washington University
St. Louis, MO

President,
The Marketing Advantage, Inc.
71 Strawberry Hill Ave., Suite 709
Stamford, CT 06902

The authors describe PEP (Planning Expert Promotions), a rule-based marketing expert support system designed to investigate the planning of consumer sales promotion campaigns for mature consumer packaged goods. The system was designed to utilize information from multiple knowledge sources, including survey data collected from 34 promotion experts, and empirical information from scanner panel data. Knowledge is represented within PEP as production rules, analytic functions, and declarative parameters with associated measures of uncertainty. The current system's performance, measured as solving graduate school promotion marketing cases, is at the level of an MBA student in marketing.

1. INTRODUCTION

A research topic currently of interest to both marketing academics and practitioners is the development of Expert Systems for marketing domains. Successes in developing expert systems in medicine, mass spectrometry, geological exploration, and other areas have been impressive. If researchers are able to duplicate these successes in marketing, they will develop valuable managerial tools and advance our knowledge of marketing phenomena. The main purpose of this paper is to introduce an expert system developed for the marketing domain -- PEP (Planning Expert Promotions).

PEP is a rule-based marketing Expert System designed as an aid for planning consumer sales promotion campaigns for frequently purchased consumer branded package goods in established product categories. The need for such a system is significant. Every year American businesses spend more than $153 billion promoting branded consumer package goods (Marketing Communications 1986). These expenditures are divided between media advertising, trade promotions, and the fastest growing segment, consumer promotions, including rebates, coupons, sweepstakes, and cents-offs.

In 1964, approximately 4% of consumer package goods were being promoted at any given time -- by 1985, in some product categories sales promotions are accessible to consumers 100% of the time. The total value of consumer sales promotions currently exceeds $42 billion annually (Marketing Communications 1986) and is increasing rapidly. Aggravated by a dispersed base of expertise, multiple simultaneous objectives, and by rapid rotation of brand managers within and between companies, consumer promotion management is rapidly becoming a dominant problem for the managers of branded package goods.

In this paper, we first briefly review what an expert system is, present successful expert system applications, and discuss marketing expert systems currently under development. We then discuss the development and details of PEP.

Research goals for PEP are to:

Perform like an expert -- solve specific, complex, promotion planning problems with an ability equal to or better than a promotion marketing expert.

Create new knowledge of marketing phenomena -- codify current knowledge of promotion planning for use in a formal system, thereby accelerating the invention of new heuristics, the creation of new marketing theories, and the synthesis of multiple knowledge sources (Bayer [1]).

Develop exploratory methodology for codifying and synthesizing knowledge from non-traditional expert systems data sources (survey data and scanner data) into representations which can be used in an expert system.

2. EXPERT SYSTEMS

2.1. What is an Expert System?

A great deal of recent attention has been devoted to expert systems. Simply stated, an expert system is a computer system which, within a limited problem domain, can solve a problem with an expertise approximately equal to that of acknowledged human experts (Clifford, Jarke, Vassilious [2]). For a system to qualify as an expert system, the problem area must be both complex and require non-routine decision processes. Thus, a "hard" problem which can be completely and consistently solved with an algorithm is not suitable for solution by an expert system. An expert system must also have the ability to reason about its own reasoning (Brachman, et. al., [3]). That is, the system must be able to tell the user how it arrived at a certain conclusion. It can also update itself in terms of both new information and new decision rules. Thus it is natural for expert systems to be developed incrementally, on an ongoing basis, as learning about a problem progresses.

Other characteristics which differentiate expert systems from traditional data processing systems include the system architecture, the way knowledge is represented by the system, and the strategies used by the programs to accomplish their tasks. In expert systems, knowledge about the problem (the knowledge base), is typically separate from the formal rules of logic and the solution search strategy (the inference engine) which drives the program solution. This permits more efficient incremental system development (Nau [4]). Special search strategies have been developed within the Artificial Intelligence community to reduce the typically large problem search space. Many of these are analogous to traditional operations research methods. (For an excellent discussion of knowledge representation and search strategies, see Nau [4]. Stefik, et. al., [5] describes various types of system architectures used by builders of expert systems.)

2.2. Applications of Expert Systems

Expert systems have been successfully created in a variety of fields. Many of the systems solve diagnostic and treatment problems for limited classes of disease types in various areas of medicine (Pople [6]; Buchanan and Shortliffe [7]). It is worth noting that there are often well known causal (or at least strong empirical) associations between symptoms and diseases, and there is also a correct answer (or a set of correct answers where there is multiple disease diagnosis).

Hayes-Roth, Waterman and Lenat [8] discuss 10 types of expert system applications, many of which have relevance for marketing expert systems as illustrated below.

1. **Interpretation:** analysis of data to determine their meaning. For example, speech understanding and chemical structure analysis.

    Analyze competitor strategy based on an analysis of the competitor's advertising, PR announcements, etc.

2. **Diagnosis:** fault-finding in a system, or determination of a disease based on the interpretation of data.

    Determine the causes of new product failure.

3. **Monitoring:** interpreting signals continuously and setting off alarms when intervention is required; air traffic and patient monitoring.

   Monitor sales force; test market monitoring.

4. **Prediction:** inferring probable consequences of given situations.

   Predict new product success or failure.

5. **Planning:** designing actions.

   Plan media strategy, plan promotion campaigns.

6. **Design:** configuring objects under constraints.

   Design new products, packages.

7. **Debugging:** prescribing remedies for malfunctions.

   Prescribe remedies for inadequate store traffic in a retail location.

8. **Repair:** executing a plan to administer a prescribed remedy.

   Reposition products.

9. **Instruction:** diagnosing, debugging, and repairing student behavior.

   Train sales force.

10. **Control:** interpreting, predicting, repairing, and monitoring system behaviors.

    Conduct a test market.

2.3. Expert System Applications in Marketing

In marketing, non-propriety expert systems which either have been developed or are under development are found in the areas of:

- Consumer sales promotions (Bayer [1]; Bayer and Keon [9]; Keon and Bayer, [10]; Bayer and Lawrence [11]),
- advertising strategy (by Rangaswamy and Wind, at Wharton School of Business),
- media planning (by Arvind Sathi at Carnegie Mellon and A. Mitchell at University of Toronto)
- trade promotions (Ibraham and Lodish, 1983),
- market share analysis (Alpar [12]),
- marketing channels (by J. Mentzer and others at Virginia Polytech Institute),

- teaching marketing strategy (Cross, Foxman, and Sherrell [13]),
- analysis of marketing data (McCann 1986).

For marketing applications, however, there seem to be issues which are not only unresolved but they have not yet been thoroughly considered. (A discussion of these issues can be found in Bayer and Keon [9]).

3. PROMOTION MARKETING

3.1. Problem Space

The promotion marketing planning problem is conceptualized in Figure 1, in which the current state of a branded consumer product is transformed, by some operator, to a more desirable future state. The state of a product can be characterized by its various characteristics: i.e. current market share, level of consumer awareness, defensive position, etc. In order to improve the state of the product along some, or all, of these dimensions, brand manager responsible for a product chooses a promotion from a set of consumer sales promotions (operators). The application of promotion "operators" transforms the current state of the product market place to some new future state. Promotion planning thus bears similarity in many respects to the classic search problems long investigated in artificial intelligence and operations research.

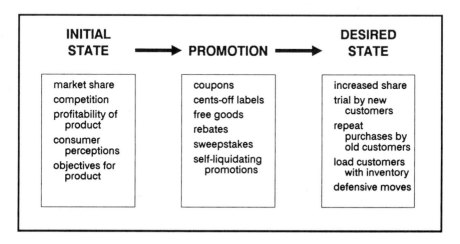

Figure 1
Promotions as Operators

However, the promotion planning problem is complicated by a number of factors. First, the search tree for the promotion planning problem is not very deep. Product managers seldom look more than one or two promotion campaigns into the future -- the promotion domain is too volatile to do otherwise. Competitors respond to the brand's promotions and initiate their own promotions -- thus making long term promotion planning unrealistic.

3.2. Search Space

Thus, instead of a deep search tree, the search tree for promotion planning is very broad. That is, the number of promotion vehicles is large, the possible values of the promotion deal is large, and the promotion can be applied to a wide variety of package sizes for the same product. For example, there are many varieties of promotions including various coupons (for example, free-standing-inserts and direct mail), cents-off deals, rebates, sweepstakes, and bonus packs. Once a particular promotion type is chosen (say a magazine coupon), the value of the coupon, the package size for which it is valid, the timing, and the duration of the promotion offer (if there is one stated) must all be considered. PEP in its present form primarily addresses promotion type and value decisions. In a broader sense, all decisions must be consistent with the goals of the promotion and the brand's competitive situation in the marketplace. Other factors of which developers of expert systems in marketing domains should be aware, which are described in Table 1, include 1) multiple operators, 2) exogenous factors, 3) multiple perspectives, 4) lack of causation, and 5) dispersed knowledge. PEP primarily addresses the last two issues.

Dispersed knowledge consists of three primary types:

1) **Experiential** -- privately held experiential knowledge held by expert practitioners, occasionally described in textbooks and practitioner literature.

Experiential expert knowledge can be efficiently represented as **production rules** (Davis, Buchanan and Shortliffe [14]). However, coding this information into a knowledge base is difficult because of the breadth of the search space. Individual promotion managers may have experience with only portions of the search space and a great deal of uncertainty often exists as to effects of promotions. This makes it desirable to collect information from multiple experts.

2) **Empirical** -- raw data, such as scanner data, collected based on purchasing behavior of consumers.

Empirical knowledge is **declarative** knowledge and can be represented either as isolated **facts** and **parameters** or transformed into implied production rules. Methodology has not, however, been developed by the expert systems research community to convert these raw empirical data into production rules with appropriate levels of uncertainty.

TABLE 1
Expert System Issues

- Multiple Operators. There are many independent players in the marketplace, each of whom will simultaneously be applying promotion operators to their own products for their own objectives. Unlike chess, competitors in consumer markets do not wait for opponents to complete their moves before countering.
- Exogenous Factors. Promotion planning exists in an open system. External factors outside of management control continuously impinge on the product marketplace. These include changes in consumer taste, government regulation, material costs, product innovation, and so forth. An additional level of factors, outside direct control but affected by management, include those related to the distribution channel -- wholesale and retail compliance.
- Lack of Causation. There exists little causal knowledge about the operation of promotions in the marketplace. Although there has been some work linking theory with promotion effects (see, for example, Dodson, Tybout and Sternthal [19]; Blattberg, Eppen, and Lieberman [20]; Rothschild and Gaidis [21]; Narasimhan [22]), available public knowledge is largely empirical and anecdotal.
- Multiple Perspectives. The focus of marketing is the exchange process -- everything that affects the interaction between the producer and the consumer. An expert promotion support system should accommodate both of these perspectives (Bayer and Keon [9]). This issue of on whom to focus -- producer or consumer -- may be unique to the marketing domain.
- Dispersed Knowledge. The knowledge that exists about promotions is dispersed among practicing brand managers, academic research studies, textbooks, and survey literature (e.g. Nielsen marketing surveys).

3) **Analytical** -- research studies that relate raw data to observed purchasing behavior in the marketplace, resulting in analytic statistical models.

Analytic knowledge can best be represented in the form of mathematical **algorithms**.

4. EXPERT SYSTEM DEVELOPMENT

4.1. Desired System Attributes

In developing PEP, a number of attributes were desired. (See Stefik, et. al., [5] and [15] for attributes of expert system development tools.) First, PEP must be able to deal with the different knowledge types described above. Second, PEP must accommodate uncertainty in an organized and efficient manner -- most statements about promotions must be heavily qualified, since few are known with certainty. Third, given the dispersed nature of knowledge in the domain of promotion planning, and in light of the multiple perspectives of the players in the domain, it is desirable that knowledge be easily partitioned allowing dispersed knowledge to be captured in an organized fashion. However, the architecture must concurrently make selected information available between partitions. Fourth, PEP must provide good explanation facilities. Both as a research tool and as an expert consultant, it is important that the reasoning processes of PEP be accessible to the user. Finally, it is desirable to use an expert system development tool that was publicly or commercially available.

After some review, it was decided to build PEP in an EMYCIN-derived language, *Texas Instruments' Personal Consultant,* running on a TI Professional Computer. EMYCIN (Buchanan and Shortliffe [14]; van Melle, Shortliffe and Buchanan [16]) is an Expert System shell which facilitates the Expert System development task by simplifying knowledge input and updating and by pre-structuring the system's inference mechanism. Using an EMYCIN based system, the knowledge engineer creates a modified production system where the problem can be separated into multiple, semi-cooperating subtasks. The characteristics of EMYCIN-type languages and their relation to the goals of PEP are described in more detail below.

1. KNOWLEDGE REPRESENTATION. Intrinsic to EMYCIN is the ability to represent the declarative, procedural, and analytic knowledge required by PEP. Declarative knowledge is simply represented within EMYCIN as parameters (variables). For example, within PEP there is a parameter, PROMOTION, which may take on values such as CENTS-OFF-PACK and DIRECT-MAIL-COUPON. Procedural knowledge is represented as production rules. An example of a production rule is illustrated in Figure 2. The third type of knowledge intrinsic to EMYCIN is analytic knowledge (mathematical algorithms) available in the form of LISP functions called by production rules. These functions can be mathematical models, statistical analysis routines, or calls to external databases.

2. UNCERTAINTY. Uncertainty is included in EMYCIN through the use of Certainty Factors associated with parameter values (Buchanan and Shortliffe [7]). Certainty factors (CF's) can range in value from -1000 (definitely not true) to +1000 (definitely true). For example, the parameter PROMOTION above might have a value CENTS-OFF-PACK (CF 750) indicating strong evidence for a cents-off-pack promotion. A value of DIRECT-MAIL-COUPON (CF -250) indicates weak negative evidence for promoting with direct-mail-coupons. Production rules exploit certainty factors to control the firing (triggering) of rules, and to modify the certainty of parameters conditioned on the premise of the rule, as shown in Figure 2. Although other methods exist for representing uncertainty (viz. Gordon and Shortliffe [17]), certainty factors give a simple, easily modified, and accessible methodology for representing uncertainty in marketing.

PREMISE: IF   possible TRADE-RESISTANCE is an important
                   consideration in planning the promotion

ACTION: THEN   there is some suggestive evidence that the
                   PROMOTION

                   IS an IN-STORE-COUPON (30)
                   IS-NOT an ON-PACK-COUPON (-40)
                   IS FREE-GOODS (60)

Figure 2
Production Rule Example - Rule 34

3. KNOWLEDGE PARTITIONING. Knowledge partitioning is accomplished by EMYCIN and its derivatives through the use of context trees (see Figure 3). The knowledge represented within a context is automatically available to its descendants (children), but is not available to antecedent (parent) contexts unless specified by the user. This use of context trees facilitates the partitioning of knowledge as required by PEP, and also supports a backward chaining search strategy. Backward chaining strategies are goal driven (rather than data driven) which means that rules are tested and fired only if they can help to solve the current problem. Since the promotion planning task is proactive (goal driven) rather than reactive (data driven), backward chaining within the structure of a context tree is a natural inference strategy for PEP.

4. EXPLANATION. Finally, EMYCIN-type systems offer an integral explanation facility which is adequate for the purposes of PEP. Explanation supports conclusions, offers on-line help, and can parse production rules into English equivalents.

5. DESCRIPTION OF PEP

5.1. System Architecture and Rule Base Context-Tree
PEP is partitioned into three primary contexts: STATE, PROMOTION, and RESPONSE. This partitioning reflects the problem solving framework of promotion planning illustrated in Figure 1. Knowledge required by all three contexts is associated with the PEP context, while local knowledge is associated with contexts lower in the tree. The use of a hierarchy of contexts also provides a convenient means of dealing with interactions between various sources of knowledge. Figure 3 is a diagram of the PEP context tree.

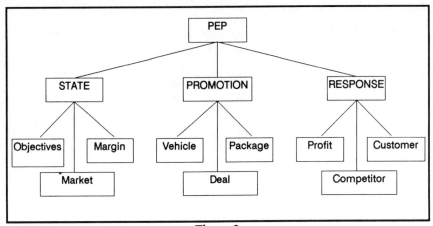

Figure 3
PEP Context Tree

The "STATE" context contains knowledge about the current marketing condition of the product being considered for promotion. The STATE context is further partitioned into three sub-contexts containing information about the managerial objectives, goals, of future promotions (OBJECTIVES subcontext), the brand competitive situation, such as market leadership and the activities of competitors (MARKET sub-context), and profitability information about the product (MARGIN sub-context). The STATE context and its subcontexts extract knowledge from the user as required, either by direct query or by assisting the user in formulating objectives, determining market situation, or calculating gross margins.

The PROMOTION context contains procedural knowledge required to make recommendations for a promotion plan. Again this knowledge is partitioned into three sub-contexts. The VEHICLE sub-context contains information needed to determine a promotion type (for example, a magazine coupon, a rebate, or a cents-off promotion). The DEAL sub-context makes recommendations for the value of the promotion. PEP determines if the value of a deal should be average, lower than average, or higher than average for this type of promotion for the product class. The system also computes an appropriate range of values for the promotion, in cents. The PACKAGE sub-context recommends that certain package sizes be promoted, or, if the system user wants to specify a package size, determines the appropriate promotion given that package size.

The RESPONSE context, partially implemented in the PEP prototype, contains procedural and analytic knowledge needed to forecast the effect of promotions in the marketplace. It is divided into three partitions containing submodels. CUSTOMER makes estimates of consumer response to promotions, such as increases in sales. COMPETITOR evaluates the likely response of competitors to promotions -- defensive counter-promotions. The PROFIT sub-context estimates the overall value of promotions to the firm.

In the current system implementation, the PROFIT sub-context contains a simple algorithm which estimates a profit index for various system-suggested promotion types and vehicles, at the system computed deal values, where:

$$(1) \quad PI_{k,v} = (RNC_{k,v} \ * \ (GM - DV_k) \ + \ RNC_{k,v}$$
$$* \ NCR_{k,v} \ * \ GM - RC_{k,v} \ * \ DV_k) \ / \ 1000$$

where:

PI	=	Promotion index
RNC	=	Redemption of product by non-current users
NCR	=	% non-current users who will repeat purchase of brand in $t + 1$
RC	=	Redemption of product by current users
GM	=	Gross margin
DV	=	deal value in cents as suggested by PEP
k	=	kind of promotion type (e.g., newspaper insert coupon)
v	=	value of deal as suggested by PEP

We use data from a survey of promotion experts, as described in the next section, to obtain estimates for RNC, NCR, and RC for different kinds of promotion types, k, and at different deal values, v.

In addition, PEP informs the user whether or not the suggested promotion is expected to be profitable in the short run. Deal value adjustments are made, should the user want it, to guarantee no losses on the promotion.

The PEP Rule-Base currently contains 77 rules embedded within 14 contexts. Declarative information is contained in 15 system parameters and 36 domain specific parameters.

5.2. Knowledge Acquisition in PEP
PEP contains knowledge from three main sources:

I) Survey of promotion experts.

A mail survey was conducted of experts in the sales promotion field (see Keon and Bayer, 1985, for details). Thirty-four promotion experts returned completed questionnaires. Promotion experts were queried about:

- preferred promotion alternatives given different product classes and brand situations,

- expectations about outcomes of choosing promotion alternatives,

- advantages and disadvantages of using a variety of promo-
  tional techniques in terms of meeting objectives, trade support, cost considerations, as well as other considerations.

Preferred promotion alternatives. Subjects were asked to fill in a matrix
of product class (coffee, soda, cookies, pet food, bar soap, and toilet tissue) by
brand situation (major brand, minor brand, new brand) with preferred promotions and values of promotions. The experts denoted their first and second
choice promotion offerings. The results were aggregated across respondents to
determine the percentage of respondents who preferred a particular promotion
and value in a given situation.

Surprisingly, preferred promotion types and values did not vary much across
product classes. However, Figure 4 shows that the brand situation sharply determined the perceived correct value for the promotion.

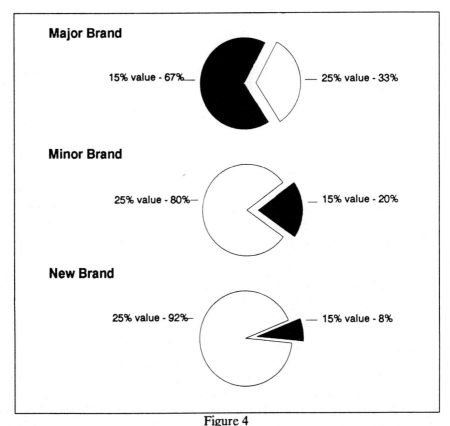

Figure 4
Promotion Preference by Market Situation: 15% Value vs 25% Value

TABLE 2

Preferred Promotion Alternatives Different Brand Situations

	% Promotion is Preferred		
PROMOTION TYPE	MAJOR	MINOR	NEW
newspaper coupon	.040	.072	.077
magazine coupon	.025	.025	.026
newspaper insert	.277	.297	.420
in-pack coupon	.280	.156	.033
in-store coupon	.072	.083	.160
rebate	.067	.038	.019
cents-off	.129	.156	.094
free goods	.109	.172	.172

Table 2 shows the percentage of time different types of promotions were preferred in different situations.

These data were combined into a set of production rules to help establish the promotion plan. The percentage of time a promotion alternative is preferred is used in establishing Certainty Factors for these rules, where:

$$CF = \% \text{ promotion is preferred X } 1000$$

For example, if the brand is a major brand, an IN-PACK-COUPON is the preferred promotion alternative with a certainty of 280 (out of a maximum of 1000). These PROMOTION and CF values would then be combined, as described in Appendix 1, with the results of firing other rules.

Expectations about outcomes. The survey instrument included several scenarios where the respondent was asked to assume certain market conditions and types of promotion offerings, and give subjective estimates of:

- redemption rate by current users,
- redemption rate by non-current users,
- percentage non-current buyers that repeat purchase,
- stock-up by current users,
- stock-up by non-current users.

Advantages and disadvantages of different promotions. The promotion experts were asked to explain the advantages and disadvantages of various types of promotions. Results were compiled to form a set of production rules associating managerial objectives, brand competitive situation, managerial constraints and retail environments with different promotions. For example, a major disadvantage of coupons is that there is a high level of misredemption. If misredemption is an important factor to consider in developing the promotion plan, then coupons become a less attractive promotion alternative. Certainty Factors (CF) for the production rules are derived based on the level of consensus among the experts.

The survey data were used to formulate a set of production rules and declarative information to help solve the promotion planning problem. As mentioned, a problem in the promotion planning area is a lack of a well defined knowledge base, leading to a high level of uncertainty. By using survey data from 34 experts we were able to utilize consensus of the experts in helping to formulate certainty factors. This multiple perspective data collection procedure also allowed us to develop an information-rich knowledge base in an efficient manner.

An example of a typical PEP rule derived from the survey data is shown in

If	1)	1) the objective of this promotion is BUILD-SHARE or
		2) the objective of this promotion is TRIAL, or
		3) the objective of this promotion is BUILD-AWARENESS,
and		
	2)	1) the objectives of this promotion is MAX-LOADING, or
		2) the objectives of this promotion is REDEMPTION, or
		3) the objectives of this promotion is DEFENSE,
Then		There is evidence that TYPES OF PROMOTION
		OFFERINGS is NEWSPAPER-INSERT (370)
		MAGAZINE-COUPON (180)
		IN-STORE-COUPON (180).

Figure 5
RULE057: Promotion Flexibility

Figure 5.

The critical belief driving this rule is that certain types of promotions offer more flexibility in meeting managerial objectives than others. When certain combinations of objectives need to be met, these promotion types would become more attractive.

As an example of how we used survey responses, and variance in responses, in constructing rules, we show the following "Agree-Disagree" question from the survey:

Coupons have a greater chance of converting non-current users to become users, than does a cents-off promotion.

STRONGLY AGREE   1   2   3   4   5   STRONGLY DISAGREE

The mean survey response to this question was 2.42, with a standard error of .204. The intent is to construct a rule which 1) reflects the ability of a coupon versus a cents-off promotion to attract non-current users, and 2) has a certainty factor which accurately reflects our level of confidence in the truth of our assertion.

Values for the "Agree-Disagree" scale were rescaled as shown:

STRONGLY AGREE   1000   500   0   -500   -1000   STRONGLY DISAGREE

Using this new scale, the mean survey response can be translated into our preliminary certainty factor, where if the value were 1, rescaled to 1000, the CF would be set to 1000.

The rescaled mean response is 290. However, there was variance in responses between subjects which should have the effect of lowering our confidence in this result, and thus give us a lower CF.

We set our Certainty Factor to represent a 90% confidence level. Using a Z-score of 1.65, the mean, and the standard error, the less certain value moves from 2.42 to 2.76. The rescaled response drops to 120, which becomes the Certainty Factor. (Note, when we set the CF to reflect the confidence level, we move the CF closer to 0. If, in this example, the value has moved above 3.0, moving the rescaled value into the negative range, the rescaled CF would be set to 0.)

The rule, assuming no overlapping information, becomes:

IF   the OBJECTIVE is to attract NON-CURRENT-USERS
THEN   consider using (COUPON 120) (CENTS-OFF -120)

The non-overlap qualification is important. We will return to this issue, and this rule, in the discussion of scanner data analysis.

II) Analysis of scanner panel data.

Scanner panel data is a highly accurate, within limited markets, source of empirical information about packaged goods. These data have good potential for incorporation into expert systems if the data can be converted to knowledge.

Towards this objective, purchase data and coupon usage data were analyzed for a panel of 2500 households over an 18 month period. Examples of analyses of interest include:

a) **the extent to which the brand's competitive situation is associated with coupon use.**

For example, medium brands are less effective in drawing non-current users. Major brands are more effective. In other words, people switch into major brands to use a coupon. This suggests that, for major brands, coupons may be good for a defensive strategy.

If the previous purchase was of a minor brand, then coupon users are more likely to be switchers than non-switchers. People switch from minor brands to use coupons.

b)   coupon use and brand switching behavior.

Switching seems to be a non-monotonic function of coupon use. People who occasionally use coupons do more brand switching than people who never use coupons or people who are heavy coupon users.

Another observation is that customers tend to switch into lower priced brands.

c)   the extent to which use of different types of sales promotions influences quantity purchased and purchase timing.

For example, the quantity purchased during a coupon use purchase occasion is less than during an occasion when no coupon is used. This suggests that if the managerial objective is loading, a coupon is not an attractive promotion alternative.

d)   characteristics of coupon users.

Heavy users (and more frequent purchasers) are more likely to use coupons. This suggests that if the managerial objective is to attract heavy users, consider using a coupon.

More frequent purchasers are less likely to be brand switchers.

e)   differences in household purchasing behavior resulting from coupon use and cents-off deals.

Results of analyses were converted to declarative information contained in parameters and production rules. Figure 6 shows an example of a typical analysis of coupon use versus cents-off and its production rule conversion.

Note that one of the statistical measures computed is an uncertainty coefficient. This is the additional level of information in the phenomenon explained by the analysis, and is computed as:

$$\text{Uncertainty Coefficient} = \frac{2\{U(Y) + U(X) - U(X,Y)\}}{U(Y) + U(X)}$$

where:

$$U(Y) = -\Sigma_j \ p(Y_j, x_k) \ \log \ p(Y_j)$$
= average uncertainty in the marginal distribution of Y

$$U(Y,X) = -\Sigma_j \ \Sigma_k \ p(Y_j, X_k) \ \log p(Y_j, X_j)$$
= joint probability of Y and X

$$p(Y_j) = \text{proportion of } Y_j$$

For non-overlapping rules, the uncertainty coefficient was used to compute the Certainty Factor where:

CF = Uncertainty Coefficient × 1000

Note that although much of the information obtained from the promotion experts and the scanner analysis was non-overlapping, some of the analysis overlapped. Occurrences of overlapping information are used to help validate the system (Bayer, Keon and Lawrence [11]), and to increase our confidence, and thus the CF.

Difference between coupons and cents-off deals in terms of consumers' switching behavior

	CURRENT BRAND	SWITCH	
COUPON	46%	54%	100%
CENTS-OFF	86%	14%	100%

Chi Squared statistic = 47.8 (p < 0.001)
Degrees of freedom = 1
Uncertainty coefficient = .080

Implication: Cents-off deals attract current users; and coupons can draw people who usually purchase another brand.

Rule: IF the OBJECTIVE is to attract NON-CURRENT-USERS THEN consider using (COUPON 80) (CENTS-OFF -80)

Figure 6
Example of Scanner Analysis

The rule generated in Figure 6 is the same as the one shown in our discussion of the survey of promotion experts where the CF was computed as 120. The algorithm used for combining the two CFs is the one shown in Appendix 1. The new CF for these values of PROMOTION, based on the combined information from the multiple data sources is 190.

III) Single expert knowledge

Knowledge from one of the authors was used to construct the overall framework for the knowledge base. Essentially, an empty shell was constructed which told us how the problem should be formulated, but, because of the lack of breadth of detailed knowledge, the shell was not filled in. The survey analysis and scanner data analysis were used to fill the shell.

6. PERFORMANCE AND VALIDATION

A major problem in performance assessment and system validation for PEP (and other expert systems) is the difficulty of ascertaining a "correct" answer. There are several ways the validation problem can be approached:

1)We can implement the suggested promotion plan and wait to see if it succeeds or fails. Aside from the fact that this is not practical from a business perspective, the plan's ultimate success or failure may occur regardless of the inherent weaknesses or strengths of the plan. The success or failure of the plan may occur because of aspects of the open environmental system which are beyond the planner's control.

2)We can plan promotions through the system utilizing a variety of scenarios. The system recommendations can then be assessed for face validity. This step is necessary, but not sufficient for system validation.

3)Published case studies, which describe actual past marketing problems and suggest promotion plans, can be simulated through the promotion planner. We ran three of these published cases through PEP. Figure 7 briefly describes the product classes and salient problem characteristics.

Company	Brand Situation	Problems
Gillette [personal care]	New Brand Established product	Selection of objectives Target audience
Legume [bean curd-tofu]	Minor Brand New product class	Stimulate trial Promote to trade or consumer Almost no money
L'Eggs [hosiery]	Major Brand Established product	Increase awareness Load consumer with product Select correct deal value

Figure 7
Cases Used for Validation

For two of the cases, Gillette and L'Eggs, PEP was able to develop a promotion plan which offered a good case solution. In the Legume case, (a new product) however, PEP's plan was not as consistent with the case results. This was an interesting finding because Legume fell outside PEP's stated problem domain -- plans for consumer sales promotions in established product categories of frequently purchased packaged goods. In the case, there is a basic issue of whether or not consumer sales promotions should even be used. Given the case facts, a strategy which incorporates trade promotions is important to consider. Also, tofu is not a well-established product class.

Future research includes incorporating additional sales promotion information, and extending the system to incorporate trade promotions, and joint advertising-promotion decisions. Based on validation, PEP currently seems to perform at about the level of expertise of an MBA student with a marketing concentration.

PEP is actually the authors' second implementation of a promotion expert system. The first version, PROMEX, was primarily designed to test ideas about system architecture and formulation of production rules from multiple knowledge sources. During this experimental phase, it was found, that on occasion, production rules would accidentally be duplicated. This occurred when expert knowledge overlapped scanner information. As described earlier, in the PEP implementation, this overlap was used to increase our certainty in portions of the rule base.

7. CONCLUSION

The authors presented PEP, a marketing expert system for planning consumer sales promotions for frequently purchased goods in mature product classes. PEP was implemented using an EMYCIN-based Expert System building tool.

PEP's knowledge base includes information from three major sources:

- a survey of 34 sales promotion experts which was analyzed, synthesized, and codified into a set of production rules,
- analysis of scanner panel data -- analysis of empirical associations between purchasing behavior, promotion use, and brand switching behavior, and
- a shell of the promotion problem.

Research issues included the exploratory development of methodology for transforming survey data and raw scanner data into production rules and associating appropriate levels of confidence in those rules. Examples were presented of how this information was incorporated into PEP.

PEP currently appears to perform at the level of an MBA student with a concentration in marketing. Future work will incorporate trade promotions into the system, bring the system up to the expertise of sales promotion experts, and more extensively incorporate the use of analytical models.

An additional use for this type of system would be to help validate theories of consumer behavior. By integrating multiple knowledge sources and multiple types of reasoning, one can use PEP to help extend current marketing theory (see Hayes-Roth and Hayes-Roth [18] for similar considerations). The current framework allows one to embed the results of academic research into the system and merge that knowledge with managerial expertise.

ACKNOWLEDGEMENTS

The authors would like to thank the Promotion Marketing Association of America (PMAA) for their assistance in collecting information from sales promotion experts. We also thank Burke Marketing Services, Inc. for allowing us to use their scanner panel data, and Texas Instruments, Inc. for allowing us to use their Personal Consultant software and computer equipment.

REFERENCES

[1] Bayer, J., "Marketing Expert Systems: Issues and Proposal for a System Architecture," working paper at Carnegie-Mellon University, 1986.

[2] Clifford, James, M. Jarke, and Y. Vassilious, "A Short Introduction to Expert Systems," *IEEE Database Engineering Bulletin,* Vol 8, No 4, (December) 1983.

[3] Brachman, Ronald J., S. Amarel, C. Engelman, R.S. Engelmore, E.A. Feigenbaum and D.E. Wilkins, "What are Expert Systems?" In *Building Expert Systems,* edited by R. Hayes-Roth, D.A. Waterman and D.B. Lenat. Reading, Mass.: Addison-Wesley, 1983.

[4] Nau, Dana S., "Expert Computer Systems", *Computer,* February, 1983.

[5] Stefik, M., J. Aikins, R. Balzer, J. Benoit, L. Birnbaum, F. Hayes-Roth,and E. Sacerdoti (1983), "The Architecture of Expert Systems." *In Building Expert Systems,* edited by R. Hayes-Roth, D.A. Waterman and D.B. Lenat. Reading, Mass.: Addison-Wesley, 1983.

[6] Pople, Harry E., "Heuristic Methods for Imposing Structure on Ill-Structured Problems: The Structuring of Medical Diagnosis." *In Artificial Intelligence in Medicine,* edited by Peter Szolovits. Boulder, Co.: Westview Press, 1982.

[7] Buchanan, B. G. and E. H. Shortliffe, *Rule-Based Expert Systems: The MYCIN Experiments of the Stanford Heuristic Programming Project.* Reading, Mass: Addison-Wesley, 1984.

[8] Hayes-Roth, Frederick, D. A. Waterman, and D. B. Lenat, "An Overview of Expert Systems." *In Building Expert Systems,* edited by R. Hayes-Roth, D.A. Waterman and D.B. Lenat. Reading, Mass.: Addison-Wesley, 1983.

[9] Bayer, J. and J. Keon, "Expert Systems in Marketing: Developmental Issues." In *Proceedings of the American Marketing Association Educators' Conference,* edited by R. Lusch, et. al. Chicago:American Marketing Association, 1985.

[10] Keon, J. and J. Bayer, "An Expert Approach to Sales Promotion," *Journal of Advertising Research,*, June-July, 1986.

[11] Bayer, J., J. Keon and S. Lawrence, "An Expert System Based on an Analysis of Scanner Data and Managerial Expertise," presentation given at 1986 Marketing Science Conference, Dallas, 1986.

[12] Alpar, Paul, "Expert Systems in Marketing," University of Illinois at Chicago, Working Paper #86-19, 1986.

[13] Cross, G., E. Foxman, and D. Sherrell, "Using an Expert System to Teach Marketing Strategy," In *Proceedings of the American Marketing Association Educators' Conference,* edited by R. Lusch, et. al. Chicago:American Marketing Association, 1985.

[14] Davis, R., B.G. Buchanan, and E.H. Shortliffe, "Production Rules as a Representation for a Knowledge-Based Consultation Program," *Artificial Intelligence,* Vol 8, 1977, pp. 15-45.

[15] Stefik, M., J. Aikins, R. Balzer, J. Benoit, L. Birnbaum, F. Hayes-Roth and E. Sacerdoti, "The Organization of Expert Systems: A Tutorial," *Artificial Intelligence,* Vol. 18, 1982, pp. 135-173.

[16] van Melle, W., E. Shortliffe and B. Buchanan (1984), "EMYCIN: A Knowledge Engineer's Tool for Constructing Rule-Based Expert Systems," in Rule-Based Expert Systems, 1984, pp. 302-313.

[17] Gordon, J. and E. Shortliffe, "The Dempster-Shafer Theory of Evidence," in Rule-Based Expert Systems, 1984, pp. 272-294.

[18] Hayes-Roth, B. and F. Hayes-Roth, "A Cognitive Model of Planning," *Cognitive Science,* Vol 3, 1979, pp. 275-310.

[19] Dodson, J., A. Tybout and B. Sternthal, "Impact of Deals and Deal Retractions on Brand Switching," *Journal of Marketing Research,* 15 (February) 1978, pp. 72-81.

[20] Blattberg, R., Eppen, and J. Lieberman, "A Theoretical and Empirical Evaluation of Price Deals for Consumer Nondurables," *Journal of Marketing,* Vol 45 (Winter) 1981, pp. 116-129.

[21] Rothschild, M. and Gaidis, "Behavioral Learning Theory: Its Relevance to Marketing and Promotions," *Journal of Marketing,* Vol 45, No 2, 1981, pp. 70-78.

[22] Narasimhan, C., "A Price Discrimination Theory of Coupons," *Marketing Science,* Vol 3, No 2 (Spring) 1984, pp. 128-147.

Applied Expert Systems, E. Turban and P.R. Watkins (Editors)
© Elsevier Science Publishers B.V. (North-Holland), 1988

DEVELOPING CONSOLIDATED FINANCIAL STATEMENTS USING A PROTOTYPE EXPERT SYSTEM

Daniel E. O'Leary and Toshinori Munakata

Graduate School of Business
University of Southern California
Los Angeles, California 90089-1421

Computer and Information Science Department
Cleveland State University
Cleveland, Ohio 44115

In the development of accounting financial statements for external purposes, firms face the problem of consolidating financial statement data across two dimensions: companies (or e.g., profit centers) and accounts. This paper presents a prototype expert system developed using Prolog, FINSTA, designed to aggregate accounts across the second dimension in order to develop financial statements. The system uses natural language account titles and account dollar amounts as inputs and prepares aggregated financial statements as outputs. In order to accomplish this task, FINSTA first processes symbolic information (e.g., account titles) and then uses that and other information from that process in the context of an analytic model that it also solves in order to develop the financial statements. Thus, FINSTA uses multiple types of knowledge and processes that knowledge in a number of different ways.

1. INTRODUCTION

Accountants face a number of judgmental tasks where the questions rarely result in yes or no or black or white responses. Tasks such as these can be addressed using expert systems. The purpose of this paper is to discuss an accounting-based prototype expert system that has been developed to address such a judgmental task.

Firms developing financial statements for external purposes face the problem of consolidating financial statement data across two dimensions: companies (or e.g., profit centers) and accounts. This paper discusses a system for use in consolidating across accounts in order to develop aggregated financial statements, FINSTA. For example, FINSTA would use as input table 1 and produce table 2 as output. FINSTA is designed to simulate the approach of a human accountant consolidating financial statements by using heuristics and other rules of thumb in the computer program in order to accomplish that task.

FINSTA was developed using Prolog. FINSTA uses a frame-based knowledge representation with an inference engine that is a combination of forward chaining and backward chaining designed to solve the specific problem. FINSTA uses natural language processing designed for this particular accounting problem. The approach is based on instantiating "accounting concept" frames that contain liquidity and time frame (e.g., "current") knowledge about the accounts. Then FINSTA uses this "qualitative" knowledge about the particular problem to formulate and analytically develop the model output. Thus, FINSTA uses multiple types of knowledge representation and analysis.

TABLE 1

An Input Example--Financial Statement Before Aggregation

BOSTON EDISON COMPANY--DECEMBER 1963

Title	Dollars	Transactions
1. Cash	$ 4,048,773	167,354
2. Special-Deposits	1,166	87
3. Working-Funds	242,495	608,959
4. Notes Receivable	53,004	911
5. Customers Accounts Receivables	17,448,883	17,392,927
6. Other Accounts Receivables	479,353	74,945
7. Fuel Stock	1,218,478	75
8. Plant Materials Supplies and Merchandise	7,176,643	8,056
9. Prepaid Insurance	369,210	894
10. Other Prepaid Items	10,028	742
11. Rents Receivable	40,607	962
12. Miscellaneous Current and Accrued Assets	61,032	1,480
13. Net Electric Plant In-Service	327,802,559	109
14. Electric Plant Construction In-Progress	21,609,430	723
15. Net Steam Plant In-Service	10,520,537	15
16. Steam Plant Construction In-Progress	179,584	76
17. Net Nonutility Property	2,167,063	201
18. Other Investments	1,758,042	1,358
19. Unamortized-Discount Series-D Bonds	41,501	80
20. Refunding-Costs Series-G Bonds	341,875	120
21. Temporary-Facilities	18,249	1,040
22. Deferred-Debits Federal-Income Tax	990,800	89
23. Deferred-Debits Miscellaneous	321,644	1,655
24. Nonutility Property Additions	82,193	842
25. Deferred-Debits Sewer-Use Tax	12,037	895

(This example is constructed by the authors for illustration purposes from information given in Lev [8]. For this example, the order of the items is rearranged and the number of transactions is added.)

TABLE 2
Output of FINSTA--An Aggregated Accounting Statement for Table 1.

Original Number	Title	Dollars
1	Cash	4,048,773
2,3	Special-Deposits and Working--Funds	243,661
4,5	Prepaid Insurance and Other Prepaid Items	379,238
6,7,8,9	Receivables	18,021,847
10,11	Fuel Stock and Plant Materials, Supplies and Merchandise	8,395,121
12	Miscellaneous Current and Accrued Assets	61,032
13,14	Other Investments and Temporary Facilities	1,776,291
15	Net Electric Plant In-Service	327,802,559
16	Electric Plant Construction In-Progress	21,609,430
17,18	Net Steam Plant In-Service and Steam Plant Construction In-Progress	10,700,121
19,20	Net Nonutility Property and Nonutility Property Additions	2,249,256
21,22	Unamortized Discount--Series-D Bonds and Refunding-Cost Series-G Bonds	383,376
23,25	Deferred-Debits Federal--Income Tax and Deferred--Debits Sewer--Use Tax	1,002,837
24	Deferred-Debits Miscellaneous	321,644

1.1. Plan Of This Paper

This paper proceeds as follows. The second section briefly describes some accounting-based expert systems. The third section describes the importance of consolidating financial statements to yield aggregated accounts. The fourth, fifth and sixth sections summarize the judgmental issues in implemented FINSTA. The seventh section discusses some of the limitations and extensions of the system. The eighth section summarizes the paper and some of the contributions of FINSTA.

2. ACCOUNTING-BASED EXPERT SYSTEMS

There are at least two accounting expert systems (AES's) that have been developed for commercial use that have been reported in the literature or at research symposiums. Peat Marwick is currently testing an AES to analyze bank loans (Willingham and Wright [1]). Coopers and Lybrand has implemented a system for tax accrual planning (Shpilberg and Graham [2]). Other AES's are prototype systems, such as the AES developed in this paper including TAXADVISOR (Michaelsen [3]), AUDITOR (Dungan and Chandler [4]) and EDP AUDITOR (Hansen and Messier [5]). TAXADVISOR, designed for use in estate planning, was developed using EMYCIN. AUDITOR, designed for auditing the allowance for bad debts account, was developed using AL/X. EDP AUDITOR, designed for use in auditing EDP systems, was developed using AL/X.

AES prototypes provide a useful tool in accounting research and in accounting practice. Accounting research can use AES prototypes to understand the judgments and heuristics used in a specific decision, to determine the feasibility of developing an AES in a specific area, and to categorize the knowledge in a specific judgmental area: if you can't program a decision making process, it is likely that it is not understood. Accounting practice can use AES to either replace or supplement decision makers.

3. CONSOLIDATION OF ACCOUNTS

Consolidation of accounts is done in order to provide a parsimonious financial statement that is meaningful to users, meet regulation constraints, conform to generally accepted accounting principles (GAAP) and yet does not disclose too much "strategic" information. First, sometimes it is thought that users of financial information should be provided with all available information. However, in his classic paper, Ackoff [6] noted this can lead to an over-abundance of irrelevant information. Second, these statements must reflect the disclosure constraints of regulation as promulgated by the Securities and Exchange Commission (SEC). For example, the SEC requires disclosure of all expenses that are greater than or equal to one percent of sales in the Form 10-K. Third, consolidated statements must conform to GAAP. For example, this means that balance sheet should reflect the liquid nature of the assets and the liabilities. Fourth, as noted in Porter [7] financial statement information can be used to analyze the strategies of a competitor. As a result, firms do not wish to disclose information that can be used to the competitive advantage of their competitors--for example, most firms probably would prefer not to disclose research and development expenditures.

3.1. Approaches to Consolidation

However, there is no generally accepted framework of knowledge for consolidation of financial statement information by aggregating accounts. Accordingly, multiple sources of knowledge are used to develop consolidated financial statements:

1. Theoretical Findings
2. Accounting/Auditing Heuristics
3. Legal Requirements

The limited theoretical work on aggregation in financial statements has suggested some judgmental heuristics. For example, Lev's [8] entropy-based analysis suggested aggregating accounts whose dollar balances are a small percentage of the total dollar balance of the set of accounts, with other accounts.

Accountants use a number of heuristics to guide their efforts in aggregating information. For example, the materiality of an account is often measured using the rule of thumb that an account is material if it is greater than or equal to 5% of some standard.

Legal requirements primarily include those disclosure requirements promulgated by the Securities and Exchange Commission (SEC), Financial Accounting Standards Board (FASB) and Generally Accepted Auditing Standards (GAAS). These requirements include, for example, disclosure of all expenses that are greater than or equal to 1% of sales in the Form 10-K.

3.2. Implementation of the Consolidation of Financial Statements

FINSTA uses three basic steps to aggregated accounts to develop consolidated financial statements:

1. Determining which accounts should be aggregated,
2. Identifying the sets of accounts that it makes "sense" to aggregate, and
3. Choosing between alternative sets of potential account aggregations.

Each of these steps requires that the system have the knowledge of an accountant. They are implemented using rules and frames. Determining the accounts that should be aggregated involves identifying those accounts that for some reason (e.g., lack of importance or for strategy reasons) should be aggregated with other accounts. Identifying the accounts that can be aggregated is the process of determining which accounts are somewhat similar so that it makes "sense" to aggregate those sets of accounts. Choosing between alternative sets of potential aggregations is the process of choosing between alternative financial reports while meeting the constraints that have been identified in the second step.

4. DETERMINING THE ACCOUNTS THAT SHOULD BE AGGREGATED

Developing a consolidated financial statement where some of the accounts have been aggregated requires determining the "important" accounts. Then the unimportant accounts can be aggregated with other accounts to develop a consolidated financial statement. The development of FINSTA lead to the recognition of three sources of information on which to base the decision to aggregate or not aggregate an account:

1. Account Balance
2. Industry/Company Importance
3. Strategy Security

4.1. Account Balance

Human accountants routinely use the dollar amount of the account to measure the importance of the account. FINSTA also uses this same measure. For those accounts where this measure is below a certain level, FINSTA indicates that they should be aggregated. FINSTA uses a heuristic-based percentage of the total dollar volume. In addition, the total is based on the category totals of the type of assets--for example, current assets. FINSTA uses percentages of the category totals based on the SEC and GAAS percentages.

4.2. Industry/Company Importance

Certain industries require the disclosure of particular accounts either due to regulation by, e.g., the FASB or because of standard industry disclosures. In these cases, those accounts should not be aggregated with other accounts. Alternatively, the company may desire that a particular account is disclosed as a "signal" to the business community or as a measure of its strength or uniqueness.

4.3. Strategy Security

A third approach used by accountants is to determine if there are any potential strategy leaks due to the disclosure of particular accounts. For example, a firm generally would prefer to not disclose research and development expenditures. FINSTA can be used to include this kind of information.

4.4. Example

The accounts from the example that have been chosen for aggregation are summarized in table 3. For purposes of this example, the accounts have been chosen for aggregation based on the number of transactions and the dollar volume of the account.

5. IDENTIFYING SETS OF ACCOUNTS THAT CAN BE AGGREGATED

Next, the human accountant must determine which accounts make "sense" to aggregate with the accounts that have been determined to require aggregation. For example, in table 1, the human accountant would likely decide that it makes "sense" to aggregate the first three items, "Cash," "Special-Deposits," and "Working-Funds," while the accountant would decide that it may not make "sense" to aggregate "Cash" and "Net Electric Plant In-Service". What knowledge would the accountant use to make such a decision?

5.1. Accounting Language Processing

The accountant has a vocabulary of accounting words that describe the accounts and an understanding of the characteristics that define the

accounts. Two primary characteristics are time frame and liquidity. For example, "Cash" is a short-term and highly liquid asset, whereas, "Net Electric Plant

		TABLE 3
		The accounts to be aggregated.
Category No.	Serial No.	Title
1	2	Special-Deposits
1	4	Prepaid Insurance
1	5	Other Prepaid Assets
1	6	Notes Receivable
1	8	Other Accounts Receivable
1	9	Rents Receivable
1	10	Fuel Stock
1	12	Miscellaneous Current and Accrued Assets
2	13	Other Investments
2	14	Temporary-Facilities
2	18	Steam Plant Construction In-Progress
2	19	Net Nonutility Property
2	20	Nonutility Property Additions
3	21	Unamortized Discount Series-D Bonds
3	25	Deferred-Debits Sewer-Use Tax
(For the purposes of this example, aggregation is based on the magnitude of the dollar and transaction expenses.)		

In-Service," is a long-term asset with very little liquidity. Because those characteristics are different it may not make "sense" to aggregate those particular assets in a consolidated financial statement. FINSTA uses an approach to natural language processing that meets the specific needs of this problem domain.

5.2. Accounting Vocabulary Representation in FINSTA

In each title there is a concept represented by a set of "keywords" and less important words. Accounting vocabulary representation in FINSTA is implemented as follows. To determine the characteristics of an account title, the concept must be found. This is done as follows. First, given an account title, the "importance level" (called the hierarchical level) of each word is determined. Level 1 is treated as the most important and Level 8, the least important--for example, "Net (Level 6), Electric (Level 4), Plant (Level 1), and In-Service (Level 2)." Such hierarchical levels are assigned to the words so the significance of the words in determining the characteristics of the account title are not equal.

FINSTA uses the hierarchical levels found in a table referred to as "Hierarchical Levels of Accounting Words" (see table 3). This table, in the form of a list, is given to FINSTA as a priori knowledge.

Not every word in the table has a unique level. For example, the word "Plant" in "Net Electric Plant In-Service" is a keyword defining the account as a fixed asset. However, the "Plant" in "Plant Materials, Supplies and Merchandise" does not represent the concept for that title. Instead, "Supplies" defines the concept for that account. The latter is identified by the fact that there is another level 1 word in the title.

This table is not the only table that could be constructed for an AES or a human accountant to represent accounting language. Because this table was designed to meet the needs of this application, it reflects the asset side of the balance sheet, general accounting knowledge and selected electric power industry knowledge required for this application.

Levels were designed to group conceptually similar accounting words that the system would encounter. As a result, there is no strict ordering of importance of the particular levels. Level 1 includes the set of concept describing keywords that FINSTA recognizes. Level 2 summarizes the state of plant assets. Level 3 defines the descriptors associated with receivables. Level 4 reflects the industry-specific descriptors. Level 5 includes the set of descriptors that are not keywords, but are the same as keywords (e.g., Plant Asset as opposed to Plant Supplies).

TABLE 4

Hierarchy levels of accounting (Level 1 is the highest)

Level 1

plant*, property, investments, equipment, cash, special-deposits, working-funds, receivables, stock, supplies, merchandise, materials, prepaid, current, accrued, unamortized discount refunding-cost, temporary-facilities, deferred-debits, inventory

Level 2

In-service, in-progress

Level 3

notes, accounts, rent, bonds

Level 4

Electric, steam, fuel, nonutility, construction, customers, insurance, series-d, series-g, tax

Level 5

plant* (if there are no other components that are Level 1)

Level 6

net

Level 7

other, items, additions, miscellaneous, assets

Level 8

(all other words that do not appear in Levels 1 through 7)

*Note. "plant" is in Levels 1 and 5.

Level 6 summarizes the descriptors deriving from the depreciation or amortiza-
tion of assets. Level 7 includes the miscellaneous asset descriptors. Level 5, 6,
and 7 words generally are not required to derive the "concept" of the particular
accounting descriptor.

Second, given that FINSTA has found the concept in a given title, it uses the
concept as represented by the appropriate Level 1 word to determine the characteristics associated with the title. The characteristics provide accounting "meaning" of the account to FINSTA. The characteristics are based on the two
dimensions of time frame and liquidity. These dimensions typically are used by
accountants to develop financial statements. Generally, the time frame determines the category in which the asset is included (e.g., Current or Long-term).
In addition, the liquidity determines the order of appearance within a category.
Table 4 shows the set of characteristics for time frame and table 5 shows the
characteristics of liquidity. Table 6 summarizes FINSTA's knowledge of the assets.

TABLE 5
Vocabulary set of accounting words for time frame
A1. Current (short term)

cash, special-deposits, working-funds, receivable, stock, supplies, merchandise, materials, prepaid, current, accrued, inventory

A2. Long term

investments, plant, property, equipment, temporary-facilities

A3. Deferrals

unamortized-discount, deferred-debits, refunding costs

5.3. Development Of Potential Aggregation Tuples

To develop the potential aggregation sets (tuples), the human accountant
may use the accounts that require aggregation and find those accounts that it
makes sense to aggregate with them. First, accounts with the same A (table 5)
and B (table 6) numbers are grouped together as "original tuples." For example,
in table 8, assets (15, 16, 17, 18) constitute an original tuple since they have the
same A number 2 and B number 10. These tuples represent one type of potential aggregation of accounts: the set of accounts that have the same time frame
and liquidity.

Second, another type of potential aggregation, with greater specificity, is
derived from the original tuples by considering their subsets. If a subset contains
at least one Level 2, 3, or 4 word in common, then the subset is a potential ag-

TABLE 6

Vocabulary set of accounting words for liquidity

B1.   cash, special-deposits, working funds

B2.   investments

B3.   prepaid

B4.   receivable

B5.   merchandise, inventory

B6.   supplies, stock, materials

B7.   current, accrued

B8.   temporary-facilities

B9.   equipment

B10.   plant

B11.   property

B12.   deferred-debits, refunding-costs, unamortized discount

gregation; otherwise, it is not considered for aggregation. For example, the subset (15, 16) is a potential aggregation tuple since both accounts 15 and 16 contain a common level 4 word "Electric." Subset (15, 16, 17) is not a potential aggregation since there is no common Level 2, 3, 4 word for all the accounts. Table 8 shows the set of potential aggregation tuples for the example.

This second process derives its rationale from using additional information in the development of the potential aggregation tuples. In particular, it allows the grouping of more closely related sets of assets. In addition, this process is frequently used in the development of aggregated financial statements.

6. CHOOSING BETWEEN ALTERNATIVE AGGREGATIONS

Given the set of potential aggregation tuples, the system must choose between the available alternative aggregations. FINSTA uses two heuristic rules to guide the search: (1) minimize the number of accounts that are aggregated, subject to the constraint of aggregating the appropriate accounts. This rule is based on the entropy approach of Lev (1969); and (2) group together similar sized accounts. This rule is based on practical experience and an analysis of the entropy approach.

TABLE 7
FINSTA's Knowledge of the Table 1 Information

A No.	B No.	Serial	Title	Dollars	Transactions
1	1	1	Cash	4,048,773	167,354
1	1	2	Special-Deposits	1,166	87
1	1	3	Working-Funds	242,495	608,959
1	3	4	Prepaid Insurance	369,210	894
1	3	5	Other Prepaid Items	10,028	742
1	4	6	Notes Receivable	53,004	911
1	4	7	Customer Accounts Receivable	17,448,883	17,392,927
1	4	8	Other Accounts Receivable	479,353	74,945
1	4	9	Rents Receivable	40,607	962
1	6	10	Fuel Stock	1,218,478	75
1	6	11	Plant Materials, Supplies and Merchandise	7,176,643	8,056
1	7	12	Miscellaneous Current and Accrued Assets	61,032	1,480
2	2	13	Other Investments	1,758,042	1,358
2	8	14	Temporary-Facilities	18,249	1,040
2	10	15	Net Electrical Plant In-Service	327,802,559	109
2	10	16	Electric Plant Construction In-Progress	21,609,430	723
2	10	17	Net Steam Plant In-Service	10,520,537	15
2	10	18	Steam Plant Construction In-Progress	179,584	76
2	11	19	Net Nonutility Property	2,167,063	201
2	11	20	Nonutility Property Additions	82,193	842
3	12	21	Unamortized Discount Series -D Bonds	41,501	80
3	12	22	Refunding-Cost Series-G Bonds	341,875	120
3	12	23	Deferred-Debits Federal-Income Tax	990,800	89
3	12	24	Deferred-Debits Miscellaneous	321,644	1,655
3	12	25	Deferred-Debits Sewer-Use Tax	12,037	895

The choice between alternative aggregations works as follows. First partition the set of tuples in table 8 into groups of tuples so no elements in one group ever appear in other groups. For table 8, the groups are partitioned as follows (here [] represents a group): [(1,2,3), (1,2), (1,3), (2,3)], [(4,5)], [(6,7,8,9), (7,8)], [(10,11)], [(15,16,17,18,), (15,16), (15,17), (16,18), (17,18)], [(19,18)], [(21,22,23,24,25), (21,22), (23,25)]. After partitioning, an optimal solution may be obtained for each group. Since few tuples are in each group, the number of possible solutions will be relatively small. The set of optimal solutions for all the

TABLE 8

The set of potentially tuples for aggregation.

(The elements in the tuples are the Serial Numbers in Table 1.)

(1, 2, 3)	(1, 2)	(1, 3)
(2, 3)	(4, 5)	(6, 7, 8, 9)
(7, 8)	(10, 11)	(15, 16, 17, 18)
(15, 16)	(15, 17)	(16, 18)
(17, 18)	(19, 20)	(21, 22, 23, 24, 25)
(21, 22)	(23, 25)	

groups gives an optimal solution for the entire problem. To obtain an optimal solution for a group, the following "elimination search" is used. This search is an efficient exhaustive search that constructs a tree of all possible solutions excluding those tuples whose elements have appeared before. The following are the algorithm and an example of its use.

6.1. Elimination Search Algorithm

Construct a tree of all possible solutions. The root of the tree is a dummy node, called "start." Every other node represents a particular tuple, "X" (crossed out) or "N" (No solution).

A1. Place the root "start." For each account to be aggregated that has not been picked up, perform A2 through A3.

A2. Connect all the tuples that satisfy the following to the previous tuple node:

i. the tuple contains the account to be aggregated and

ii. none of the other elements in the tuple has appeared in the partial solution so far.

If there is no such tuple, write "N" in the node.

A3. For each tuple in A2, check whether it contains other accounts to be aggregated. If so, cross out the other accounts in the subtree whose root is the tuple.

A4. After all the accounts to be aggregated are picked up in steps A2 and A3, count the number of aggregated accounts for all the solutions. Choose the smallest number solution. If there is a tie, select the one with the smallest difference between the dollar amounts.

6.2. Computational Illustration of Algorithm

Consider the following set of aggregatable tuples in one group (different than the one in table 1): (1,2,4), (1,4,5,6), (2,3), (3,5,6,9), (3,5,7,8), (7,8,9), where the following accounts require aggregation, 2*, 5*, 7*.

The search is as follows.

2*	5*	7*	No. of Aggregated Accounts
-(2*,3) —	-(1,4,5*,6)—	-(7*,8,9)	9
-(1,2*,4)┬	-(3,5*,6,9)—	(N)	
└	-(3,5*,7*,8)—	(X)	7(Optimal)

Start-

In order to meet the constraints of aggregating the three accounts, 2, 5 and 7, either four other accounts or six other accounts could be used. The algorithm chose the solution where four other accounts are aggregated.

6.3. Example

Using the information in Table 1 as input, with the accounts in Table 3 requiring aggregation, leads to Table 2. In order to aggregate the 15 accounts in Table 3, only 5 additional accounts were required. However, there was one account, number 12, that should have been aggregated, but was not aggregated. This resulted because no tuples were developed that included account number 12.

7. LIMITATIONS AND EXTENSIONS OF FINSTA

Since FINSTA is a prototype there are necessarily a number of limitations of the system that could be addressed if the system were to be developed for commercial application. However, each of these limitations is easily remedied and does not require further development in this proof of concept.

First, the approach used in this paper is only for the asset portion of the balance sheet. This does not include the income statement or the liability/capital section of the balance sheet. This limitation can be remedied by increasing the scope to include these other areas of financial statements.

Second, as with all natural language like systems, FINSTA has a relatively limited vocabulary. The set of accounting words in the knowledge base can be extended to mitigate this difficulty.

Third, FINSTA does not contain client information. This type of knowledge can improve the match between the financial statements designed by FINSTA and the user's needs. The more specific the information that can be used by the system, the more likely the financial statements will meet the user's needs. FINSTA can be changed to include client information by interfacing the user with FINSTA or building that information into the knowledge base.

Fourth, FINSTA could be extended to lead to consolidation across companies, rather than just accounts. Although conceptually similar to the aggregation of accounts, there are a number of regulations and rules that require adherence.

8. SUMMARY AND CONTRIBUTIONS OF FINSTA

FINSTA is an AES developed to provide consolidated financial statements The basic contribution is that FINSTA is a computer program that can perform some of the activities of a human accountant. As an example of its capabilities, FINSTA can take table 1 and develop table 2 as the final output. However, FINSTA is an AES that has made five particular contributions. First, FINSTA is the first expert system developed for the design of financial statements. Second, this is one of the first AES designed using Prolog. Third, this is one of the first AES designed using a frame-based knowledge representation. Fourth, this AES provides a first step in the analysis of natural accounting language to aid the solution of the consolidation problem. Fifth, FINSTA summarizes in computer program form much of the current theoretical and practical knowledge of the use of aggregation in accounting.

ACKNOWLEDGEMENT

The authors would like to acknowledge the programming assistance of James Petro, formerly a graduate student in Computer Science at Cleveland State University.

REFERENCES

[1]   Willingham, J. and W. Wright, "Development of a Knowledge-based System for Auditing the Collectability of a Commercial Loan." Paper presented at the TIMS/ORSA Meeting, Boston, Mass., April, 1984.

[2]   Shpilberg, D. and L.E. Graham, "Developing ExperTAP: An Expert System for Corporate Tax Accrual and Planning." Unpublished paper presented at the University of Southern California, Symposium on Expert Systems, February, 1986.

[3]   R.H. Michaelsen, "An Expert System for Federal Tax Planning," *Expert Systems,* 1 (2), (1984), pp. 149-167.

[4] Dungan, C. and J. Chandler, "Auditor: A Microcomputer-based Expert System to Support Auditors in the Field," *Expert Systems,* October, 1985.

[5] Hansen, J.V. and W.F. Messier, "Expert Systems For Decision Support in EDP Auditing," *International Journal of Computer and Information Sciences,* 11 (5), (1982), pp. 357-379.

[6] Ackoff, R.L., "Management Misinformation Systems," *Management Science,* 14 (4) (1967), pp.147-156.

[7] Porter, M.E., *Competitive Strategy.* New York: The Free Press, 1980.

[8] Lev, B., *Accounting and Information Theory.* American Accounting Association, 1969.

Applied Expert Systems, E. Turban and P.R. Watkins (Editors)
© Elsevier Science Publishers B.V. (North-Holland), 1988

EXPERT SYSTEMS FOR USE IN FINANCE

Paul R. Watkins

Director, Expert Systems Program
School of Accounting
University of Southern California
Los Angeles, CA 90089-1421

Finance has been forecast by some to be the major area outside of medicine as having the greatest potential for serious expert systems development. Finance is a broad term encompassing many different sub-domains. This chapter identifies some of the application areas where expert systems are being developed in finance and develops a framework for evaluating areas of potential promise for developing new applications. Selected examples of expert systems work in some of the sub-domains of finance are described.

1. INTRODUCTION

Finance is a broad and diverse domain with many sub-domains which appear to have potential for many applications utilizing applied artificial intelligence techniques especially those deriving from expert systems methods. Finance may be sub-divided into three broad areas: corporate, financial institutions, and securities, financial markets. Within each of these areas can be identified current and potential applications for applied expert systems work.

Finance, unlike many other business domains such as business management, has a number of structured areas which naturally mesh with the formalisms required by expert systems. Since much of finance is numbers oriented and a number of paradigms, methodologies, approaches, policies, procedures and other techniques exist for approaching current problems within finance, the utilization of expert systems tools is just a logical extension of these existing approaches. The ability to reduce human effort, to better manage high volumes of transactions such as through use of monitoring expert systems, and to better deal with uncertainty are just a few of the reasons given for extending current solution approaches in finance to utilize ES techniques.

In this chapter, a number of example expert systems are described from each of the three major areas of finance. Then, a framework is developed which provides guidance on selecting areas within finance for future ES work. The chapter concludes with a brief summary and conclusions concerning the future of ES in finance.

2. APPLICATIONS OF EXPERT SYSTEMS IN FINANCE

2.1. Corporate Finance

A number of applications are being utilized and/or developed in the domain of corporate finance. These include the following systems:

Cash Management

Financial Analysis

Leasing/Financing Options

Insurance Underwriting

Insurance Claims Processing

Credit Granting

Each of the above systems is now briefly described. CASH MANAGER [1],[2],[3] is a general system designed to choose an optimal portfolio from a set of possible financial elements. The current scope of the system is focused on short-term financial instruments, although it may easily be expanded for other situations. Typical short-term financial instruments that the system handles are money market securities, certificates of deposit, banker's acceptances, commercial paper, money market funds and daily repurchase agreements. The heart of the system is an operations research network model (similar in concept to a linear programming model) which is tied into a knowledge base containing knowledge of an operations research expert and a cash management expert. The operations research expertise consists of knowledge of how to formulate an embedded network problem and how to solve the network problem and interpret the results. The cash management expertise consists of knowledge of the set of financial instruments and the methods used by cash managers to solve cash management problems without the network system. CASH MANAGER was developed using a first principles approach to structure the knowledge about the financial instruments. Thus, the system does not use the traditional rule-based approach to capture knowledge but rather uses a frame-based approach which is congruent with human models of professional judgment. The content of the frames vary, depending on the type of instrument. The user of the system can add new frames as necessary during the life of the system. CASH MANAGER also contains procedural knowledge about how to apply the network algorithm to the financial instrument frames without any intervention on the part of the user. The system is written in the C programming language and is implemented on an IBM-PC using the Microsoft Windows graphical interface to facilitate the user/system dialog.

Although the system is currently a working prototype, the authors are continuing to enhance, improve and extend the system.

SAFARI is a prototype expert system developed for use in financial analysis. It has been tested in several institutions in France including the financial department of la Lyonnaise des Eaux and by professors at Hautes Etudes Commerciales. This system is designed for analysts who may have little or no computer experience. It is designed and implemented in the Symphony package of Lotus Development Corporation and through use of Turbo Prolog. Since the system was designed and is being used in France, the materials normally available to financial analysts in France were used as components for analysis. These items consist of financial statements and industry ratios. The Symphony component of SAFARI is designed to allow development of projections, trends, and to display the various financial data through a series of tables, graphs and figures. For example, typical graphical output includes cash flow analysis, cost breakdown and quarterly results for receivables, inventory and payables. This graphic output allows the user to make preliminary judgments prior to entering into a consultation with the expert system. The consultation with the expert system component may be in one of two modes. One mode consists of writing a file from the Symphony worksheet and then having the expert systems component read the file and perform an analysis. The second mode, the consultation mode, the user must have pre-calculated ratios available and must enter these values at the appropriate point in the dialog with SAFARI. This mode is more flexible and allows for more comprehensive sensitivity analysis. The knowledge base of SAFARI is rule based and consists of about 75 rules that transform quantitative rules into qualitative information, intermediate rules which refine the analysis and conclusion rules which determine the final comments to be delivered by SAFARI. The expert system provides a comparative analysis of selected values to industry averages or to normative standards developed by influential financial institutions such as the Banque de France. Thus, the system can be used to evaluate competitors' positions or by investors contemplating investment decisions. Benefits of this systems are its simplicity and the general familiarity of the environment (SYMPHONY) by the users. The financial analysts who use the system have been most complimentary and now plans are being made to market the system commercially in France. Extensions will likely include a communications link, and a larger knowledge and data base.

In Italy, an expert system has been developed to evaluate leasing operations. This system was developed to run on an IBM-AT using the expert systems shell SAVIOR. In the leasing operation, the soundness of the client company, the nature of the equipment to be leased and the proposed terms and conditions of the lease all need to be evaluated along with a number of other facts which are elicited during the consultation. The output of this system is a written narrative of about 6 to 8 pages which explains in detail the expert system's assessment of the leasing situation. This written narrative has enabled the company to obtain very high levels of user confidence and satisfaction with the ES. The ES has the ability to re-negotiate certain terms and conditions of the lease to attempt to obtain more favorable conditions. During a typical consultation, the ES elicits about 100 facts from the user which includes accounting data and other more general types of facts such as company characteristics and conditions of the operation. This system consists of about 1200 rules and is being used on a frequent basis by the Italian company at over 15 branch offices.

The insurance industry has begun to implement a large number of expert systems to handle a variety of tasks from underwriting to claims processing. At least half of the largest 28 insurance firms in the U.S. are actively engaged in ES development activities. Coopers and Lybrand, the large international accounting firm, has developed a Marine Umbrella Liability Insurance Underwriter for one of its clients. This system has industry specific knowledge as well as general insurance knowledge. The major benefit of this system is in consistently applying underwriting standards to the clients being considered. Blue Cross/Blue Shield has experienced a dramatic reduction in labor costs (in excess of 80%) for claims processing. The monitoring of claims forms processing by an expert system can evaluate a specific claim in context of prior claims for the same client and other clients and can identify spurious or missing information.

American Express has operational an expert system to render an opinion as to whether or not credit should be granted for a specific purchase for a given customer. Typically, American Express has no purchase limits on its card and previously a human had to retrieve information from a number of databases and make a quick decision while the merchant was still online. Now the Authorizer's Assistant (AA) can monitor the databases and reach a decision in just a few seconds. AA can also interact with a human authorizer in difficult cases to help resolve the problem quickly. Details of this system may be found in [4].

TRW Information Services has developed an expert system called DISCOVERY which focuses on discovering anomalies in credit reporting by merchants who report to the credit files of TRW. This system has knowledge of merchants and individuals and can detect unauthorized queries into the credit information system. It has general knowledge of bank and other merchant credit processing tendencies and constantly updates its knowledge base. For example, computer bulletin boards are monitored for information available to hackers on how to gain unauthorized access to the TRW system.

2.2. Financial Institutions
Financial Institutions such as banks have been quite active in the development of a variety of expert systems based systems. Some of these applications include:

Commercial Loan Analyzers

Credit Approval Systems

Commercial Account Rating Systems

Credit Application Systems

Processing of Administrative Documents

Automated Teller Control

The commercial loan analyzer and credit approval systems are smart systems designed to evaluate credit applications for commercial and consumer credit, respectively. Detailed knowledge of the potential clients' background is evaluated such as might be contained in a credit history report. In the case of commercial customers, additional information is evaluated by the system such as financial statements and other client and industry information. Tentative judgments are reached which then can be reviewed by human loan officers to reach a final judgment.

Banks are often asked by other credit granting institutions for an evaluation of a customer's banking relations, particularly a rating on the customer's bank account. An expert system has been developed that has client knowledge and history of banking activity available for assessment. Items such as the number of late charges, the number of returned checks, the number of overdrafts, the frequency of such occurrences and other information can be assessed as well as the size of the client, the type of banking relationships and other information. This enables relatively low level employees of the bank to enter into a dialog with the system and make judgments of account quality that previously had to be rendered by an officer of the bank.

Banks, in some areas, have potential exposure to fraudulent activities. One such area is in the area of electronic banking, especially with the use of Automated Teller Machines (ATM). One of the largest US banks is currently developing a system which monitors ATM transactions on a real time basis and has knowledge of customer habits and trends with respect to ATM usage. This knowledge and monitoring system can then detect unusual patterns in ATM use, such as might occur with stolen ATM cards and then automatically freeze the account or retrieve the card to prevent further abuse, particularly on weekends.

2.3. Securities/Investments/Securities Markets

The investments area has also seen a great deal of activity with attempts to develop high level expert systems to deal with the complexities of investment management and securities trading. Examples of expert systems from these areas include:

Prediction of Stock Market Behavior

Acquisition of Trading Rules

Global Financial Markets Analysis

Program Trading

Decision Analysis in Securities Trading

Risk Assessment: New Venture Capitalization, Financing

Braun and Chandler [5] describe an artificial intelligence based rule-induction approach to the analysis of stock market prediction. Stock market analysts use many techniques in making their predictions such as trend analysis, charting and historical data analysis. Experienced analysts can integrate a great deal of such information but have difficulty in describing exactly how each piece of information is weighted and combined to yield a stock market prediction. Braun and Chandler [5] demonstrate the use of ACLS (Analog Concept Learning System), a tool for learning from examples, to develop decision rules based on induction from stock market analysts actual behaviors. Based on their study, the researchers found that the rule induction system produced predictions as good as those of an expert market analyst. Such a tool can be used to supplant the expert market analyst's decision behavior or to extend the expert's capabilities in making stock market predictions.

Holsapple, Whinston and Tam [6] also describe inductive approaches to acquiring trading rules. These authors argue that rules used by securities traders have evolved through years of trading activities and are difficult to elicit through conventional methods such as might be used to elicit knowledge for expert systems development. Two methods are described for automated acquisition of these rules which, once obtained, can be used for developing and expert trading system.

Globalization of financial markets has led to a more complex environment in which financial decision making must take place. The need for better, quicker and more accurate information has never been greater. Many firms are now moving toward in-house management of corporate investment and portfolios and thus greater attention toward performance is required. Racioppo [7] identifies six areas where artificial intelligence systems can be of direct benefit in global financial markets. These include: (1) financial statements analyzer for multinational firms. This expert system would contain regulatory requirements for each particular country involved and also and expert's knowledge on the firm's performance. For example, this knowledge might be of the form that would know that a specific return on assets in one country might be inadequate where in another country it might be very acceptable. (2) Traderless, 24-hour trading programs. Individual human traders are not available on a 24-hour basis. Thus, it may be desirable to capture a trader's rules and have these available on a 24-hour basis. Smaller firms may have greater access to markets through use of such systems. The traderless system may yield benefits in providing more con-

sistent decisions. (3) Financial and Strategic Models which account for uncertainty. Many of the international markets are more volatile than domestic
markets and many decisions are made on limited and restricted information.
Thus expert systems which can deal with uncertainty can provide more realistic
financial models. (4) Hedging strategies for foreign securities and currencies.
Expert systems can be developed to take advantage of hedges that limit risk.
Many different types of hedges are possible such as interest-rate swaps, curren-
cy swaps, equities, options and futures. An expert system can analyze a trader's
position and based on various regulations suggest possible hedging options to
limit the trader's market exposure. (5) Arbitrage Systems. Expert systems can
directly act on market information to exploit arbitrage situations. The expert
systems would act in a monitoring role, monitoring large volumes of transactions
and would look for an price discrepancies between the market index and the underlying securities. Then the ES could place automatic buy/sell orders to exploit
the opportunities. (6) Real time monitoring. Real time expert systems can more
accurately assess the volumes of financial data and transactions than humans.
Thus, a wide variety of real-time financial monitoring expert systems may be
beneficial.

3. Framework for Assessment of Expert Systems Opportunities in Finance.

The domain of finance is broad and contains many opportunities for expert
systems development as described in the examples of the prior sections. Characteristics of the finance domain in general include: volatile, dynamic problem environments, particularly in investments and financial markets; the need for real
time systems in many cases ranging from the credit monitoring to the arbitrage
systems; integration of expert systems into existing systems -- very few of the existing systems in finance are standalone systems -- they are integrated with existing information systems; the need for a variety of expert systems ranging from
monitoring, to diagnostic, to planning, to intelligent checklists. In discussions
with many of the firms utilizing ES technologies in the financial area, several issues have been identified. One major trend is to have the domain experts do
much of the ES development. That is, many firms are finding best results when
utilizing the domain expert or experts to handle the knowledge elicitation, the
basic ES design (user interface, structure), and the validation of the system.
Thus, in many cases, the so-called AI experts may not be directly involved in
developing many of the finance applications; rather, if involved at all, they may
do some of the programming but in many cases, traditional information systems
departments are providing the programming and integration of ES technologies
into existing systems. Further, much of the work in finance is being implemented

using expert systems shells, both mainframe and micro, which greatly reduces the need for AI-Experts proficient in computer science skills.

Another trend appears to be the integration of expert systems into traditional or conventional information systems. The ES is just an extension of an existing decision support tool although a variety of new issues arise [8]. From the standpoint of the firm, it is beneficial to be able to use existing technology and skills to develop and implement ES. On the other hand, firms are finding the need for new skill positions such as a knowledge base manager. This position may be somewhat analogous to a database manager but with broader responsibilities requiring knowledge of the problem domains for which the knowledge base is to be maintained. Another issue arising in some firms embracing ES technology is in dealing with management. Typically, traditional information systems development projects have a finite development cycle and closure can be obtained with respect to completion of the project. Often, in the financial applications area, ES are rarely ever finished. This is largely due to the dynamic nature of the financial environments and the need for constant attention to the updating and maintenance of the knowledge bases. In some cases this lack of closure on a system causes some discomfort at the management level as they see a continuous stream of resources being directed towards ES activity. Other issues include the maintenance and quality of the knowledge base. Firms are finding that standards, policies and procedures need to be established for monitoring the quality of the knowledge base. This means that internal audit departments must develop the skills to audit and evaluated complex financial domains for which they may have little background or experience. But from a management control standpoint, many strategic decisions in the firms are financial in nature and reliance of ES without assurance of the quality of advice being rendered may open up exposures to litigation and regulation. Clearly the auditability and continual validation of knowledge bases will be a major issue confronting management dealing with ES technologies.

4. Conclusions and Summary

Expert Systems work in finance is quite diverse and provides opportunities for better effectiveness and efficiency in dealing with financial matters. From monitoring systems to detect anomalies in credit reporting to labor savings in insurance claims processing to dynamic trading systems for securities, financial expert systems have great potential to change the manner in which firms do business. This change does not come without cost and many of the costs are going to be in the establishment of new procedures and policies for managing and dealing with the technology. Areas that were once perceived to be of high cost such as standalone workstations running Lisp or Prolog based custom expert systems does not appear to be as much of a cost problem since much of the development work is taking place on micros or mainframes with high-quality expert systems shells. Indeed some firms, such as Dupont, have taken an approach which allows end users to obtain low cost shells and experiment with developing ES for individual decision making support.

Benefits from ES work in finance appear to be in better managing and dealing with huge volumes of transactions (e.g., insurance claims processing), dealing with extremely dynamic and volatile environments (arbitrage systems), and in managing complex finance based projects (cash management). Indeed, several leading AI forecasters view finance as the coming Mecca for ES development and opportunity.

REFERENCES

[1] McBride, R.D., O'Leary, D.E. and G.R. Widmeyer. "A System for Supporting Cash Management Decisions", working paper, Center for Accounting Research, University of Southern California, March, 1988.

[2] McBride, R.D., O'Leary, D.E. and G.R. Widmeyer. "CASH MANAGER: A Knowledge-Based DSS for Cash Management", working paper, Center for Accounting Research, University of Southern California, October, 1987.

[3] McBride, R.D., O'Leary, D.E. and G.R. Widmeyer. "A Knowledge-Based System for Cash Management with Managemtn Science Expertise", working paper, Center for Accounting Research, University of Southern California, January, 1988.

[4] Newquist, H. "American Experess and AI: Don't Leave Home Without Them", AI Expert, vol. 2, no. 4, April 1987, pp. 63-65.

[5] Braun, H. and J.S. Chandler. "Predicting Stock Market Behavior Through Rule Induction: An Application of the Learning From Example Approach", Decision Sciences, vol. 18, no. 3, Summer 1987, pp. 415-429.

[6] Holsapple, C.W., Whinston, A.B., and K.Y. Tam. "Inductive Approaches to Acquire Trading Rules", Proceedings of the First Annual Conference on Expert Systems in Business, November 1987, pp. 103-120.

[7] Racioppo, S.G. "Expert Systems in Global Financial Markets", Proceedings of the First Annual Conference on Expert Systems in Business, November 1987, pp. 201-208.

[8] Turban E. and P.R. Watkins, "Integrating Expert Systems and Decision Support Systems", MIS Quarterly, 1986, vol. 10, no. 2, pp. 121-136.

Applied Expert Systems, E. Turban and P.R. Watkins (Editors)
© Elsevier Science Publishers B.V. (North-Holland), 1988

EXPERT SYSTEM-BASED
ROBOT TECHNOLOGY

Efraim Turban and Donna M. Schaeffer

Systems Management Center
University of Southern Calif.
Los Angeles, CA
90049-0021

Programs in Information Sciences
The Claremont Graduate School
Claremont, CA 91711

Many of the limitations of today's robots can be removed by using expert systems technology. This paper outlines a framework for the integration of expert systems into various activities performed by robotics. First, the importance of robotics is highlighted followed by some of their major limitations. The integration of expert systems into robotics is examined next, both in the areas of planning and design as well as in the area of operations. Improvements in speed, capabilities, quality, maintainability, and safety are the major targets of the integration. The state-of-the-art of such an integration is presented. Finally, practical applications in assembly lines, material handling, and welding are presented.

I. INTRODUCTION

Countries in the Pacific Basin have dominated manufacturing in the last two decades with high product quality and low labor costs. In order to out-compete factories in the Pacific Basin, United States' factories must improve productivity and product quality. One of the most promising ways of doing this, which has been explored during the last few years by the manufacturing sector, is the use of robotics. Many manufacturing executives and experts believe that robots offer a chance for American industry to regain its supremacy. Robots play a key role in the "factory of the future", where material handling, maintenance, design, engineering, assembly, and quality control will be integrated and controlled by computers.

Robotics is now considered a serious area of industrial endeavor, with research, design, manufacturing, and sales conducted worldwide by such major firms as Fanuc, Fujitsu, GE, GM, IBM, NEC, Olivetti, and Volkswagon. Several American firms have formed joint ventures with foreign partners for developing and commercializing robots. There are also a number of small corporations producing and selling robots. Several major universities (e.g. Carnegie-Mellon, Massachusetts Institute of Technology, Purdue, and Stanford) have research laboratories dedicated to robotics. The government does research through public and private research institutions such as the National Bureau of Standards, Standard Research Institute, and the Jet Propulsion Laboratory.

Robots usually transport or assemble products with greater consistency and higher quality than human workers can. They sometimes use less resources, have less waste, and have greater output capabilities than human workers do. Robots can also be used to execute jobs in hot and hazardous environments as well as those jobs that are monotonous.

Despite these advantages, today's robots have many limitations which slow down the development of the robotics industry. The purpose of this paper is to explore how some of these limitations might be removed or lessened through the integration of expert systems' technology with robotics.

2. BASIC ROBOTICS CONCEPTS

2.1. Definitions.

According to the Robotics Institute of America, robots are reprogrammable, multi-functional manipulators designed to move materials, parts, tools, and specialized devices through variable programmed motions for the performance of a variety of tasks. Some robots can be viewed as being intelligent.

Intelligent robots are designed to perform complex tasks, imitate the reasoning processes of humans, and hopefully to solve problems that develop in the areas they operate in by identifying problems and taking the necessary corrective actions.

2.2. Types of Robots.

Robots are classified by their control methods which can be either nonservo or servo.

Nonservo robots perform in open loop sequences to complete their tasks. There is no feedback mechanism. Pick-and-place robots which transfer items from one point to another are nonservo robots.

Servo robots incorporate feedback into their operations and provide a limited means of correcting their actions.

2.3. Robot's Components.

The major components of a robot are: manipulator, controller, and the power unit.

The manipulator performs the task the robot is programmed to complete. It is similar to the fingers and wrist of a human's hand.

If the manipulator is considered to be like a hand, then the controller may be thought of as the brain of the robot. It controls the motions the manipulator moves through in completing the robot's task.

The power unit works through actuators to move the manipulators. Pneumatics, hydraulics, and electricity are the most commonly used sources of power.

3. SOME LIMITATIONS OF TODAY'S ROBOTS

Most of today's robots are described as being clumsy, slow, and stupid. They are geared towards performing highly specialized tasks under entirely controlled conditions. No robot, for example, can tie a pair of shoelaces or understand as much language as a two-year-old child can. It is incredibly difficult to teach a robot to perform even the simplest human tasks. The major reasons for these limitations, according to Nitzen [1] are:

3.1. Insufficient material-handling capability
Workpieces and other objects can be handled only if they are indexed within tolerances that match the accuracy of the robot manipulator. Today's robots have very limited capabilities and flexibility in this respect.

3.2. Open loop control
Tasks that require closed-loop feedback control to correct local errors cannot be performed by many of today's robots.

3.3. Inability to detect and correct errors
Detection of unexpected errors and recovery from them cannot be achieved by most of today's robots. A robot system cannot usually verify that all the robot's actions have been executed as planned.

3.4. Restricted mobility
The locomotion of today's robotic carts is restricted to fixed guidance; these carts cannot navigate freely, avoid obstacles, or find their targets in an unstructured environment.

These and other limitations can be alleviated, at least to some extent, with the aid of expert systems.

4. THE POTENTIAL INTEGRATION OF ES AND ROBOTICS

The field of robotics has been closely related to the field of Artificial Intelligence (AI). Some people view robotics as an applied AI area. Expert systems are also considered as being a type of applied AI. Therefore, there are many potential interactions between the two fields.

In order to identify the potential areas in robotics that are candidates for expert systems integration, we used a systems life cycle approach. Figure 1 shows a schematic view of a typical systems life cycle of robotics.

If one analyzes the ten generic areas for which expert systems were found to be most successful (control, diagnosis, design, debugging, instruction, interpretation, monitoring, planning,prediction and repair), one can see a natural fit with many of the robot's life cycle activities.

Most ES efforts are found in the various areas of robotics operations where extensive research has been conducted and several ES were fielded. The following sections provide details of these efforts.

5. PLANNING AND DESIGN

Here are a few examples of activities (based on Soroka [2]) in the area of robotics planning and design that can be enhanced by the use of expert systems:

5.1. Kinematics and Design.

A basic problem of robot kinematics is going from a desired Cartesian position and orientation back to the joint angles required to achieve it. Each kinematically new robot requires its own unique arm solution. Producing such solutions is tedious work and error prone. Nonetheless, existing solutions have been obtained by using only a few simple heuristics for searching a set of relevant equations. An ES can probably be implemented to replace the human expert at this difficult task. Such a program could also be designed to explore the space of possible robot configurations, looking for designs which satisfy input criteria such as workspace shape and size.

5.2. Robot Selection.

Many robot applications involve replacing a human operator with a robot. Rather than designing an ideal robot from scratch, it is frequently possible to find a robot which fits the application. An ES can aid in this process.

The program would prompt the user for important parameters required in the robot, including reach, speed, number of program steps, payload capacity, repeatability, and accuracy. Additional constraints could also be described, such as maximum space available and clean-room considerations. When selecting a robot, the human expert - the applications engineer - considers all these factors in determining cost, payback, and return on investment. Experienced application engineers are in short supply today. An ES could be useful in diffusing robotic applications among a wider community (see the March 1987 issue of Industrial Robots).

5.3. Workplace Layout.

Sometimes robot workplaces are designed de novo,either for a new factory or for a new line. Clearly, applications engineers cannot try out all possible machine placements in laying out robot lines. There is little science for this task, but presumably planners use some rules of thumb which can be translated into heuristics for an ES to guide the search for useful factory layouts. Expert systems will eventually be able to prepare the most appropriate workplace

layout and even to discover major layout manufacturing principles (for a prototype application, see Kumara et al. [3]).

6. OPERATIONS

Expert systems are integrated with robots in an effort to improve robots' operations in the areas listed in Figure 1. We will describe here only two: reliability and safety.

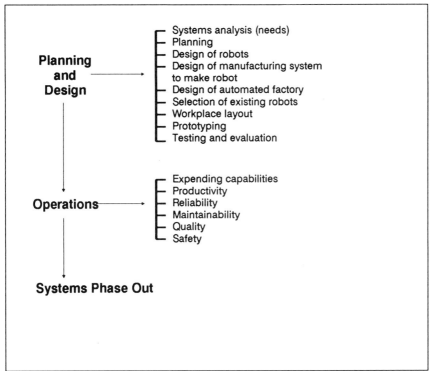

Figure 1
System Life Cycle for Robotics

6.1. Improved Reliability

Robots' reliability is an important issue that restricts the growth of robots' applications. Errors could develop in the robots themselves or in the environment they operate in. For example, at IBM's automated PC assembly plant (in Austin, Texas), a major problem is that the feeders that deliver the screws to the assembly robot frequently provide the screws in an incorrect position. The results are that parts are jammed or assembled incorrectly. The products may be of a poor quality and extensive reworking might be required. The handling of such situations is called error recovery. It involves the detection of errors and the execution of corrective actions. Applying corrective actions can be difficult in applications with real-time systems. The process involves monitoring the robot's operations, detecting the error, diagnosing the cause, and recommending a corrective action to a human operator or commanding the robot's control to execute one. This process can be automated completely or in part with the use of ES, as shown in Figure 2. However, there is a technical difficulty here: most ES are not designed to operate in a real-time environment.

A prototype ES-based error recovery system for off-line programming systems was developed at the University of Minnesota. This rule-based system is still fairly limited in its capabilities; a stronger inference is planned (e.g. by using ES frames representation and object-oriented programming). For further details see Smith and Gini [4].

The Ford Motor Company System. ES can also play a partial role in the automation of the processes shown in Figure 1. Such a case is evidenced at Ford Motor Company. Robots play a major role in the automotive industry, yet one sometimes hears about robots going askew, painting windshields or one another. Today's state- of-the-art technology involves human expert intervention in such cases. However, the human expert may not always be available when things go wrong. Ford Motor Company developed an ES that is used by inexperienced technicians via a PC. The technician responds to a series of questions generated by the ES. The system makes a diagnosis and suggests a corrective action. For further details consult Ford Motor Company at its Essex and Sterling Heights plants and the April 21, 1986 issue of American Metal Market. (For other fault diagnostic ES, see Robot, special issue of October, 1985.)

6.2. Improved Safety

Safety problems do occur from time to time. Accidents can result in severe damages including the loss of human life (as has happened in both Japan and the United States). Accidents could occur due to several reasons. For example, one safety regulation for working with robots is that human employees will not enter the robot's working environment (called work envelope). However, some employees do enter the work envelope. They are either unaware of safety regulations or ignore them. Another possible reason for accidents is that the employees

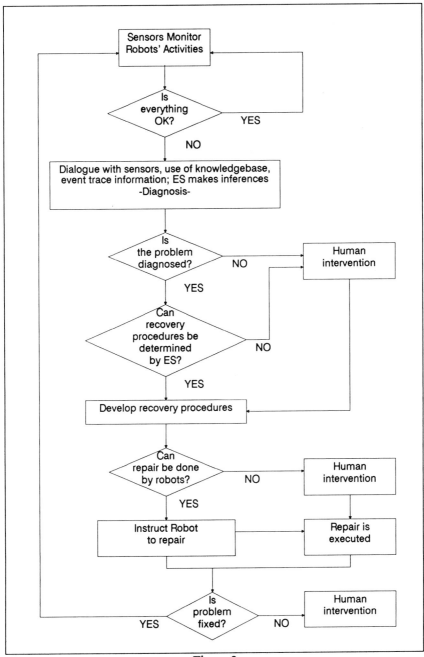

Figure 2
Expert Systems and Robots

may have commanded the robot to stop operating, but there is a malfunction and the robot continued to operate. By integrating an expert system, like the Robotic Intelligence Safety System (RISS), with robots, such accidents can be prevented.

RISS is built with rules like the following:

IF: The robot was commanded to be deactivated, and a person is inside the work envelope, and the robot remains active

THEN: Cut off the main power circuit breaker.

RISS constantly monitors the environment for failures or abnormalities. If any are detected, they are diagnosed and corrective actions are executed. Information is being gathered from several sources in the environment, including the robot's components (i.e. end effector and controller), sensors, other computers and machines, and human operators. Corrective actions for possibly dangerous situations are outputted to the robot's controller, the controllers of other machines, or to a display. Corrective actions may also be outputted to relays or alarms. The robot's next scheduled actions can then be modified or halted.

RISS's knowledge base contains information on the robot's "world", including its elements, their functions, their interactions, and the rules that govern activities (see Figure 3).

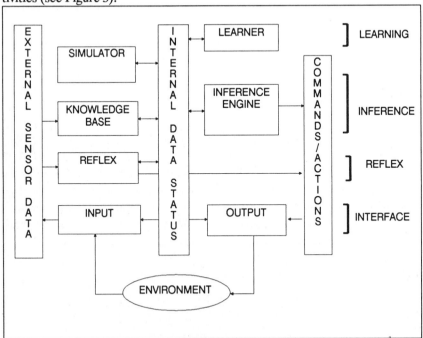

Figure 3
Overall Systems Diagram of the RISS

RISS was developed by Martin Marietta Aerospace Company for NASA's Space Shuttle (for more information, see Ramirez [5]).

7. ROBOT PLANNING AND PROGRAMMING

Robot planning, programming, and reprogramming are important both during the planning and design as well as in the operations of robots. The following are potential areas for ES integration:

7.1. Robot Planning Expert Systems

Robot planning refers to the automatic decision making and planning carried out by a robot as a response to changes. Robot planning can be done at various levels. For example, the most obvious level is where a robot might have to plan a sequence of actions on the basis of signals obtained from changing conditions in its environment. These signals may, indeed, be quite complex, for example the input of visual information from a television camera. Within this level there are four sublevels of planning: actuator (at the lowest level), end effector, object, and task (the highest).

At another level, automated planing may be required to schedule the entire work cycle of a plant that includes many robots as well as other types of automated machinery.

Robot planning activities are fairly complex; therefore they require expert engineering and they last a considerable amount of time. Several attempts to automate the process with AI technologies such as general purpose search heuristics, semantic networks, and first-order predicate calculus, resulted in limited success. For example, PULP-1, which uses analogy as an approach to introduce learning capabilities,is still slow (see reference #). Other programs are effective only for small robotic systems with few independent tasks.

Recently, ES have been used for robot planning and programming. Most of these systems are still in a research phase, but the results are encouraging. An example of such an experimental system is reported by Cai and King-Sun [6]. Their experimental system titled ROPES was successful in improving the planning performance and in increasing the planning speed. Furthermore, ROPES can generate multiple possible solutions for a task and assist in evaluating them. The architecture for this system is shown in Figure 4. The basic control strategies for ROPES are searching, matching, and backtracking.

Another AI-based robot that contains robot planning is Freddy 3. Its inventors (see Mowforth and Bratko [7]) attempted to create a flexible and efficient robot programming environment featuring:

- automatic robot planning
- inductive programming capabilities for the expert system

- AI-based processing of sensory information
- flexible use and transformation between different representations of the robot's world, tasks, and knowledge
- Human transparent communication between robots

This system is one of the most sophisticated ES-based robotics ever constructed. It includes several robots, minicomputers, local area network, and sensors. It was constructed with several ES building tools including the RuleMaster shell which provides the inductive learning capability.

An example of an ES that helps in robot planning as a part of an automated plant is ISIS II. The system, for example, reschedules work in case of malfunctions. For details see Fox and Smith [8].

7.2. Robot Programming

A major difficulty in robot technology exists in the translation from a task specification to a robot program that executes that task. Special dedicated robot languages are used. These languages include customized special features (e.g.for kinematic control of a robot's manipulator). Extensive training and experience are required in order to be a robot programmer.

Because of this and some other difficulties, programming languages are estimated to be used with only 10% of the robots currently in place in factories (Kirschbrown and Dorf [9]). The majority of robots are manually guided through the necessary motions to complete the desired task. The robot later "remembers" the motions and executes them. This method takes a great deal of time and is very cumbersome.

KARMA is a knowledge-based system under development that seeks to eliminate the need for manually instructed robots. For example, when used with an assembly robot, KARMA would take the product's specifications, the components, and a goal statement such as "assemble this product". The result would be a complete and error-free program.

KARMA includes a communication interface enhanced with graphics, pointers, and non-keyboard input devices. This interface communicates back to the user, reporting error conditions, offering additional options, requesting additional information, and making suggestions. KARMA also includes a justifier that explains its actions to the user.

The knowledge base includes facts that are specific to the robot's working environment (e.g. "bottles are made of glass") and rules that apply to assembly operations in general (i.e. "do not drop items").

While still in a developmental phase, KARMA has the potential of reducing the amount of time it takes to make a robot productive (for more information, see Kirschbrown and Dorf [9]).

Another effort to improve robot programming is reported by Cai [10]. The project developed at Purdue University is based on an extension of the "C" programming language.

8. OTHER AREAS

Several other potential areas of integration are discussed in the literature. Some representative samples are:

8.1. Teams of Robots

Most of today's robots are individually programmed for each particular task. This approach works well enough, but the robots must be painstakingly reprogrammed or replaced when the task is altered. In computer integrated manufacturing, (CIM) robots may be organized in a team and may be required to perform any number of tasks. For example, IBM's lap top computer is assembled by a team of three robots, each of which performs some assembly operations. In addition, there is a robot that provides material handling and one that performs tests. Expert systems could direct the robots to communicate and reason with each other. Work is currently being done at the Institute for Robotics and Intelligent Systems at the University of Southern California, in an attempt to equip teams of robots at work on an assembly line with a high order of decision making capabilities. For example, the robots would be able to decide among themselves how best to accomplish a particular task. Thus, if a supply of parts arrives late, several robots (rather than one) could be assigned to the task of inspecting and preparing the parts so that the work team can catch up with the schedule.

8.2. Control

A considerable amount of efforts were invested in attempts to make the robot's control device more intelligent. One attempt in this direction involves the construction of an ES whose knowledge base contains information regarding the system to be controlled. For example, if the robot operates on an assembly line, the knowledge base comprises information relating to the robots and their environment and is used to determine the control signals required to obtain the desired response from the robots and their environment. The control methodology devised has been used to achieve motion control of a single axis electric module in a robot.

8.3. Maintenance by Expert Systems

(Source: Ayres and Miller [11]). The maintenance and repair of mechanical systems is very labor intensive and requires a high level of expertise when performed by humans. There are indications that the automotive industry may lead the way in using robots to perform this type of maintenance. For example, several years ago, Volkswagen introduced a diagnostic system for some of its models, in which an automatic electronic diagnostician was plugged into a specially designed connector built into the car. With expert systems capability, the automated diagnostician could guide a human or even a robot through the needed repairs and adjustments step by step, reducing the need for skilled human labor.

One can foresee ambitious robotic application in automotive maintenance considering the number of automobile parts that are commonly rebuilt. These range from carburetors and alternators up to automatic transmissions. In the future, robotic systems will combine the precision and dexterity developed for assembly operations with inspection capability. With the addition of an ES that can recognize parts needing replacement, a robot could perform the entire repair task, requiring only the old unit and a kit of replacement parts.

8.4. Computer Vision

Expert systems have been applied to improve computer vision as well as the interpretation of information collected by other sensory devices. For further information, see the Proceedings of the Fourth International Conference on Robot Vision and Sensory Control (London, 1984).

9. ACTUAL APPLICATIONS

While it makes sense that ES could provide the technology for future intelligent robots which will be able to cope with unstructured environments, and while there are extensive experimentations going on in research institutions, there are very few commercial robots/ES systems currently in use. However, as can be seen from the examples which are summarized below, there is tremendous potential for such commercial systems.

9.1. IBM's Assembly Plant

IBM's lap top PC Convertible is the first computer to be assembled entirely by intelligent robots. The factory uses a process called flexible automation, which makes use of modular workstations that are programmed to perform a variety of tasks. From the receiving dock to the shipping dock, the PC is assembled, tested, packaged, and shipped by robots. The robots use extensive sensory systems (such as computer vision) to execute tasks as well as to detect errors. Once errors or malfunctions are detected, the information is transmitted to an expert system which diagnoses the situation and reports the results to a human supervisor (there is only one such person in the entire plant). At the present time, the corrective actions suggested by the ES are executed by humans.

The plant assembles over 100,000 PCs a year and is currently being upgraded for increased output and reduced costs. For further details, see Saporito [12].

9.2. Knowledge-Based Expert Welding

Adaptiweld Systems (manufactured by Adaptive Technologies, Inc., Sacramento, California) is one of the first commercially available intelligent robot welding systems. It incorporates the knowledge of skilled welders. This knowledge is used for robot planning once the characteristics of a seam to be welded are collected by a 3-D vision system. Based on these characteristics the ES plans the welding task to be performed without direct human supervision. The rules in the knowledge base allow the system to best respond to particular welding conditions. For further information see Kerth [13] and Thompson et al. [14].

9.3. DEC's Automated Materials Handling System

DEC has implemented a materials handling system in two of its manufacturing facilities. These systems control factory inventory and generate timely, accurate reports on work progress and quality. Key elements of each system are a pair of robots that transport assembly items, and two expert systems that determine when and to where items should be dispatched.

The expert systems, named Dispatcher and Mover, are the controlling software for the entire materials handling system. Dispatcher determines the order in which work-in-progress (WIP) items are dispatched, and to which workstations they will be sent. Mover coordinates and drives WIP items via the robots' carousels and conveyors.

Dispatcher uses information in its knowledge base to select the best work item(s) to dispatch to a workstation, depending on current work status and demand on the factory floor. The knowledge base was created initially with interactive utilities that are part of the system. New work is entered into the system either by automatic utilities or iterative routines. Dispatcher performs updates automatically, but any exceptions that arise can be handled manually with interactive utilities.

Dispatcher's knowledge base contains information about four components that enable it to make decisions: workstations, route list, unit load, and WIP. These elements, along with the validation table that verifies valid workstations, operations, parts and classes, represent the state of the factory floor. Since its implementation at DEC's Marlborough, Massachusetts, facility in 1985, the materials handling system has been in operation six days a week for three shifts per day. During the first month, it reduced inventory by 50%, and inventory accounts increased in accuracy to 99.9%. DEC estimates that this system saves $25 million annually.

10. CONCLUSION

Intelligent robots will play an increasingly significant role in industrial, service, and military settings in the future. Just how much of a role and how soon is a question that cannot be answered now. The answer depends on several variables, all with economic, technological, and sociological impacts.

Expert systems are being integrated with robotics technology along several dimensions. This integration may include other AI technologies (such as machine vision and voice recognition). Such an integration can result in a much wider use of robotics which could be propelled by a constructive synergy among the systems' elements.

This paper pointed out some initial efforts in the integration of the two technologies; the prospects are bright, but the road to mature integration may be lengthy. However, advances in computer technology, VLSI, parallel processing, and ES shells coupled with the appearance of reasonably priced AI workstations and expert systems on a chip, could accelerate the integration and make it technically and economically feasible in many settings in the very near future.

REFERENCES

[1]   Nitzan D., "Developing of Intelligent Robots." In *The World Yearbook of Robot R&D*, edited by I. Alexander. London: Konan Page, 1985.

[2]   Soroka, B.I., Expert System and Robotics; PROC. *Robots 8*, June 1984.

[3]   Kumara, S.R.T. et al., "Application of AI Techniques to Facilities Layout Analysis and Planning - Development of an Expert System," *Proceedings of the Intelligent Systems and Machines Conference.* Oakland University Center for Robotics & Advanced Automation, April, 1986.

[4]   Smith, R. E. and M. Gini, *Robot Tracking and Control Issues in an Intelligent Error Recovery System,'* IEEE, 1986.

[5]   Ramirez, C. A., "Artificial Intelligence Applied to Robot Fail Safe Operations," *Robots 9*.

[6]   Cai, Z. and F. King-Sun, "Robot Planning Expert Systems," *IEEE*, 1986.

[7]   Mowforth, P. and I. Bratko, "AI and Robotics; Flexibility and Integration," *Robotica*, Vol. 5, 1987.

[8]   Fox, H.S. and S.F. Smith, "ISIS - A Knowledge-Based System for Factory Scheduling," *Expert Systems*, Vol. 1, No. 1, 1984.

[9]   Kirschbrown, R.H., and R.C. Dorf, "KARMA: A Knowledge-Based Robot Manipulation System: Determining Problem Characteristics," *Robots 8*.

[10] Cai, Z., "Some Research Work on Expert Systems in AI Courses at Purdue," *IEEE*, 1986.

[11] Ayres, R.U., and S.M. Miller, *Robotics and Flexible Manufacturing Technology.* Park Ridge, N.J.: Noyer Publishing Company, 1985.

[12] Saporito, B., "IBM's No-Hands Assembly Line," *Fortune*, 15 September, 1986.

[13] Kerth, W.J., Jr., "Knowledge-Based Expert Welding," *Robots 9.*

[14] Thompson, D.R., et al., "A Knowledge-Based System for Continuous Seam Welding in the Autonomous Manufacturing Environment." In *Knowledge-Based Expert Systems in Manufacturing,* Proceedings of the American Society of Mechanical Engineers, edited by S.C. Lu and R. Kumanduri, 1986.

Applied Expert Systems, E. Turban and P.R. Watkins (Editors)
© Elsevier Science Publishers B.V. (North-Holland), 1988

TOWARD AN EXPERT/DECISION SUPPORT SYSTEM IN BUSINESS VENTURING

Professor Burton V. Dean

Chairman
Department of Organization and Management
School of Business
San Jose State University
San Jose, California 95192

Expert systems and decision support systems applications in firms are increasingly of interest to both managers and management scientists. Current developments in such systems make it possible to apply these techniques to a wide variety of managerial situations and industrial sectors.

Business ventures require financing, technology transfer, and manufacturing capabilities to achieve corporate goals. Similarly, suppliers of funds, knowledge, or facilities often need to review and evaluate such business ventures on an ongoing basis. At the present time there is a significant mismatch between demand and supply of these resources, with many unsatisfied needs occurring throughout U.S. industry.

This chapter reports on the results obtained at an early stage in applying expert systems and decision support systems (EDSS) methodologies in the case of business venturing. The chapter presents 1) the key sources of information concerning business ventures in the form of a business plan and associated business profiles, 2) the essential characteristics and associated relative weights of importance for a business venture to be successful in achieving its business goals, and 3) the methodology to be used to evaluate and score business ventures as to their magnitude and chance of success.

Analysis of results achieved in the case of a firm developing a prototype EDSS in business venturing is presented, along with future requirements for full-scale implementation.

1. INTRODUCTION AND BACKGROUND

This chapter reports on an area of business venturing in which a business venture requires financing to undertake manufacturing and/or marketing activities (Dean and Lee [1], and Kozmetsky, Gill and Smilor [2]). Many technology startup firms fail, and the results of such incidents are usually devastating because of the capital, time, and number of individuals involved. In spite of this, major amounts of venture capital are being committed to high technology startup firms (Pratt and Morris [3]). The magnitude and trend of such investments suggests the need for an advanced methodology to match high technology-based startup firms with a variety of users at early stages. Clearly, the success of a business venture depends on many factors (Tyebjee and Bruno [4]). The successful development of a new business venture is influenced by factors related to the business venture itself as well as to the external relationships with investment firms, manufacturers, and the marketplace (Dean, [5]).

Sourcenet, a California based two year old firm, addresses investment/business opportunity sourcing needs of high technology based firms. Sourcenet maintains a computerized database that contains profiles of business venture investment opportunities. Currently, it is envisioned that Sourcenet will have approximately 4,000 firms on file in the data base. At the present time, Sourcenet has approximately 1,000 firms in the database, with the remaining expected to be entered in 1988. For each firm, Sourcenet will have a set of characteristics (questions) listed and data elements (answers) (Dean and Lee, [1]).

Coincident with the work reported on in this chapter, Sourcenet developed a conceptual model for providing specific detailed information, as represented in Figure 1. Although Sourcenet receives information from business ventures, financing sources, and technology users, the data that is collected on the Sourcenet designed form will also be processed using an expert system developed by Sourcenet. At the present time a prototype of this system, Sourcenet Expert/Decision Support System for Business Venturing (SESBV), is under testing and evaluation. Sourcenet, in developing its EDSS, believes that no other firm has a working system of this type. The flow diagram in Figure 1 indicates that SESBV is planned (1) to utilize large volumes of data, with know ledge to be developed by the EDSS, and (2) to disseminate this information to a variety of different types of users indicated at the bottom of Figure 1. The central objective of SESBV is to provide both an efficient and an effective means of providing successful matches of business ventures with related organizations.

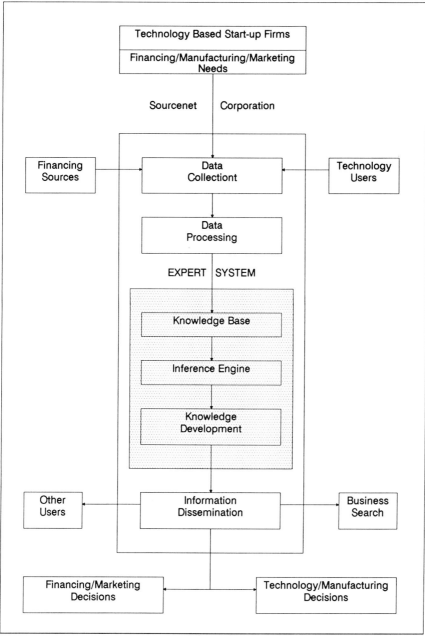

Figure 1
The Conceptual Model of Sourcenet's SESBV

2. PROBLEM STATEMENT

At the present time, Sourcenet has the capability to assemble data and to transform its data files, which contain detailed information concerning characteristics of technology-based startup firms. Sourcenet's problem is to develop an expert system to match needs of technology- based startup firms with the requirements of users representing a variety of business venturing interests. Examples of users are venture capital firms, pension funds, investment bankers, manufacturing firms, investment brokers, acquisition firms, and other organizations interested in capitalizing on potential opportunities occurring through investments, technology transfer, or technology acquisition associated with high technology-based startup firms.

Although a technology-based startup firm may be seeking financing, usually from a number of potential sources, an investment firm is often deluged with more opportunities than it can handle. The excess demand for funds over the available supply provides numerous opportunities for a mismatch and/or a reluctance on the part of investors to receive adequate expert information concerning opportunities. In fact, investors are able to consider only a fraction of the potential opportunities available to the particular investment firm.

It is envisioned that each user will periodically receive a packet of new venture opportunities tailored to meet the user's specific investment criteria. Upon evaluation of the venture opportunities, the user is encouraged to contact those venture applicants in which there exists an interest.

SESBV will provide a particular user with a ranking, if so desired, of all business venture opportunities in accordance with user needs and priorities. Furthermore, the user will have the capability to access the specific choices, along with the relative factor scores provided by the expert system. Finally, the user will have the capability to notify the expert system as to those business ventures that are of immediate interest to the user and to obtain the associated business plans and profiles.

3. ROLES OF SESBV

Senior management at Sourcenet recognizes that its corporate future depends on automation of its business venture matching process. Import ant roles of such automation are (1) the improvement and increase of managerial productivity, (2) the reduction in clerical costs and (3) the elimination of delays and lost time in carrying out the business venture matching requirements. The tasks that SESBV will automate are the following:

1) Accessing large amounts of information concerning technology-based startup firms in a systematic and integrated manner;

2) Evaluating potential business ventures using a mathematical
model based on factors and weights provided by the user or
suggested by SESBV; and

3) Selecting those business ventures that meet prescribed user
needs and interests, or allowing the user to suggest desired
characteristics of technology-based startup firms to be requested for further searching.

As documented by Harmon and King [6] and Turban and Mock [7], SESBV
should yield significant results for Sourcenet by (1) accumulating knowledge
over a number of users of the Sourcenet data, (2) being consistent in providing
information, (3) documenting its results, (4) replicating and duplicating expert
human users, and (5) operating at a reasonable cost over years of use. SESBV
is an industrialization of knowledge acquisition and dissemination concerning
business ventures and will allow future users to benefit from previous experience
in analyzing business ventures.

SESBV will enable the Sourcenet computer to aid users in the decision
making process. The know-how of the human expert is used to instruct the Sourcenet computer on solving a user problem or making a user decision. The attractiveness of SESBV is that it utilizes the expert know ledge of the humans who
develop and use the Sourcenet system, as well as the computer's ability to store
large amounts of information and to consider all possibilities at high speed.

SESBV will utilize the Sourcenet computer to interact with the user's questions and arrive at a conclusion based on the answers provided. The Sourcenet
user may ask the Sourcenet computer why certain information is desired and the
SESBV will explain its need for data and how the data will be utilized. The
SESBV will state how it arrived at its conclusions; it will not only give advice but
also justify the opinion it offers.

Figure 2 presents the essential structure of the SESBV. SESBV, in its role
at Sourcenet, must provide the following capabilities:

(1) The means to manage information and/or data (business venture profiles),

(2) Logic management (decision model and rules), and

(3) Dialogue management (involving multiusers business venture
needs as indicated in Figure 1).

Sourcenet has already developed an excellent capability in the area of (1)
above by utilizing a written questionnaire to obtain a profile for a business venture to be listed in the Sourcenet database. The questionnaire contains 33

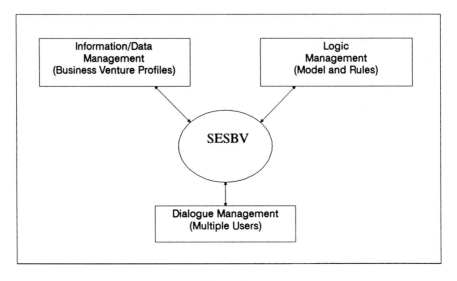

Figure 2
Basic Interrelationships and Structure of the Sourcenet SESBV

detailed questions, classified into eight sections, as presented in Table 1. In addition, a Business Plan, if available, is entered into the Sourcenet file.

In the case of (3) above, an approved user may access the Sourcenet database and request that it provide answers to a number of questions, as listed in Table 2. The user-friendly mode of operation allows the user-computer dialogue to take place in accordance with the specific needs of the user. The user may wish to utilize SESBV to obtain numerical evaluations of specific characteristics, as well as an overall weighted score of those business ventures of particular interest to the user. Users may also receive special reports and analyses concerning specific business ventures. Accordingly, a user receives the data and information concerning business ventures that meet the user's needs for investment, technology, and/or manufacturing opportunities.

The following section presents the methodology utilized for accomplishing (2) above.

4. METHODOLOGY

The central element in the logic management program of SESBV is a decision model - a set of equations and parameters which are used in the business venture evaluation process. Modeling is necessary when a combination of human judgment and a computer can be more effective than the person alone. A model is an idealization of a real situation, which permits one to conduct trial

Table 1
Business Venture Profile Data and Information

I. Overview Company identification, date listed, business type, number of employees, location, annual sales, type of relationship sought, range of financial commitment preferred, reason for seeking development resources.

II. Corporate History Year company founded, corporate year end, stage of development, last year's profit, percentage of sales growth, debt obligation.

III. Product or Service Title of project, company activities, industry trends, valuable characteristics, stage of development, distribution, development schedule.

IV. Technology Description Technology or expertise offered, description of application, areas of application, how technology will improve the market penetration, further expansion plans.

V. Management Team Background of chief executive officer, senior engineering manager, senior marketing manager, and other key executives.

VI. Marketing Information Target market and customer, market strategy tools, unique marketing or sales strategies, competition.

VII. Financial Information Date of current statement, net sales, cost of goods sold, selling and administrative expenses, net income, debt-equity ratio, liquidity ratio, availability of financial statements, auditor.

VIII. Balance Sheet Current balance sheet, listing current and fixed assets, current liabilities and long-term debt, total assets and liabilities, loans from shareholders, capital stock, retained earnings, total liabilities

---

experiments on a computer while obtaining relatively valid results. Obviously, the Sourcenet computer and its data base concerning a business venture will not be an exact replica of the actual business venture represented by a profile. However, if Sourcenet is capable of (1) capturing the essential elements of a business venture in its profile and (2) processing information utilizing an accurate model to arrive at a qualitative assessment of the relative value of a business venture, then SESBV would be of significant economic value to both Sourcenet and its users.

We should further point out that a decision support system usually requires a mathematical model to be developed that represents senior management's view in the process. In the field of business venturing the final decisions concerning

Table 2
User Dialogue Management

I. Company Profiles   The user is asked to state preference in having the expert system search for opportunities on the basis of business type, location, or level of financing involved. The system prints reports by reference number.

II. Relationship Preferred   Choices for relationships include capital placement, corporate partner, joint venture, licensing, technology transfer, or no preference.

III. Keyword Search   Users may search for types of businesses or technologies on the basis of keywords entered. An extensive data dictionary of important terms is provided to the user.

IV. Location   Users may restrict the location of opportunities to countries, regions or states.

V. Level of Financial Interest   The user enters the range of financing available for a transaction (minimum and maximum amounts).

VI. New Opportunities   New business ventures are listed weekly. Users may page through the list, search using keywords, or use reference numbers to select business venture opportunities.

---

business venture evaluation, selection, and acquisition are always the responsibility of senior management at the highest level.

In SESBV, the author is utilizing the Delphi Method involving the use of expert members of the Advisory Board of Sourcenet, to arrive at consensus evaluations (Linstone and Turoff [8]).

The Sourcenet structured research effort in developing SESBV is based on the use of a Scoring Model and incorporating the Delphi Method (Dean and Nishry [9]). SESBV represents a body of experience with business ventures and is subject to incremental learning as a result of knowledge acquisition. The following steps are being followed in building SESBV:

(1) Obtaining the relevant facts concerning business ventures and associated Sourcenet procedures,

(2) Refining the means for acquiring facts and developing procedures for processing this information,

(3) Constructing a prototype of SESBV,

(4) Structuring the knowledge domain consistent with the basic Scoring Model,

(5) Developing the first working model of SESBV,

(6) Testing, debugging and refining further SESBV, and

(7) Conducting experimental applications with actual users.

Knowledge is being built up incrementally as a result of experience with the EDSS and utilizing the above seven steps.

Sourcenet has assembled a Delphi Panel, consisting of its Advisory Board, whose chairman is the author, to carry out the following steps in SESBV development:

(1) Utilize the Delphi Panel in applying the Delphi Method to reach consensus decisions on all aspects of the SESBV model development.

(2) Develop a set of categories which are of major importance in evaluating a business venture.

(3) Derive a set of six factors, (F1, . . ., F6) based on the categories in (2), which can be quantitatively assessed from available information in the Sourcenet computerized database (profiles) or subjectively evaluated by experts utilizing such information as written business plans. Each Fj is evaluated on a scale of five values, 1 (very low) - 5 (very high).

(4) For each F_j, $j = 1, 2, . . ., 6$, develop a weighting value, W_j, which assesses the criticality of the corresponding factor F_j in the business venture, and its importance to the potential user (Sourcenet subscriber). We stipulate that each W_j is to be a numerical fraction and that the sum of the W_j equals 1.00.

(5) SESBV considers business ventures (i), where i may range over integer values of 1 through 4,000; Sourcenet is interested in evaluating as many as 4,000 business ventures in its database depending on user interests.

(6) SESBV calculates (A_{ij}), a matrix of values associated with the assessment of the ith business venture with respect to the jth factor, F_j. The values of the A_{ij} will range between 1 (very low) - 5 (very high). The A_{ij} are estimated by human experts at the present time.

(7) SESBV calculates the relative score, or overall strength, of the ith business ventures using a Scoring Model, as follows:

$$S_i = \sum_j \left(W_j \right) \times \left(A_{ij} \right)$$

A perfect (ideal) business venture will have a maximum score of $(1.00)(5) = 5.00$. Other ventures will have smaller proportional values.

(8) SESBV will also have the opportunity to conduct preliminary screening on the basis of particular factors specified by a user. Accordingly, certain business ventures would not be evaluated using (7).

(9) A user may wish to stipulate that certain additional factors be considered, beyond those normally evaluated by Sourcenet, which will be easily incorporated into SESBV.

Table 3 presents a list of the SESBV factors and corresponding weights, which were derived by the Delphi Panel. The Delphi Panel reached consensus concerning the six factors, as well as the associated factor weights. In SESBV a user may decide to add or modify the factors, as well as change the associated weights.

TABLE 3
SESBV FACTOR WEIGHTS

SESBV FACTORS	NORMALIZED FACTOR WEIGHTS
1. Organization/Personnel Characteristics	33
2. Market Analysis	20
3. Business Strategy/Policy	18
4. Technology Characteristics	11
5. Product Characteristics	10
6. Marketing/Sales Operations	8
TOTAL	100

The Appendix presents the individual criteria, which are to be utilized for evaluating each of the six factors presented in Table 3. The method used for developing these criteria is as follows:

(1) Each member of the Delphi Panel was requested to generate a set of criteria for each of the six factors.

(2) The associated criteria were reviewed and categorized by a member of the Delphi Panel, Professor Les Jankovich, Department of Organization and Management, School of

Business, San Jose State University, San Jose, California
95192 and the author.

(3) After several rounds of consensus seeking the categories and
classifications were developed as presented in Appendix A
and approved by the Delphi Panel.

5. SESBV IMPLEMENTATION

At the present time an expert system for business venturing methodology is
being instituted utilizing the Sourcenet database of business venture profiles and
its user dialogue management. To fully implement SESBV, Sourcenet would require the following steps to be performed:

(1) Conducting a manual evaluation of a sample of Sourcenet
business ventures applying the SESBV which has been
developed-to-date. The purpose of this test and evaluation
would be to determine the adequacy of SESBV, as compared to human experts. In fact, this step has been completed at the present time.

(2) As a result of the completion of (1) above, a computer
software package needs to be developed to carry out the
scoring model calculations. In this regard, matrix multiplica-
tions are to be performed, based on the factor weights and
the business venture assessments corresponding to the associated factors,as provided by human experts.

(3) A small sample of business ventures and associated lead users
should be used to test, evaluate and modify the prototype
SESBV.

(4) Based on the successful accomplishment of (3), introduction
of the SESBV service could be provided.

(5) Actual users' experiences would provide the means to
upgrade SESBV and allow the expert system to become a
cost-effective means of matching business ventures with user
needs.

In summary, this chapter has presented the steps being followed to develop
an expert system in business venturing in the case of one firm's undertaking of
this effort (Dean and Lee [1]). In conclusion, SESBV is an intelligent decision
support system incorporating a rule-based expert system within it, as shown in
Figure 1. Increasingly, the combination of expert systems and decision support

system methodologies is being utilized (Sprague and Carlson [10] and Turban and Mock [7]).

ACKNOWLEDGMENTS

The author acknowledges the contributions made by the following in developing an expert system in business venturing:

(1) Sourcenet Corporation, Belmont, California

(2) The senior members of the management team of Sourcenet Corporation, including Peter McCracken and Edward Myers.

(3) The Advisory Board of Sourcenet Corporation, and

(4) Professor Les Jankovich, Department of Organization and Management, School of Business, San Jose State University.

Responsibility for the basic methodology and approach in developing SESBV rests with the author.

REFERENCE

[1] Dean, B.V., and D.R. Lee, "Growing a Venture Capital Expert System," *INTERACT*, November 1987, pp 126-128.

[2] Kozmetsky, G., M.D. Gill, and R.W. Smilor, *Financing and Managing Fast-Growth Companies: The Venture Capital Process*. New York: Lexington Books, 1985.

[3] Pratt, S.E. and J.K. Morris, *Guide to Venture Capital Sources*. Wellesley Hills, Mass.: Venture Economics, Inc., 1984.

[4] Tyebjee, T.T. and Bruno, A.V., "A Model of Venture Capitalist Investment Activity," *Management Science*, volume 30, Number 9 (September 1984) pp. 1051-1066.

[5] Dean, B.V., "The Project-Management Approach in the 'Systematic Management' of Innovative Start-up Firms," *Journal of Business Venturing*, Volume 1, Number 2, 1986.

[6] Harmon, P. and D. King, *Expert System--Artificial Intelligence in Business*. New York: John Wiley Press, 1985.

[7] Turban, E. and T.J. Mock, "Expert Systems: What They Mean to the Executive?" 1988.

[8] Linstone, H. and M. Turoff, *The Delphi Method*. Reading, Mass.: Addison-Wesley Publishing Company, 1975.

[9] Dean B.V. and M.J. Nishry, "Scoring and Profitability Models for Evaluating and Selecting Engineering Projects," *Operators Research*, Volume 13, Number 4, July-August, 1965, pp. 550-569.

[10] Sprague, R.H. and E.D. Carlson, *Building Effective Decision Support Systems*. Englewood Cliffs, N.J.: Prentice-Hall, 1982.

Appendix A - SESBV FACTORS AND CRITERIA

Table A1
Technology Characteristics

1. Technology Specifications

- Is the technology well defined?
- Is an advanced or me-too technology being used?
- Is it a single technology or a re multiple technologies being used?
- Is it high/low technology?
- What is the state of development of the idea, prototype, and manufacturing?
- Is this a state of the art product development efort? Or is it uniqueness that is being stressed?
- Is the prototype completed?
- Is the product difficult or easy to produce?

2. Company's Position in the Technology

- Does the firm have sufficient strength in the underlying technology?
- How does the firm's base of technology compare to its competition?
- What is the quality and capability of the firm's technical staff?
- Do the proprietary features of the technology reside in the firm?
- Are the technological risks for the firm high or low?
- Does the firm have the technological experience to move the prototype into production?
- What is the relative standing of the firm within the particular technology field?

Table A2
Market Analysis

1. Market Potential: Size and Profitability
- Is the future market large or small?
- does the market grow at a sufficiently high rate? How long will the market continue to grow?
- What is the size in total dollars of the market, as well as the firm's current and anticipated market share?
- Is the market potential of sufficient size and such that the firm may become highly profitable?
- Does the proposed development constitute a new market, or is it an extension of an existing market?
- Does the market contain extreme price sensitivity?
- What is the profitability of the market niche?
- Where is the market located - local, national, international?
- Are there a few or a large number of customers?

2. Competition: Strength and Vulnerability
- What is the competition?
- How many competitors are there?
- Are the competitors' strengths sufficient to dominate this particular firm?
- What are the significant competitive factors in the market - price, service, quality, availability, response time to customers?
- What is the possibility of a substitute product appearing in the market?
- What is the competitive advantage of the firm's product?
- What are the costs, product differentiation, and patent positions?

3. Firm's Role in the Market
- Is the firm aware of the specific niche market it intends to serve?
- What is the value added by the firm?
- Is there a systematic means for analyzing the market, as presented by the firm?
- What is the relative position of the firm within the marketplace?
- What is the firm's potential expansion into new markets? Into related markets?
- Has the firm worked closely with the major customers in the market?
- Does the firm demonstrate a detailed knowledge of the market?
- Has a market research study been performed, and what is the quality of the study?
- What is the supporting data for the Market Analysis and how accurate is it?

Table A2 (Continued)
Market Analysis

___

4. Product Need
- Does the market view the proposed product as being unique?
- Is this a required product versus a discretionary product?
- What are the social implications of the product?
- What are the prerequisites for success of the firm's product(s)?

Table A3
Product Characteristics

___

1. Product Strength
- Will there be a number of products in the line, or only a single product?
- What is the relative importance of cost factors?
- What is the percentage value added by the firm?
- What are the global implications of the product?
- Are the product's characteristics described in sufficient detail?
- What has been the track record of the firm's previous products?
- What is the function performed by the product from the user's point of view?
- Is the product a component or a system?

2. Product Life Cycle
- Are there a sufficient number of customers?
- Does the product have a long-term utility and viability?
- What is the user risk versus the advantages to the user?

3. Product Development Stage
- Does the company have a good idea of what its product's characteristics are?
- Can the product's characteristics be modified with a changing market/or competition?
- What is the possibility for multiple sourcing of components, or of finished goods?
- Is the prototype working satisfactorily?
- Is the prototype ready for demonstration, or ready for production?
- Are there any liability or legal issues of concern?
- What is the patent/trademark/copyright position?

Table A4
Marketing/Sales Operations

1. Sales/Staff Efforts
- Does the product require specialized marketing staff?
- What are the sales/marketing staff requirements?
- Are marketing costs low or high relative to price?
- What are the support/service requirements for the product?
- What is the nature and prior experience of the marketing and management staff?
- What are the characteristics of the sales staff?
- What is the service/support element?
- Does the firm have detailed intelligence gathering system concerning its customers?

2. Marketing Strategy
- Is the firm's marketing strategy clearly stated?
- Is there a marketing study? Is there is one, what are the quality and results of the study?
- What is the firm's selling plan and its unique features?
- What are the detailed plans for prioritizing potential customers?

3. Distribution
- How does the firm plan to distribute its products?
- Is the Product to be marketed through existing channels? If not, how does the firm propose to access the new channels?
- What are the distribution requirements?

4. Customers
- What are the inherent difficulties in obtaining access to markets?
- Is the firm working with lead users in the case of a start-up?
- Does the firm know its primary customers? If so, how has this been validated?
- Are the target customers specified?

Table A5
Organization/Personnel Characteristics

1. Organization Structure
- Is the organizational structure appropriate to the current stage of the firm?
- Are all corporate positions filled in each key area? If not, why not? If not, can the gaps be filled when needed?
- Has the firm addressed all factors?
- What is the management/staff mix?
- What has been the staff growth and turnover?
- Is the firm in a union or non-union environment?
- What is the level of the human resource management function in the organization?

2. Joint Team Activities
- How experienced is the management team? What previous positions have the management held, and at what level?
- To what extent has the management team worked together in the past and for how long? What have been the results?
- To what extent has the management team demonstrated leadership capability?
- What has been the previous performance of the management team in similar situations?
- What has been the track record of the management team? What is the quality of the track record?
- What has been the team-building experience and capabilities of the management team?
- What is the current position and mix of talent? Is the age distribution of the management team appropriate?
- What is the duration of the joint association of the management group?

3. Individual Performance and Background
- What has been the academic backgrounds of each of the key executives? Are they related to the positions of each executive?
- Are the management team members highly dedicated and motivated?
- What is the diversity of previous organizational activities?

4. Financial Implications
- What is the upside potential/downside risk and to what extent is it carried by the management team?
- To what extent are the key executives likely to leave in the near future? What incentives exist(or stock options) not to leave?

Table A5 (Continued)
Organization/Personnel Characteristics

- What are the credit ratings of the team members?
- What is the current financial position of the members of the management team?
- What is the salary level of the management team and is it appropriate?

Table A6
Business Strategy/Policy

1. Strategic Planning process
- Does the plan have a well thought out business strategy?
- Has the firm proposed sound R&D, manufacturing, and market plans?
- Is there a mission statement for the firm?
- Has the firm identified the key competitive factors for success?
- What is the corporate strategy and to what extent can it be implemented?
- Is the firm engaged in strategic planning and how successful has it been?
- What is the process of strategic planning and management including systematic updating?
- How are environmental changes considered in the strategic management process?

2. Business Plan Quality and Specifics
- Is the business plan complete?
- How well is the business plan organized?
- Is the business plan reasonable and achievable?
- Is the business plan sound in its approach?
- What is the quality of the business plan?
- Is there a consistency in the logic of the business plan?
- What is the overall quality of the plan's presentation?

3. Financial Analysis
- What are the financial projections for the future, and to what extent are they realistic?
- What size investment is required, and is this consistent with the firm's proposed needs?
- How will the capital investment be used by the firm?
- What will be the ROI of the proposed capital investment?
- In what detail do the proformas exist? Are the proformas realistic?

Table A6 (Continued)
Business Strategy/Policy

- How detailed is the explained use of funds? have the contingencies been recognized?
- Has the firm conducted any ratio analysis or economic investigations?
- What is the book value of the firm at the present time?
- Is there a profitability and valuation analysis of the proposed investment?
- What are the economic returns for an investment?
- What is the planned equity structure and the estimated ROI?

4. Historical Performance
- How successful has the firm been in achieving its goals to date?
- Who has already invested in the company to date?
- How long has the firm been seeking funding?
- How old is the firm and to what extent has there been an increase in its value over the recent five year period?
- What are the revenues and investments to date?

Applied Expert Systems, E. Turban and P.R. Watkins (Editors)
© Elsevier Science Publishers B.V. (North-Holland), 1988

OASES: AN EXPERT SYSTEM
FOR OPERATIONS ANALYSIS

Michael Oliff and Gautam Biswas

Department of Management Science
University of South Carolina
Columbia, S.C. 29208

Department of Computer Science
University of South Carolina
Columbia, S.C. 29208

An application of knowledge based systems in the area of Operations Analysis is presented. OASES, the diagnostic system, is designed to function as an intelligent assistant and aid management in analyzing problems in production processes such as fiberglass manufacturing. The system uses a partitioned rule base representation for the domain knowledge base and a combination of forward and backward inferencing mechanisms to interact with users in a mixed initiative format. This paper discusses in detail the OASES system architecture, its implementation, and the knowledge acquisition process adopted in building the system knowledge base.

1. INTRODUCTION

Recent advances in artificial intelligence have led to its application in many real world settings. Notable strides have been made in applications of expert systems to medical diagnosis, signal analysis, machine failure analysis, geology, and chemical data interpretation [1]. There is growing evidence that researchers can greatly enhance the capability of management support systems within the business domain [2,3]. Knowledge based systems have appeared within the business domain to address issues in configuration, diagnosis, planning and scheduling [4].

Complete diagnostic systems within manufacturing perform five primary tasks: sensing, comparing, analyzing, decision making and corrective action - the basic elements of operations analysis [5]. In this paper we discuss OASES (Operations AnalySis Expert System), an expert system designed to deal with problems in the steady state phase of the operations analysis domain. This domain is described further in Section 2. In OASES, diagnosis is divided into two parts: general cause analysis and specific cause analysis. General cause analysis is based on general principles of operations analysis and general characteristics of production processes. Once the general cause for a problem is identified, specific cause analysis develops a more detailed model of the pertinent components of the production process and attempts to derive a specific cause for the problem. OASES is currently tailored to deriving specific causes in a fiberglass manufacturing process.

The next section gives a brief overview of the operations analysis domain, illustrates the expert's approach to problem solving, and introduces the application area of fiberglass manufacturing. Section 3 describes the design and implementation of OASES, while Section 4 presents the summary and conclusions of this research.

2. EXPERT'S APPROACH IN THE OPERATIONS DOMAIN

In this section, we focus on the domain of operations analysis and discuss the expert's approach to solving problems. The specific problem domain, fiberglass manufacturing, is also introduced.

2.1. The Operations Analysis Domain

Within the operations management domain, managerial activities entail selecting, designing, operating, controlling and updating a production system [5]. These activities span the life cycle of the production system as illustrated in Figure 1. The first blocks refer to the **startup** phase of a production system: selection of product based on marketing and profitability studies, design of the production process, building the facilities, purchase of equipment, staffing the functional groups and initiating production. After the startup phase is complete, the system enters the **steady state** phase. During this state, day to day problems occur in the form of losses in efficiency, off quality, process bottlenecks, and a host of other recurring ailments. In addition, steady state operating conditions are perturbed as: new products and services are offered, new developments and changes in technology render current methods obsolete, existing equipment fails, markets shift, and so on. If the system cannot adjust to these stimuli, the enterprise declines and ultimately ceases to exist. This implies that even in the steady state phase of the system, production managers are constantly involved in problem solving and planning. Problems arise from sources that are both internal and external to the system. Sources within the production system include the production process itself, personnel, and control systems. Sources external to the system include corporate policy, other functional areas of the firm, suppliers, unions, competitors and customers.

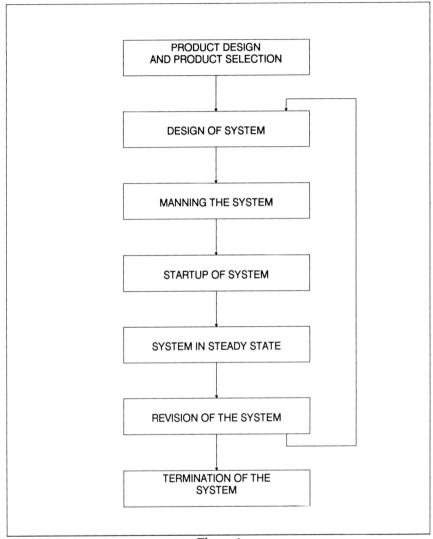

Figure 1
The Operations Analysis Domain

The domain of operations analysis spans the steady state level discussed above. The possibility of many sources of malfunction implies that there is need to continually monitor, evaluate and adjust system performance to ensure that desired goals are met. For the management staff this implies five primary tasks: sensing, comparing, analyzing, decision making and corrective action. Sensing involves data gathering to determine the status of the system. The comparison process involves matching operating data to predetermined standards of performance. Analysis determines the cause of the malfunction. Decision making involves choosing the appropriate corrective action from among some specified set of alternatives. Corrective action implements the adjustment decision and may be composed of single or multiple actions.

2.2 The Expert's Approach

The opportunities for improving performance within steady state operations arise in two very general contexts. First, the perturbations that occur and their root causes must be efficiently identified. In other instances, actual alternatives (choices) for improved performance present themselves via new technologies or methods, and decisions must be made. In group settings, such as manufacturing meetings, corrective action meetings, or quality improvement meetings, these opportunities are often ignored or confused.

OASES focuses on the cause analysis phase of the expert's reasoning process where the expert tries to match observed deviations in performance to a primary cause or a set of causes that best describe the problem. To under stand the expert's reasoning process we discuss the inherent knowledge he possesses. A typical expert in production/operations management has an in- depth understanding of different manufacturing processes. These process types can be classified into continuous flow, batch flow, machine-paced or worker- paced assembly line, job shop and hybrid processes [6]. Each of these processes demonstrate unique patterns that involve product features, process characteristics, inventory features, information-oriented features, labor- oriented features and management features. Within the operations domain, these patterns often imply or give rise to certain problems. For example, raw material sourcing is a common challenge in continuous flow environments, while shifting bottlenecks and scheduling are often the main concerns of job shop management. From experience, the expert also accumulates a list of causes that relate to observed symptoms and process characteristics. Problems, defined as observed deviations from a norm, manifest themselves in the form of symptoms such as changes in efficiency or effectiveness, reductions in quality, etc. This judgmental knowledge used by the expert forms the core of the reasoning process in general cause analysis.

Establishing general cause categories enables the expert and management staff to quickly focus on a broad problem area and then obtain specific evidence directly related to the problem at hand. This process begins with the identification of the process type involved, often obvious from the user's initial problem statement. For example, if the product is steel, paper or fiberglass, the underlying process is often flow manufacturing or some type of hybrid. On the other hand, if the product is automobiles, it is likely that a machine paced flow process is involved. Similarly, industrial machinery typically implies either a job shop or a worker paced process.

Characteristics that differentiate process types include the type of processing layout (e.g., unstructured, partially structured, rigidly structured), and key factors that influence output yield (e.g., workers, machines, raw materials). Once the process type is isolated, the expert seeks further evidence to establish the general cause (or causes), i.e., raw material sourcing, process design, technology, scheduling, maintenance, capacity planning, etc. A prototypes of OASES developed for general cause analysis is discussed in [7].

After establishing a primary or general cause category, the expert's emphasis is on finding specific causes for the observed problems. Specific cause analysis is not only tied to the type of production process under consideration (e.g., textiles, fiberglass, machine tools, automobiles) but also to the most likely cause category derived by general cause analysis. The aim now is to gather much more refined and relevant evidence than previously possible. For each type of general cause category, using knowledge of the process itself, the expert can begin to ask highly technical, cause specific questions. Unsolicited, ambiguous and incomplete data presented earlier, can now be interpreted with a higher degree of confidence as well. With directed probing, the expert is able to elicit sufficient evidence (symptoms) and then select the specific cause that "best explains the effect". A matching and elimination process is employed to build the case for certain causes and rule out others entirely. If insufficient evidence exists, and a "best cause" cannot be determined, the expert returns to general cause analysis or shifts gears entirely to choice analysis.

The importance of general cause analysis can be readily seen. If the initial "high level" cause category is incorrect, a substantial amount of time will be wasted focusing on the wrong part of the process, and may ultimately require backtracking to the general cause analysis phase. Once a specific cause or set of causes is known one can decide on the best possible scheme to solve the problem, i.e., to pursue corrective action. In this paper, the OASES architecture is applied in the context of fiberglass manufacturing, specifically within the highly volatile forming operation. A brief description of this environment follows.

2.3. Fiberglass Manufacturing Process

A fiberglass manufacturing process consists of continuous forming operations as well as batch flow fabrication processes. Molten fiberglass is formed, the glass is spun onto various sized spools and then transported to specific fabrication areas for further processing. These operations produce a variety of products including chopped strands, matting, tire chords and others. Ultimate end users are found in the marine, corrosives and construction industries.

The general manufacturing process is illustrated in Figure 2. The vast percentage of quality problems found in end products (boat hulls, pipes, automobile

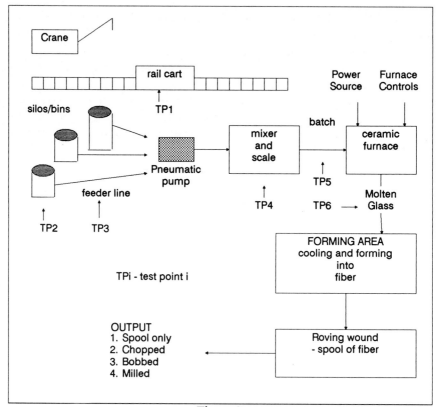

Figure 2
Fiberglass Manufacturing Process

components, residential fixtures, etc.) can be traced to this original forming process. The furnace formation of glass is by nature a high volume and often volatile operation with conversion efficiencies that range from 60-95%. Rail cars deliver the required raw materials, which are checked for chemical conformance (the percentage of fluorine, boron, etc.) and then pneumatically fed into bins or silos. Not only is the physical chemistry at delivery critical, but so is the proper maintenance of bin levels. Wide fluctuations in material bin levels and the resulting impact on compaction ratios can have a dramatic effect on each ingredient's particle density, and, therefore, on its ultimate physical chemistry.

Various types of fiberglass require different ratios of raw materials (silicate, dolomite, probertite, etc.). Batch formulas provide the specific percentage of each raw material required. Bin ingredients are mixed and fed to the furnace for melting. A scale weighs the mix content and acts as a control to confirm that feeders are functioning as specified. After initial melting, the glass is channeled from forehearths and is gravity pulled through bushings, cooled and then often wound on spools or chopped directly.

A series of tests are made throughout the process to gauge the quality of the glass as well as the performance of all intermediate system components. TP1 tests the metallic oxide content of all basic raw materials. TP2 tests the compaction ratio of each bin (density of material in the bin). TP3 tests the feeder pressure for each line in PSI. TP4 is the scale audit weight test that verifies the accuracy of the scales. TP5 verifies physically that the batch contains appropriate proportions of all input material for the type of glass selected. Finally, TP6 tests the viscosity level, a vital characteristic of the molten glass. Viscosity can be defined as the friction within a fluid resulting from molecular attraction and making the fluid resistant to flowing.

Each of the key variables measured have target levels that must be maintained within specified control limits. However, these values are neither static nor independent and vary based on type of glass and operating conditions.

The diagnostic process in this domain requires a combination of fault elimination and detection based on determination of mutually supporting evidences that lead to specific problem areas. These problem areas include: IRM - inconsistency of raw materials, BLF - bin level fluctuation, IBF - incorrect batch formula, PMF - physical malfunction of feeders, IB - inaccurate batching, PMS - physical malfunction of scales, PSC - post scale contamination, and IMM - improper melting mechanics.

2.4. The Need for an Expert System

The need to quickly and accurately diagnose problems in a manufacturing process, a forming process in fiberglass manufacturing for instance, is of critical importance. Not only does such diagnosis require a high level of technical expertise, but if not carried out in a timely fashion, can cause major losses to the company. For example, one hour of contaminated forming output can result in immediate losses of tens of thousands of dollars. Due to the high volume of production, the luxury of tracking down a "company expert" is not always available. Access to an expert system with quasi real time performance for each forming location is, therefore, a desirable objective.

3. THE SYSTEM FOR CAUSE ANALYSIS

Like many other diagnostic expert systems [8,9,10], OASES adopts an **evidential** approach to reasoning. Rather than develop a detailed causal model, the system uses key process and product characteristics along with observed symptoms (deviations from expected performance) to establish causes for the problem. Expert supplied relations between process characteristics, problem symptoms, and cause categories are based on the expert's judgmental knowledge, and are expressed as **production rules**. As discussed in Section 2, experts first use process, product, and general problem characteristics to infer a general cause category. Using the general cause as a focal point, they engage management in a progressively directed dialogue based on a specific process model (e.g., the fiberglass manufacturing process) to derive a specific cause for the problem. This suggests the use of a **partitioned knowledge base** where individual partitions contain expert rules based on one of several process types. This structure mirrors the expert's reasoning process and makes the directed dialogue and inferencing scheme simpler to implement.

Another important characteristic of the expert's judgmental relations is the degree of uncertainty associated with them. An **observed** problem cause (e.g., decrease in efficiency, set up times, inventory level) usually implies a number of possible causes, each one with a different degree of belief. Therefore, **inexact reasoning mechanisms** are incorporated into the evidential decision making framework.

The drawbacks of the Bayesian and related adhoc schemes [11,5,12] have drawn attention to the Dempster Shafer theory of evidence combination [13]. The key advantages of this theory are its abilities to explicitly incorporate the concept of ignorance in the decision making process, assign belief to subsets of hypotheses in addition to singleton hypothesis, and model the narrowing of the hypotheses set with the accumulation of evidence. OASES adopts this framework for modeling the human expert's reasoning process. Belief functions and their combining rules defined by the scheme are well suited to represent the incremental accumulation of evidence and the results of its aggregation.

The Dempster Shafer formulation is based on a frame of discernment, Θ, a set of propositions or hypotheses about the exclusive and exhaustive possibilities in the domain under consideration. Two concepts that relate the impact of evidence on judgmental conclusions are the measure of belief committed exactly to a subset **A** of Θ and the total belief committed to **A**. Exact belief relates to the situation where an observed evidence implies the subset of hypotheses, but this evidence does not provide any further discriminating evidence between individual hypotheses in **A**. The measure of **total** belief committed to a subset **A** is defined as:

$$\text{Bel}(\mathbf{A}) = \sum_{\mathbf{B} \subseteq \mathbf{A}} m(\mathbf{B}),$$

where m represents the exact belief function, and the summation is conducted over all B that are subsets of **A**. Given an exact belief function m,

if $\quad \sum_{\mathbf{A} \subset \Theta} m(\mathbf{A}) < 1,$

then $\quad (1 - \sum_{\mathbf{A} \subset \Theta} m(\mathbf{A}))$

defines a measure of ignorance, denoted by $m(\Theta)$. In other words, $m(\Theta)$ is the extent to which the observations provide no discriminating evidence among the hypothesis in the frame of discernment Θ.

Judgmental rules provided by experts basically represent individual pieces of evidence that imply subsets of hypotheses from Θ with belief values that correspond to exact belief functions (details of rule structure are given in Section 3.1). Corresponding to two different pieces of evidence e_1 and e_2 with corresponding exact belief functions m_1 and m_2 over the same frame of discernment, Dempster's rule of orthogonal products is applied to combine the effects of observing the two pieces of evidence and compute a new exact belief function, m, that is given by

$$m(C_k) = \frac{\sum\limits_{A_i \cap B_j = C_k} m_1(A_i)\, m_2(B_j)}{1 - \sum\limits_{A_i \cap B_j = \Theta} m_1(A_i)\, m_2(B_j)}$$

A_i represents hypotheses subsets that are supported by e_1, B_j represents hypotheses subsets supported by e_2, and C_k represents the hypotheses subsets that are supported by the observation of both e_1 and e_2. The denominator is a normalizing factor to ensure that no belief is committed to the null hypothesis. More detailed discussions on the Dempster Shafer theory of evidence combination appear in [14,13].

The overall architecture of OASES is illustrated in Figure 3. The front-end is made up of a simple language processor and an explanation mechanism. The language processor uses a combination of Augmented Transition Tree and simple pattern matching techniques to interpret user input in restricted natural language (i.e., natural language terms and constructs pertaining to production and manufacturing processes). Further details of the language processor are presented in Section 3.3. Evidence extracted from the user's response is placed in working memory for use by the inferencing mechanism. Working memory acts as a scratch-pad where intermediate results and conclusions are stored.

A directed question-answer technique makes the evidence gathering process efficient; the system avoids annoying the user with too many irrelevant or redundant queries. The system adopts a mixed-initiative format in interacting with the user. User responses are not restricted to the context of the system query; the language processor is flexible enough to accept additional process information and not limit users to specific responses.

Thus the user can shift focus by providing information on other aspects of the problem that are not connected to the query. A simplistic explanation or help mechanism is provided where the system displays a list of meaningful responses when a user expresses his inability to understand a query.

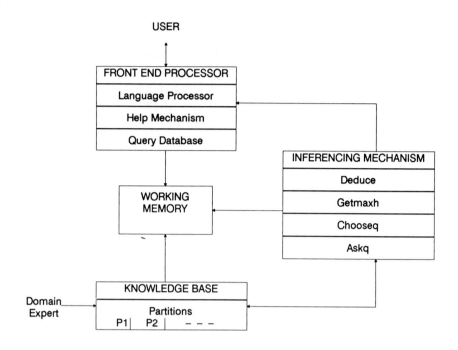

Figure 3
OASES System Architecture

The inferencing mechanism combines forward and backward reasoning to achieve the mixed-initiative form of interaction. The forward chaining mechanism includes the D-S evidence combination function (equation 2) for updating belief values as evidence is accumulated. The backward chaining function ranks candidate hypotheses according to their belief values, and attempts to extract from the user those pieces of evidence that would lend most support to the top ranked hypothesis.

Section 3.1 presents the details of the organization of the knowledge base while Section 3.2 discusses the inferencing mechanism. Section 3.3 discusses the language processor used in the front-end.

3.1. Knowledge Base

From a knowledge engineering standpoint, the ability to construct a rule base that represents the expert's judgmental rules requires, first of all, the identification of both process and product characteristics and problem symptoms. Based on prior experience in similar situations the expert associates degrees of importance to different pieces of evidence. He also associates certain degrees of belief in the relationships between observed symptoms and hypothesized causes.

The judgmental or heuristic information acquired from the expert is compiled into a rule base. The format of a rule appears below:

$$\{ <attribute> \ <value> \} => \{ [(cause_i) (bf_i)]$$
$$[(cause_j) (bf_j)]$$
$$[(cause_k) (bf_k)] \}$$

Therefore, a rule links a pattern on its left hand side (LHS) to one or more conclusions on its right hand side (RHS), i.e., the LHS pattern represents relevant evidence for conclusions on the RHS. Single pieces of evidence are represented as attribute-value pairs. Attributes can be process parameters or characteristics, product characterizations, or problem symptom descriptions. For example, the three patterns [(process type)(continuous flow)], [(process input)(mixed)], [(process layout)(unstructured)], refer to process parameters or characteristics, [(product type)(steel)] is an example of a product characterization, whereas [(problem occurrence)(all days of week)] is an example of a problem symptom description.

Cause in the rule refers to individual causes or subsets of causes. Causes are basically of two kinds: general cause categories such as capacity planning, process design and raw material sourcing; and specific causes such as contamination, bin level maintenance, inconsistency in raw materials, and improper melting mechanics. bfi's are numbers that refer to the expert's confidence, or degree of belief in the relationship between cause categories and the pattern.

To accommodate uncertainty in the rule structure, OASES associates an expert supplied belief value with every conclusion on the RHS. Belief values are modeled as a bpa (basic probability assignment) function in the Dempster-Shafer (D-S) framework. Note that belief values may also be associated with individual pieces of evidence in the LHS pattern. They may be derived from user input or computed values for intermediate conclusions. BF is a Lisp function that computes the overall belief value for the LHS pattern of a rule.

If multiple pieces of evidence are involved, the belief value associated with the LHS pattern is the minimum of the belief values of each piece of evidence on the LHS of the rule.

The following rule illustrates the rule structure:

$[(<process-type> \ <continuous \ flow>) \ bf_a$ and
$(<insufficient \ capacity> \ <late \ in \ process \ flow>) \ bf_b] \rightarrow$
$\{[(<cause> \ <process \ design>) \ 0.5]$
$[(<cause> \ <(raw \ materials, \ technology, \ maintenance) > 0.3]\}.$

The expert may also supply evidence that negates the belief in a conclusion. Consider the following expert supplied heuristic:

if   (continuous flow fiberglass manufacturing process) &
                 (molten glass viscosity is not nominal)&
                 (all ingredient compaction ratios are within limits)

then   (rule out bin level fluctuations as the cause for the raw
                        material sourcing problem)

Such heuristics enable the expert to apply the process of elimination in the diagnostic process. In the D-S framework, evidence against a hypothesis is treated as evidence in favor of the negation of the hypothesis in the set theoretic sense. Therefore, if Θ = { bin level fluctuations, inconsistency of raw materials, post scale contamination } then the above rule translates to:

if   (continuous flow fiberglass manufacturing process) &
                 (molten glass viscosity is not nominal)&
                 (all ingredient compaction ratios are within limits)

then   (inconsistency of raw materials or post scale contamination
                        is the cause for the raw material sourcing
                        problem)

Partitioning the knowledge base results in breaking down a large set of rules into separate sets or units thus resulting in a more efficient computational system. In addition, partitioning facilitates modeling of the expert's reasoning process. Conceptually, partitions represent the breakdown of a complex problem solving process into a sequence of component subproblems. For example, R1 [15], a system for configuring VAX computer systems given customer orders, divides the problem solving process into six sequential steps: (i) determine if order is improper or incomplete, i.e., check for mismatched items or missing prerequisites, (ii) put the appropriate components in the CPU and CPU expansion cabinets, (iii) put panels in the Unibus expansion cabinets and put the appropriate components on the bus, (iv) put panels in the Unibus expansion cabinets, (v) lay out the system on the floor, and (vi) do the cabling. This step-by-step process makes problem solving manageable and more efficient.

In OASES partitioning is used to implement the two sequential steps in problem analysis: general cause analysis followed by specific cause analysis. The component partitions of the OASES knowledge base are illustrated in Figure 4. At the general cause analysis level, partitions correspond to the five different process types in the production spectrum. Each of these processes imply unique symptoms and cause hypotheses. For example, machinery speed and size is an important factor in machine- and worker-paced processes, whereas process flow and raw material characteristics are key factors in continuous flow processes.

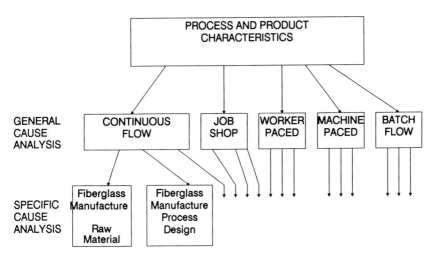

Figure 4
Partitions in the OASES Knowledge Base

The next level of partitions deal with specific causes directly related to individual general causes (e.g., bin level fluctuations is a specific cause related to the general cause, raw material sourcing). Rules at this level are also tailored to specific process and product types (e.g., forming area of a fiberglass manufacturing process). These partitions are sequential in nature in that the problem solving process moves from one partition to another successively until a problem solution (i.e., a specific cause) is obtained. The division of the knowledge base into partitions is an attempt to streamline and make efficient the inferencing mechanism by imposing a structure on the problem solving process.

In summary, the partitioning approach provides an efficient way to model the expert's reasoning process. As a result, the knowledge acquisition process acquires more structure, thus simplifying an otherwise arduous task. In addition, it provides an elegant means of implementing the directed interaction with the user. Lastly, it fits well with the Dempster Shafer scheme for evidence combination. The technique adopted for extracting confidence values from the expert and translating them into belief functions in the Dempster Shafer framework follows.

Knowledge Acquisition and Refinement Belief values are extracted fon the basis that each pattern (left hand side of a rule) corresponds to an independent piece of evidence, and therefore, has a corresponding belief function m associated with it. The expert's belief in the confidence of conclusions regarding causes needs to be expressed in this framework. Expert rules relate patterns of the type described above to a group of possible cause categories; typically the main concern is the relative ordering of these cause categories. This was expressed by assigning numbers on a scale of 0-1 to indicate the confidence levels. A typical rule provided by the expert is:

[(amount of process affected)(high)] = > [(raw material sourcing) 0.4]
                  [(process design) 0.3]
                  [(technology) 0.3]
                  [(capacity planning) 0.2]

However, the Dempster Shafer framework allows for an explicit representation of ignorance $\{m(\Theta)\}$. Therefore, in addition to the information obtained above, the expert is specifically queried as follows "On a scale of 0-10, what is the importance of this evidence in determining a problem cause?". The value provided by the expert in response to this query is used to compute the $m(\Theta)$ value for that evidence. The confidence factors for the implied cause categories are then updated using:

$$(bf)_{new} = (bf)_{old} * \frac{1 - m(\Theta)}{\Sigma \ (bf)_{old}}$$

Regarding "high percentage of the process being affected" the expert, when asked the above query, reiterates that this piece of evidence has an importance of 6 on a scale of 0-10. Therefore, = 0.4. When applied to the above rule the resultant belief values are as follows:

[(amount of process affected)(high)] = > [(raw material sourcing) 0.2]
                  [(process design) 0.15]
                  [(technology) 0.15]
                  [(capacity planning) 0.1]

How is the validity of these belief values verified once the process of knowledge acquisition is complete? A series of representative case studies provided by the expert were run on OASES and a relative ordering of causes was obtained. If the ordering did not agree with that of the expert's, an iterative fine tuning process was undertaken where the belief values (and sometimes rules themselves) were modified so that OASES's results would conform with the expert's.

3.2. Inferencing Mechanism

The overall inferencing mechanism for OASES has four main components: the evidence combination scheme, the procedure for selecting the top ranked hypothesis, the query selection mechanism that directs the user-system dialogue based on the top ranked hypothesis, and a top level controller that is related to the selection of partitions within the rule base. The system adopts a mixed-initiative form of control. Initially, the user may provide facts and evidence that he/she considers relevant to the problem. The system forward chains on this evidence, establishes intermediate conclusions, and then ranks goal hypotheses (i.e., causes) based on some criteria, e.g., the belief values associated with each goal hypothesis. The Dempster Shafer scheme is used to update the belief values of hypotheses depending on the evidence provided by the user. The shell then goes into the backward chaining mode, identifies the top ranked hypothesis, and then the best question to ask the user to try and establish this hypothesis. If the user considers the current query to be irrelevant, he/she may provide additional facts and evidence, unrelated to the query, which switches the system back into the forward chaining mode. This approach illustrates mixed initiative control.

The overall flow of control for the inferencing mechanism is shown in Figure 5. The user interface is directed by the ASKQ routine. In the initial step, the system goes through questions in the top level partition, i.e., the partition that has

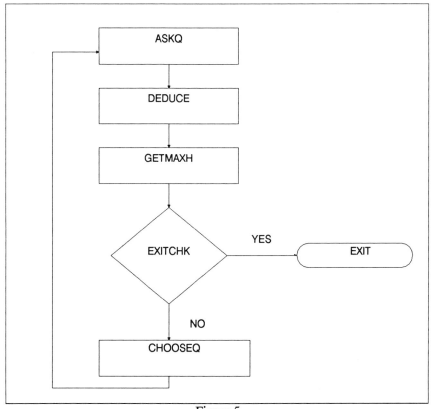

Figure 5
The Inference Control Structure

the initial set of queries that establish process and product characteristics, and a set of plausible general causes (corresponds to partition 1 in Figure 4). The first four questions in the case presented in Section 3.4 are examples of initial queries. User responses are converted into appropriate evidence patterns and stored in working memory. Depending on the responses, the partition controller transfers control to an appropriate partition (continuous flow partition in the case of Section 3.4). Forward chaining and evidence combination is performed by the DEDUCE function. This establishes intermediate conclusions upon which the ranking of the goal hypotheses is based. The function GETMAXH is invoked to select the leading hypothesis. Next the backward chaining process is initiated, and CHOOSEQ selects appropriate queries based on the top ranked hypothesis. At each step, the exit condition is checked by an EXITCHK function. Before querying the user for more information, the system determines if, based on the current belief values, it can come to some definite conclusions. To elaborate, the following conditions:

(i)   the ignorance factor, $m(\Theta)$ is below a certain threshold;

(ii)   the belief value committed to the top ranked hypothesis exceeds a second threshold; and

(iii)   the difference in belief values between the two top hypotheses exceeds a third threshold

were checked in the EXITCHK routine for the lower level partitions of OASES to establish the leading hypothesis beyond reasonable doubt. A combination of the first two conditions ensures that further corroborating evidence will change the belief in the leading hypothesis only marginally, whereas the third condition ensures that the belief in the next leading hypothesis cannot be greater than the leading hypothesis. The inferencing mechanism is explained in greater detail in [16].

To illustrate the evidence combination scheme and the query selection mechanism in more detail, a part of the user-OASES dialogue from Section 3.4 is presented in greater detail. After the initial set of queries, OASES determined the following general cause categories as plausible hypotheses:

$$\text{process design} = h_1 \text{ (belief value} = 0.358)$$
$$\text{technology} = h_2 \text{ (belief value} = 0.329)$$
$$\text{raw material sourcing} = h_3 \text{ (belief value} = 0.221).$$

This corresponds to the exact belief function:

$$m(h1) = 0.358$$
$$m(h2) = 0.329$$
$$m(h3) = 0.221$$

Based on these values, GETMAXH establishes as the leading hypothesis, and CHOOSEQ is invoked to pick an appropriate query to obtain more evidence from the user. CHOOSEQ examines the rule base partition for continuous flow processes and picks (excess capacity or insufficient capacity) as the most appropriate evidence on which to query the user. (An affirmative response to this evidence would provide maximum support for the cause process design). The user response to both these questions were negative, and this caused rule032 to fire and the belief values updated according to equation 2 as shown below.

m_{rule32} m	$\{h_2, h_3, h_4\}$ (0.5)	h_1 (0.2)	$\Theta(0.2)$ (0.3)
$h_1(0.358)$	Φ (0.179)	$h_1(0.072)$	$h_1(0.107)$
$h_2(0.329)$	$h_2(0.165)$	Φ (0.066)	$h_2(0.099)$
$h_3(0.221)$	$h_3(0.111)$	Φ (0.044)	$h_3(0.066)$
Θ (0.092)	$\{h_2, h_3, h_4\}(0.047)$	$h_1(0.026)$	Θ (0.08)

The updated belief function is:

$$m(\{h2\}) = 0.371, m(h1) = 0.288, \text{ and } m(h3) = 0.249$$

This time the GETMAXH function identifies h_2 as the leading hypothesis, and, therefore, it modifies its line of questioning. To increase belief in h_2, CHOOSEQ determines it has to establish evidence corresponding to investment in process technology. It queries the user about this characteristic, and the user response again results in the recomputation of belief values, and a new ranking of the plausible hypotheses. This continues till EXITCHK determines that the system has established a general cause category (raw material sourcing) with a sufficiently large degree of belief.

3.3. The Language Processor

The language processor for parsing user input to OASES is based on a list of Augmented Tree Transition (ATT) structures described in Whinston [17]. For efficient processing, separate ATT's were defined for each user query. A sample ATT, an associated help message and pattern list is shown for the type of products in Figure 6. Responses can be in the form of complete statements such as "we produce fiberglass for the automotive and marine industries", or curt phrases such as "fiberglass" or "fiberglass products". Statements that contain multiple evidence, e.g., "we produce fiberglass products and our is based primarily on the quality of the raw materials used" are also parsed successfully.

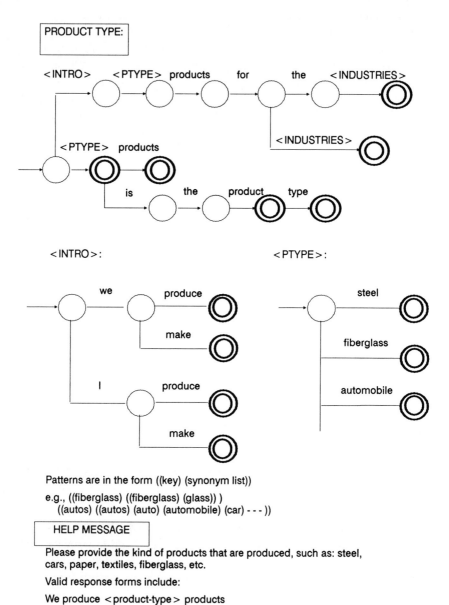

PRODUCT TYPE:

Patterns are in the form ((key) (synonym list))

e.g., ((fiberglass) ((fiberglass) (glass)))
     ((autos) ((autos) (auto) (automobile) (car) - - -))

HELP MESSAGE

Please provide the kind of products that are produced, such as: steel,
cars, paper, textiles, fiberglass, etc.

Valid response forms include:

We produce < product-type > products
or just, < product-type >

Figure 6
Partial ATT Semantic Grammar Product Type

For a given user response, the language processor first attempts to apply its corresponding ATT semantic grammar. If the ATT fails to parse the input statement, a pattern matching scheme is invoked to find key patterns in the input statement. For each query there is a pattern list of keywords and key phrases that correspond to appropriate responses for the query. The vocabulary of the system is enhanced by incorporating a number of synonymous patterns. If one or more are found, the user is asked to verify if what the system derived is valid or not. This is necessary since a pure keyword approach may produce incorrect results. Lastly, if both the ATT and pattern matching schemes fail, the system prints a help message and asks the user for a new response. Responses such as "i dont understand" or "help" trigger the same help message.

3.4. An Example Case

The operations analysis expert system general cause analysis component described above has been implemented in Franz Lisp on a VAX 11 780 computer system running Berkeley 4.2 Unix. A partial transcript of a case run on this system appears below and illustrates the nature of the dialogue between the user and OASES, resulting in the determination of a specific cause for an observed problem. The systems queries and remarks appear in bold font, whereas the user responses are in italics. Explanatory comments appear within square brackets ([...]). Additional output provided by the system is omitted for the sake of brevity and clarity.

[OCF is a major producer of fiberglass products. They have been experiencing efficiency and quality problems recently at one of their largest manufacturing locations. The factory manager and furnace supervisor interact with the expertsystem OASES as outlined below.]

-- OASES

OASES is ready.
Type "help." if a question is not clear or a valid response is unknown.
Diagnostic commands are "show facts." "show hypotheses." "show rule #."

What type of products services does your company provide?
We produce fiberglass products for the automotive, corrosives and marine industries.

[From the above response the system picks ((product type) (fiberglass))].

What is the process type involved?
I'm not sure what you mean. Our forming area is involved.

[Again no direct response is obtained, but the keyword forming enables the system to make some conclusion about the type of process involved. OASES asks a few more questions such as "What is the type of layout" and "On what basis do you operate in the marketplace". The responses convince the system that it is dealing with a continuous flow process. It now queries the manager for general symptoms.]

When do you observe the problem?
We have been experiencing a gradual decrease in efficiency over all shifts.

[The system cannot parse this response directly using the defined augmented transition tree [8]. It resorts to a pattern matching approach and finds two pieces of evidence, which it then asks the user to verify.]

OASES has extracted the following evidence. Confirm (y.) or disconfirm (n.).
((trouble occurs) (all shifts))?
y.
((problem symptom) (decrease in efficiency))?
y.

[As expected, the user confirms both symptoms. Otherwise, the system would have just ignored that part of the statement but the user would be aware of it. This concludes the top level partition of the system. OASES has come to the following preliminary conclusions:]

Possible cause categories
(i) process design (belief value = 0.358)
(ii) technology (belief value = 0.329)
(iii) raw material sourcing (belief value = 0.221)

[Other cause categories with belief values less than 0.05 are ignored.
The next set of queries pertain to the continuous flow partition of the knowledge base. Note that process design is the top ranked hypothesis.]

Are you experiencing excess capacity early in the process flow?
No, I don't think so.

Are you experiencing insufficient capacity late in the process flow?
No, there are no bottlenecks in the process.

[The above responses have ruled out "process design" as the top ranked hypothesis. The current ranking is: (i) technology (belief value: 0.371), (ii) process design (belief value: 0.288) and (iii) raw material sourcing (belief value: 0.249).]

When was your last major investment in process technology?
Two years ago we built state of the art forming tanks.

[The knowledge base includes by process product the expected competitive lifetime of various critical technologies. In forming, OASES knows that forming tanks and furnaces are key elements in the process, and that useful life is greater than two years. So OASES concludes technology is not the problem cause. The current ranking is: (i) raw material sourcing (belief value: 0.358), (ii) process design (belief value: 0.335) and (iii) technology (belief value: 0.215).]

Do your input raw materials meet specifications?
I think so.

[This response causes the system to set aside this query for later. Actually the system considers this evidence to be very important, so it tries to obtain it in a different way.]

Have you changed vendors for any major raw materials recently?
Yes.

[This causes belief in raw material sourcing to increase. The current degrees of belief are: (i) raw material sourcing (degree of belief: 0.544), (ii) process design (degree of belief: 0.238) and (iii) technology (degree of belief: 0.155). The system proceeds --]

Is there any difference between the physical characteristics of the materials supplied by the new vendors and the old ones?
[This question is a follow up on the one before the previous one, where the system got no response.]
Yes, both the dolomite and probertite have smaller particle densities.

[This piece of evidence enables the system to draw its final conclusions about the most likely cause category based on the peak degree of belief 0.65 and difference between first and second belief values 0.3). Also, the m(@) value .05). The system's conclusions for general cause analysis are --]

The two top ranked cause hypotheses are:
(i) raw material sourcing (degree of belief : 0.771)
(ii) process design (degree of belief : 0.12)
The following facts strongly supported the top ranked hypothesis:
(i) fiberglass products. (ii) rigidly structured layout.
(iii) output depends mainly on raw materials. (iv) change of vendors.
(v) change in raw material quality.

[At this point it is very likely that a more specific cause is at the heart of OCF's efficiency problem. OASES now focuses on each area of the forming process sequentially (see Figure 2). The batching operation is the first in a series of rigidly connected operations. Here, raw materials stored in silos, are pneumatically pulled, mixed and weighed. They are then fed to a ceramic furnace through feeders. The staff obtain various physical chemistry measurements throughout this process and note unacceptable readings as symptomatic of specific causes. These measurements involve physical properties such as the viscosity at the pre-winder level, and finished goods chemistry (e.g., tensile strength at the end of the winder level). The chemical properties of the mix and the working condition of the feeder are also monitored continually. As in general cause analysis, rules relate observed symptoms to specific causes. For example, some of the specific raw material problems in forming are: (i) inconsistency of the raw material, (ii) scaling errors, (iii) mechanics of the batching process, (iv) contamination, (v) insufficient bin level maintenance, and (vi) poor melting mechanics. Correct formulae must be used to set up the batch and it's consistency must be insured. Scaling refers to accuracy of the batching or weighing process. Mechanics of batching deal with the working condition of the pneumatic feeders and mixers. Contamination frequently occurs after the batch passes the scale. Bin level maintenance relates to a constant volume and assumes that the resulting compaction ratios remain constant. Finally, melting mechanics deal with the temperatures and actual conditions of the melt in the furnace. Most experts agree that the first five cause categories account for about 80% of the problems in forming. An expert supplied rule enables OASES to order specific causes shown below and proceed to invoke related queries.

1. inconsistency of raw material (.384)   5. physical malfunction of feeders (.198)
2. incorrect batch formulas (.251)   6. post scale contamination (.185)

3. inaccurate batching (.248)   7. bin level fluctuation (.158)
4. physical malfunction of scales (.211)   8. improper melting mechanics (.152)]

Please enter the ingredient and its tested physical characteristics.
Dolomite

% Iron	*.0023*
% Calcium	*.0125*
% Titanium	*.0016*
% Boron	*.0270*
% Fluorine	*.0321*

[Measurements are also given for probertite, fluorspar, clay, silica and limestone].

All physical properties check to within 0.01 of control limits except Boron content in Fluorspar (within 0.02 of control limits) but still within our product specifications.

[Therefore, OASES disconfirms inconsistency of raw materials].

Please tell me the current viscosity levels
28.81

[OASES compares the observed viscosity to the predetermined statistical process control limits and determines that it is above the upper control limit. The top two specific causes now are: (i) incorrect batch formulas (degree of belief: 0.441), and (ii) physical malfunction of scales (degree of belief: 0.233). OASES proceeds --]

The level is 2.43 points above nominal and exceeds the upper control limit. What other information is available?
We have already matched scheduled batch formulas to actual and they check.

[OASES regards matched batch formulas as important evidence, and double checks --]

Are you certain that batch formulas are correct?
Yes .

[This disconfirms incorrect batch formulas and the top two specific cause hypotheses now are: (i) physical malfunction of scales (belief: 0.381) and ii) physical malfunction of feeders (belief: 0.362)]

Please provide the two most recent scale audit weights.
49.82, 49.9

OASES compares these to the standard 50 lb. weight and comes to the conclusion below. The new top two hypotheses are: (i) physical malfunction of feeders (belief value: 0.428) and (ii) bin level fluctuations (belief value: 0.364)]

Both measures are within 50% of nominal, the scales appear o.k. Please provide the PSI for each feeder.
   F1 *206* **F2** *191* **F3** *188*

[OASES compares these values to control limits, finds them satisfactory, and determines the new top ranked hypotheses: (i) bin level fluctuation (degree of belief: 0.52), and (ii) improper melting mechanics (degree of belief: 0.41)]

The pneumatic systems check within 0.42 %. Have you observed any wide fluctuations in bin levels recently?

The dolomite bin was almost empty yesterday .

[This strongly confirms bin level maintenance problems (degree of belief: 0.721). OASES wants to make sure.]

Was the dolomite compaction ratio less than 3.72?

yes.

[OASES is convinced beyond doubt that it is a bin level maintenance problem (degree of belief 0.93).]

I believe the primary cause for our problem is bin level maintenance. The following facts within specific cause analysis support this hypothesis:
(i) raw material chemistry did not change
(ii) the physical characteristics did,
(iii) batching, scales and feeders o.k.,
(iv) wide day to day fluctuations occurred in dolomite unloadings, and
(v) compaction ratio for the dolomite bin was very low.

Once bin levels were stabilized via smoothed batch unloading, viscosity values fell back within control limits.

The above dialogue between the system and the user illustrates the characteristics of both the language processor and the inferencing mechanism. The dynamic nature of the query selection mechanism is apparent. The line of questioning and the intermediate results obtained, generally agree with the case study provided by our domain expert.

The current prototype is in many ways aiding the knowledge acquisition process for cause analysis. Case studies and results are compared to the expert's solutions with observed deviations leading to the fine tuning of current rules, by changing belief values, and the creation of new rules to fill gaps in the knowledge base. The knowledge refinement is performed manually using a step by step procedure. A test case created by the expert is run on the system. At each step, the expert is asked if the current system query is relevant and if the relative ordering of the causes is consistent. If the expert disagrees, the related rules are checked, the knowledge engineers explain the system's mode of operation, and then either the current rule is modified, or new ones are created.

4. CONCLUDING REMARKS

In this paper we have demonstrated the use of expert system techniques in the field of business decision making. Specifically OASES, a system for cause analysis in the operations analysis domain has been designed and implemented. Preliminary results are encouraging and indicate this framework is an appropriate model of the expert's reasoning process. The modular property of rule based architectures allows easy modification and update of the rule base. The partitioning scheme simplified the addition of specific cause partitions under the general cause partitions (see Figure 4). Therefore, the current version of OASES has played a significant role in fine tuning existing rules and generating new ones. This has led to both enhancement of system performance and expansion in the system's capabilities. From the design viewpoint, we have successfully integrated the Dempster Shafer evidence combination scheme into a mixed initiative diagnostic reasoning system.

The current version of OASES incorporates a number of specific cause partitions under continuous flow processes. Efforts are now underway to integrate additional specific cause analysis components into the existing system, e.g., a diagnostic system for operations analysis in the printed circuit board industry. This development will test the system's ability to deal with multiple experts. We envision that OASES and similar systems will provide substantial productivity and profitability improvements within the manufacturing domain.

ACKNOWLEDGEMENT

We wish to thank the referees; their suggestions have contributed greatly to improvements in the contents and presentation of this paper.

REFERENCES

[1]   Harmon, P. and D. King, *Expert Systems: Artificial Intelligence in Business,* John Wiley, New York, 1985.

[2]   O'Connor, D.E., "Using Expert Systems to Manage Change and Complexity in Manufacturing." In *Artificial Applications in Business*, edited by W. Reitman. New Jersey: Ablex Publishers, 1984.

[3]   Power, "Using the Systems, Diagnosis, and Treatment Framework to Structure Knowledge for Management Expert Systems", *Working Paper MS S 84-206*, Dept. of Management Science and Statistics, Univ. of Maryland, 1984.

[4]   Oliff, M. ed., *Proc. of the International Conference on Expert Systems and the Leading Edge in Production Planning and Control,* Charleston, S.C., May 10-13, 1987.

[5] Chase, R.B. and N.J. Aquilano, *Production and Operations Management*, Homewood, Illinois: Richard D. Irwin, Inc., 1977.

[6] Schmenner, R.W., *Production Operations Management: Concepts and Situations*. Chicago: Scientific Research Associates, 1984.

[7] Biswas, G., R. Abramczyk, and M. Oliff, "OASES: An Expert System for Operations Analysis - The System for Cause Analysis", *IEEE Transactions on Systems, Man, and Cybernetics*, vol. SMC-17, pp. 133-145, 1987.

[8] Buchanan, B.G. and E.H. Shortliffe, eds., *Rule-Based Expert Systems: The MYCIN Experiments of the Stanford HPP*. Reading, Mass.: Addison-Wesley, 1984.

[9] Kahn, G. and J. McDermott, "The MUD System", *IEEE Expert,* vol. 1, pp. 23-35, Spring 1986.

[10] Pople, H., "Heuristic Methods for Imposing Structure on Ill-Structured Problems." In *Artificial Intelligence in Medicine,* edited by P. Szolovits. Westview Press, pp. 119-190, 1982.

[11] Barclay Adams, J., "Probabilistic Reasoning and Certainty Factors", *Mathematical Biosciences,* vol. 32, pp. 177-186, 1976.

[12] Szolovits, P. and S.G. Pauker, "Categorical and Probabilistic Reasoning in Medical Diagnosis", *Artificial Intelligence,* vol. 11, pp. 115-144, 1978.

[13] Shafer, G., *A Mathematical Theory of Evidence*. New Jersey: Princeton University Press, 1976.

[14] Gordon, J. and E.H. Shortliffe, "A Method for Managing Evidential Reasoning in a Hierarchical Hypothesis Space", *Artificial Intelligence*, vol. 26, pp. 323-357, 1985.

[15] McDermott, J., "R1: An Expert in the Computer Systems Domain," *Proceedings of the American Association for Artificial Intelligence*, vol. 1, pp. 269-271, 1980.

[16] Biswas, G. and T.S. Anand, "Using the Dempster-Shafer Scheme in a Diagnostic Expert System Shell", *Third Workshop on Uncertainty in Artificial Intelligence*. Seattle, Wash.: American Association for Artificial Intelligence, pp. 98-105, 1987.

[17] Winston, P.H. and B.K.P. Horn, *Lisp*. Reading, Mass.: Addison-Wesley Publishing Company, 1984.

Applied Expert Systems, E. Turban and P.R. Watkins (Editors)
© Elsevier Science Publishers B.V. (North-Holland), 1988

EXPERT SYSTEMS IN INDUSTRY: ACTUAL AND POTENTIAL APPLICATIONS

Brian E. Barkocy and Robert W. Blanning

Systems Analyst
The Proctor & Gamble Company
6250 Center Hill Road
Cincinnati, Ohio   45224

Associate Professor of Management
Owen Graduate School of Management
Vanderbilt University
Nashville, Tennessee 37203

Much of the existing literature on expert systems suggests that the most productive industrial applications of these systems will be in the area of decision support. That is, it is assumed that expert systems will be used by managers, staff analysts, and other professionals (such as lawyers, engineers, etc.) to assist them in decision making. In this respect an expert system is assumed to be similar to the plethora of causal models found in most of the decision support systems currently being implemented, although the way in which these new systems will support decision making (e.g., by means of explanation facilities) and the way in which they will be constructed (e.g., by means of protocol analysis) will differ. However, there are two other possible industrial uses of expert systems, and these may prove to be of even greater importance. First, an expert system may help a manager, staff analyst, or other professional to organize and manage the variety of information sources at his disposal and thus, may serve as an "intelligent" information management system. Second, an expert system may increase a company's competitive advantage by reducing the cost of producing a product or providing a service and/or by increasing the value of the product or service to its customers. We will attempt to provide a comprehensive view of the potential industrial applications of expert systems by examining these three application areas.

1. INTRODUCTION

During the past 25 years an increasing number of expert systems have been developed to help certain professionals and other specialists--such as doctors diagnosing and treating infectious diseases and geologists exploring for mineral deposits--to make more effective decisions. The purpose of these systems is to capture the specialized knowledge and experience of their subjects and make it available to less experienced persons. This has led to suggestions that expert systems and other applications of artificial intelligence (such as natural language query processing) may find profitable application in industry [1, 2, 3, 4, 5, 6, 7, 8, 9].

The principal application of expert systems suggested in the literature is in the area of decision support [10, 11, 12]. It is suggested that just as many decision support systems contain causal models, they may also contain models of the decision processes of experienced managers and certain specialists (such as financial analysts and engineers). Applications of this type are expected to be similar, but not identical, to the non-management applications of expert systems thare are well documented in the literature. However, this is not the only potentially useful application of expert systems in industry. There are two others.

The first application is in the area of information management. Most staff specialists have access to a large number of information sources, such as data files, statistical analysis packages, and decision models. Since these specialists have acquired expertise in organizing and managing information, it seems reasonable to develop systems that capture this expertise and help their users to manage more effectively the information at their disposal.

The second application is suggested by several recent observations that some conventional information systems are being used to increase a company's competitive advantage--that is, to improve the company's financial and market positions relative to other companies in the same industry. This is being accomplished by helping the company to reduce costs, by improving the quality of the product or service being offered by the company, and by helping the conpany to differentiate its products as perceived by its customer's from those of its competitors. Since this is true of the more traditional applications of information processing technology, it may also be true of expert systems. For example, a company that offers its customers a diagnostic expert system for the rapid and convenient maintenance and repair of its products may find that it has achieved a competitive advantage relative to other companies in its industry.

Our purpose here is to provide a comprehensive description of the industrial applications of expert systems by examining each of these three application areas. In so doing, we will also attempt to distinguish between potential and actual applications by making appropriate reference to the literature. However, at the time of this writing (July, 1987) much of the literature in these three areas describes prototypes being developed at universities and industrial research laboratories and projects still under development in the operating divisions of industrial firms. However, there are apparently a few hundred expert systems in productive use in industry and government [13]. Thus, our purpose is to examine the potential applicability of expert systems in industry and the degree to which this potential is currently being realized.

2. EXPERT SYSTEMS AS DECISION SUPPORT SYSTEMS

Much of the seminal literature on decision support systems (DSS) emphasized the need to support the making of semistructured decisions by providing convenient user access to stored data and decision models [14, 15, 16, 17]. Thus, many of the early DSS were user-friendly front ends to files, data analysis procedures, and models. More recently it has begun to appear that the goal of supporting decision processes can also be accomplished by constructing models of the decision processes of knowledgeable and experienced managers and staff analysts--that is, by constructing expert systems based on protocols elicited from these managers and analysts [18].

There are three problem areas in which expert systems have been developed for management decision making [19]. The first is *resource allocation*. The earliest published account of an expert system (although it was not called an expert system at the time) described a system that simulated a bank trust officer preparing a portfolio of stocks for a client [20]. The system contained a set or rules for determining the client's risk preference and other information about the client (e.g., his tax status) and for selecting stocks most appropriate to a particular type of client. The rules were obtained by eliciting protocols from a (single) trust officer, and the conpleted system compared quite favorably with the performance of the (same) trust officer. Another resource allocation system, in this case a rule-based system for capital budgeting, is reported in [21].

A problem area closely related to resource allocation in the context of manufacturing is product and process design, and expert systems have been developed for problems of this type as well. An example is ALADIN, developed by the Intelligent Systems Laboratory at Carnegie Mellon University for ALCOA [22]. The system helps metallurgists to design new aluminum alloys that will meet certain constraints on their physical properties. In addition, PRIDE is an expert system designed by Xerox to help engineers to design paper handling systems inside copiers [23], and IDRILL was developed by Ingersoll to assist engineers in the design of drilling stations for production processes [24].

The second problem area is *problem diagnosis*. An example of a system of this type is AUDITOR, an expert system for auditing trade accounts receivable-

-that is, for determining whether delinquent industrial customer credit accounts should be reported in a company's financial statements as collectable [25]. The system was constructed by taking protocols from several auditors in a public accounting firm, and the system was compared with the behavior of auditors in another public accounting firm. The results were almost identical. Another example of an expert system of this type is one that simulates a financial analyst examining the publicly available financial statements of a company and making narrative comments about the financial viability of the company [26]. Yet another example is TOAST, which helps electric power station operators to diagnose the causes of sudden power system transitions and critiques any corrective actions they intend to take [27].

The third problem area is *scheduling and assignment.* Systems that have been developed in this area are similar in certain respects to the causal logistical models that have been constructed by operations researchers and management scientists during the past thirty years, in that they help managers to schedule complex networks of activities. They differ in that their purpose is not to simulate the consequences of a proposed schedule nor to identify an optimal schedule; rather, they help a manager to prepare a feasible schedule. These systems begin with a description of a scheduling or assignment problem that may be infeasible as stated, and they help their users to identify an "intelligent" relaxation of the problem constraints so that the revised problem can be solved. Examples of such systems are (1) Omega, a system for personnel assignment [28], (2) ISIS, a system for factory scheduling [29, 30], (3) Odyssey, a system for scheduling business trips [31], (4) Nudge, a system for scheduling business meetings [32], (5) CUTTECH, a system for the planning and scheduling of machine operations [33], and (6) an unnamed system for FMS (flexible manufacturing system) scheduling [34].

We note that these systems are innovative applications of artificial intelligence technology some of which are commercially available and some of which are prototypes that were implemented for purposes of illustration rather than profitability. However, we may expect that systems such as these will be successfully implemented in the future [35], that they will be integrated with more traditional DSS [36, 37], and that they will provide useful insights into managerial decision processes [38].

3. EXPERT SYSTEMS AS INFORMATION MANAGEMENT SYSTEMS

One of the consequences of the widespread use of computers in industry is that line manager's (such as plant managers and brand manager's), staff analysts (such as financial analysts and market researchers), and other specialists (such as engineers and lawyers) have access to a variety of computer-based information sources. These sources include the following:

1. Stored data, in the form of files and databases,

2. Data analysis procedures, in the form of statistical packages and report writers containing simple calculations procedures,

3. Decision models, ranging from simple spread sheet generators to large-scale optimization models,

4. Knowledge bases of the type discussed in the preceeding section,

5. Files containing less structured information, such as text and sensory information.

One of the problems faced by the users of these systems is that they must integrate information from these sources and from other, noncomputerized sources to respond to specific queries--for example, what would be the impact on profits of introducing a certain new product? If the information consists entirely of stored data that is being controlled by a single database management system, the problem of integrating the data can be solved with exciting technology (i.e., that of database management). When other types of information are present, the problem is more difficult.

If the information base consists only of the first three types of information listed above (i e., quantitative information--rather than non- numeric symbolic, text, and sensory information), it may be possible to use expert system technology to perform the integration. Several articles have appeared in the literature suggesting ways in which this might be accomplished. In each case the problem is assumed to be one of drawing inferences from descriptions of the available files and programs, where the inference corresponds to the query to be answered. Several methods have been suggested for representing and processing knowledge about the available information (i.e., for determining how it should be integrated to respond to the query), as follows:

1. First-order logic.

The available information is described by a set of logic statements (e.g., a model is described as a logical implication between its inputs and outputs). The query is also formulated as a logic statement, and an attempt is made to derive it from the logic statements describing the available information. The approaches suggested for this purpose are resolution programming [39, 40, 41, 42] and connection graphs [43, 44].

2. AND/OR graphs.

In this case the AND nodes represent complementary data sources (each of which must be present to perform a calculation or to prepare a report), and the OR nodes represent alternative information sources. Information integration is accomplished by searching the graph [40].

3. Semantic nets.

The nodes in the net represent entities (e.g., products, factories and warehouses) and activities (e.g., the act of shipping products from a factory to a warehouse), and the arcs represent relationships between the nodes. Information integration is accomplished by traversing the net [45, 46].

4. Frames.

In this case a frame represents a model or a component of a model, and the slots in the frame contain model parameters, statements about the model (e.g., that an objective function is linear), or references to other frames (e.g., a reference to another frame would be necessary if the output of one model is an input to another model). The collection of frames is processed to integrate the model bank [47, 48].

5. Situation-action rules.

Each rule corresponds to a data source: the situation corresponds to the input to the source (e.g., the key of a file or the input to a model), and the action corresponds to the output of the source. When the sources, ordered by their inputs and outputs, form a partially ordered set (i.e., when there are no cycles in the set), information integration is accomplished by backward chaining from the query to the available information [49].

There are three research topics of current interest that may contribute to the success of efforts such as these. The first topic is coming to be called "expert database systems" [50, 51, 52]. This research attempts to combine artificial intelligence and database management in order to produce "a system for developing applications requiring knowledge-based processing of shared information" [53, p. K2]. Implicit in this statement is the assumption than the information being described is stored data, but it might include other types of information as well [49, 54] The second research topic is the extension of relational database theory to encompass the management of decision models [55, 56] and text files [57], which suggests that it may be possible to develop a single (relational) theory for the management of a variety of information sources. If this extended relational theory can be combined with the ongoing research on expert data base systems described above, it may be possible to apply expert system technology to the "intelligent" management of may different kinds of information. The third topic is the development of explanatory front ends for spreadsheet generators [58, 59] and linear programming models [60] explain to a user on request how different components of a decision model have been integrated to produce a given result.

When the information base consists of more complex types of information- -such as photographic information or videotext--and especially, when this information is to be integrated with the more structured types of information identified above, it may still be possible to use expert system technology to help a user to manage the information [61]. For example, expert systems may be useful in drawing inferences from incomplete data [62], in managing real- time interaction with the information base [63], and in helping a user to select relevant messages from a large number of messages available in an information network [64]. However, at present this area is rather speculative.

4. EXPERT SYSTEMS AND COMPETITIVE ADVANTAGE

Recent observers of the industrial applications of information systems (such as file processing systems and telecommunications systems) have suggested that the way in which these systems are being used is changing. Some companies are using these systems not only to do mandated data processing and to provide management information, but also to improve the competitive positions of their companies relative to other companies in their industries. Our purpose here is to examine this phenomenon as it applies to expert systems.

Several frameworks have been presented in the recent literature for analyzing the impact of information systems on competitive advantage. First, information systems may be used to support the fundamental competitive strategies of cost leadership and product and service differentiation [65, 66]. Second, they may be used to improve customer service in various stages of the customer resource life cycle [67]. Third, they may increase the value of an activity within the value chain of activities performed by a firm [66]. These three frameworks will be discussed below, along with examples of expert systems currently in use or under development which affect competitive advantage according to each of these frameworks. In each case we will examine briefly the ways in which conventional information systems have contributed to competitive advantage, and we will then examine the actual and potential impact of expert systems.

4.1. Cost Reduction and Product Differentiation

There are two ways in which firms have used information systems to enjoy a competitive advantage over their rivals [65, 66]. The first approach is to use information systems to reduce costs, which results in pricing and profit margin advantages. Examples are process control systems used to reduce manufacturing costs, inventory control systems used to reduce inventory costs, etc. The second approach is to use information systems to help in product or service differentiation. This may be accomplished by improving the quality of the product or service or by offering unique product/service features. An example is the integrated Cash Management Account developed by Merrill Lynch & Co. This system combines information on several customer asset accounts and automatically invests idle funds, and it is credited with asset increases of billions of dollars [68].

Some expert systems are being used for cost reduction and product differentiation. An example is Digital Equipment Corporation's XCON, an expert system that configures computer orders for customers [69]. This task was formerly done by human configurers at slower speeds and higher expense. By one estimate, the system saves DEC $18 million each year [70]. DEC also reports savings from an expert system that schedules production at a printed circuit board facility, making some of the decisions formerly made manually by dispatchers [71]. Other examples are an expert system for process control at a Texaco oil refinery [70] and one for process engineering at Campbell Soup Co. [72].

Cost savings may come from several sources. For example, Garland Corporation, a producer of knitted sweaters for retail distribution, developed an expert system, coupled with a material (i.e., yarn) trading system for inventory control in a receiving warehouse [73]. Although the company did not attempt to quantify a cost savings, it reported several savings in time, cost, space, and error rates. For example, by using simple rules to find optimal locations for incoming materials, which avoided the problem of having to split shipments among several locations, the company was able to reduce unloading and receiving time from four hours to an hour and a half, with 99% accuracy in locating material for subsequent use. By using the system to allocate materials to production runs, the company was also able to eliminate multiple handling of the same lots and to reduce storage space 30% (by eliminating holding areas). In addition, by automating the materials selection process (i.e., deciding what combination of yarns to use in what sweaters), the company was able to reduce the time needed for selection from approximately one hour to 30 seconds and reduced the number of people needed from six to one.

Examples of expert systems used for product differentiation are (1) an expert system used by the Hartford Steam Boiler Inspection and Insurance Company to analyze the coolants of large electrical transformers as part of its loss prevention program [74] and (2) an expert system used by Digital Equipment Corporation to diagnose failures in tape drives by analyzing system error logs [69, 75].

4.2. The Customer Resource Life Cycle

The second framework for analysis of competitive advantage--the customer resource life cycle--offers a different perspective on competitive uses of information systems [67]. Conventional information systems have been used to help firms become competitive in various phases of their customer relationships, including establishing requirements for products and services, acquiring products, using and maintaining products, and disposing of products after they are no longer needed. In the requirements phase, one commercially available expert system offers assistance to personal financial planners in determining which investment vehicles are best suited to a client's needs and wishes [72, 76].

In the acquisition phase, the task of selecting a source from which to obtain a product or service has been addressed by a system called K:Base, developed by Lehman Brothers [77]. K:Base is used in arranging interest-rate swaps, a complex financial maneuver in which a firm with a certain type of loan, such as one with a fixed interest rate, seeks another firm with a different type of loan, such as one with a variable interest rate. Depending on the conditions in each firm's industry, it may be possible for the two firms to exchange interest payment obligations so that each firm's interest payments are reduced. By inferring general rules for such transactions from the previous decisions of experienced brokers, the program was able to contribute to two swaps representing over $1 million in revenue during a two-month period.

Several expert systems have been developed for the use and maintenance phase. For example, the General Electric Company has developed a system, variously called DELTA or CATS, to assist in the maintenance of diesel electric locomotives [75, 78]. AT&T has developed a system called ACE that recommends maintenance activities for telephone networks [79]. Finally, IBM has developed a system called YES/MVS that helps computer operators using the MVS operating system to schedule jobs and alerts them to certain potential problems [80].

4.3. The Value Chain

In the third framework--the value chain framework--a firm's activities are analyzed in stages such as acquisition, production, distribution, marketing/sales, and service [66]. Traditional information systems have helped to increase the value of activities performed within each stage to create competitive advantage. For example, when American Airlines made its automated customer reservations system available to travel agents, it greatly enhanced its market position relative to its competitors [68]. In addition, several expert systems have been developed at American International Group and several other firms to do commercial insurance underwriting, a complex task requiring expertise in risk analysis and access to such information as data on the property to be insured, company history, and requested term [81, 82, 83, 84, 85, 86]. Other firms are developing expert systems to assist in commercial lending decisions, which require knowledge of financial data, management competence, competitive position, and operating performance 81, 87, 88].

One location in the value chain that may be especially fruitful for expert systems and other artificial intelligence applications is manufacturing [89], and several examples of manufacturing applications have been described above. In addition, expert systems have been developed for process planning and control. An example is OPGEN, an expert system for helping industrial engineers to plan the installation of electrical components on a printed circuit board [90]. Given a physical layout diagram and a bill of materials file for a particular circuit, OPGEN recommends which components should be installed by hand and which by machine, when, where (i.e., at which work center) the installation should take place, and any special conditions (e.g., special tooling) that the assembly technicians should anticipate. An example of a process control system is HCVM (the Heuristic Virtual Control Machine), developed by Tecknowledge and used by FMC Corporation for process control in chemical reactors [91]. The system uses its expertise to maximize reactor yield and minimize waste while keeping operating conditions within appropriate ranges and minimizing downtime.

4.4. The Future

We have seen that expert systems are already starting to affect competitive advantage as expressed in the frameworks of (1) cost reduction and product and service differentiation, (2) the customer resurce life cycle, and (3) the value chain. We now ask: what will be the impact of these systems in the future? One possibility is that expert systems will follow the pattern of conventional information systems in altering competitive forces within various industries. Information systems have been used to change three major competitive forces: (1) buyer power and supplier power (by electronically linking firms to buyers and suppliers), (2) potential industry entrants (by raising or lowering barries to entry), and (3) potential substitutes for a product or service (by allowing creation of new information-based products) [65, 92, 93]. Expert systems may affect these same forces in the future. For example, an expert system which evaluates simultaneously a large number of potential investment vehicles may shift power from the suppliers to those vehicles to the buyers, since prices, rates of return, etc. could be compared in detail by the investor. Expert systems which are expensive to build, such as diagnostic systems for the maintenance of electrical and mechanical products, could become investment barriers to potential industry entrants. Conversely, expert systems which allow distribution of expertise to many geographically dispersed locations could reduce some barriers to entry--such as personnel hiring and training--for firms expanding into new geographical areas, in the same way that automated teller machines have allowed banks to enlarge their geographic presence. Expert systems could also substitute for certain services offered by knowledge workers such as the giving of financial and legal advice, although the performance requirements for such systems would be very high. Although expert systems have not yet led to significant changes in industry structures and competitive forces, potential applications of the type described above suggest that certain changes are possible and perhaps likely.

Another way in which expert systems may affect competitive advantage is by assisting in the development of competitive strategies. In addition to using expert systems as part of a product or service, a firm may use expert systems to help develop and execute the strategies upon which its product line is based [94, 95, 96]. Systems could assist in strategy development by analyzing information on markets and competitors, by modelling strategic problems through simulation and scenario generation, and by improving communication between decision makers [94].

There is one commercially available expert system that performs some of these tasks. An expert financial advisory system, developed by a vendor to perform sophisticated analyses of investment projects, is currently in use or testing at several major corporations [73, 76]. Additional applications of expert systems to strategy formulation are being developed at other major industrial and consulting firms in such areas as strategic planning, market analysis, and acquisition analysis [97]. In addition, expert systems may be used to assist in the execution of strategy, by providing the information necessary to monitor performance relative to the critical factors in a firm's strategic plan, such as achievement of market [96]. For example, a commercially available expert system in this area analyzes the impact of promotions on sales in the packaged goods industry [98].

4.5. Competitive Advantage - A Summary

During the past five years there has been a growing interest in the impact of information system technology on competitive advantage. It is now well understood that information systems have improved the competitive positions of many business firms. We have seen that this is true not only of traditional information systems but also of some expert systems. We may expect that this trend will continue and that expert systems will increasingly be used by some leading edge companies to improve their competitive positions.

5. CONCLUSION

We may summarize the state of the art in the industrial application of expert systems as follows:

1. Expert systems as decision support systems. A number of systems have been developed for (1) resource allocation, (2) problem diagnosis, and (3) scheduling and assignment.

2. Expert systems as information management systems. Almost all of the work in this area is theoretical, with the exception of the work being done on expert database systems and explanation systems. However, this is an area of growing interest and importance.

3. Expert systems as tools for increasing competitive advantage. T h i s area has received little attention in the theoretical research and practitioner literature, but a number of firms are currently developing and implementing systems of this type, and the preliminary results are encouraging.

In order to understand more fully how expert systems projects are progressing in industry, we conducted (in April, 1986) a telephone survey of several industrial managers and technical specialists responsible for expert systems projects. The projects were those being reported in the business press at that time. We asked them what they were doing and what problems they were encountering. Our respondents generally felt that expert systems would eventually be used productively in their firms, but they were finding it far more difficult to construct these systems than they were initially led to believe. Specifically, they described three problems:

The first is the *cost* of developing a useful expert system. This can be quite large, and some managers are unwilling to make a commitment until their competitors have done so. For example, an executive in a leading insurance company told us that the first firm to develop a personal life insurance underwriting system would have a great advantage relative to its competitors, because it would reduce the time and cost of underwriting. This would benefit the company, its agents, and its customers. His firm had developed a prototype system that was discontinued because of the large financial commitment needed to make the system fully operational. He felt that companies, including his own, in the insurance industry were reluctant to incur the costs and risks of building such a system until forced by competitors to do so.

Because the commercial development of expert systems is still in its infancy, it is difficult to estimate accurately the risk, duration, cost, and benefits of a new expert system development effort. Some data is available for the early pioneering research-oriented systems [99, 100], but most of this data is misleading, since many of the seminal efforts were learning experiences and the information generated by these efforts is not helpful to those now developing expert systems. In addition, some mainframe inference engines [10] and many microcomputer-based expert system shells [102, 103] are now available. There is also a definitional problem: since expert systems are sometimes continually being improved, an expert system development effort may continue as long as the problem that gave rise to it continues to exist [104].

The second problem identified in our survey concerns *personnel*. It is difficult to find knowledge engineers who are competent in expert system technology and who also communicate well with domain experts. The vice president for research and development of a major bank that was developing several prototype expert systems said that the lack of interpersonal and communications skills of technical personnel charged with developing these systems was critically hindering attempts to develop the systems at his bank.

One approach that has been suggested for addressing this problem is to place on the expert system development team an intermediary who can encode domain knowledge obtained from the domain expert and make it available to the expert system specialist [105]. Another (complemntary) approach is rapid prototyping - the development of a crude and incomplete prototype early in the development effort that serves as a basis for criticism and successive refinement [105, 106].

The third problem is *misleading information.* We heard several complaints about this. The vice president mentioned above said that many of the vendor representatives that he had met were very positive about their products but did not discuss the difficulties in building expert systems of the type that he and his colleagues were encountering. A system analyst in another bank was surprised that the sales personnel of certain vendors did not adequately understand their products and could not answer simple questions about product capabilities. The analyst also felt that the business press was presenting a misleading impression of the magnitude of the effort needed to build a useful expert system.

One possible reason for this is that many expert systems efforts are unreported, both because some users wish to conceal their work from their competitors and because some users are too busy to report their efforts [13]. In addition, most successful expert systems focus on very narrow problem domains, which may give the misleading impression that a concentrated effort will produce rapid results [107].

These observations should not be surprising--they describe events that occurred during the early development of data processing, model building (i.e., operations research and management science), database managemnt, and probably many other technologies. One may expect that during the early stages of any new technology (1) costs will be high, risks will be large, and many managers will be reluctant to commit to the technology until others have done so, (2) technical specialists and the potential users of the technology will not communicate well with each other, and (3) vendors and other enthusiasts will make promises and optimistic predictions that are substantially at variance with reality. However, in the more traditional areas of data processing, decision modeling, and database management these problems have largely been overcome--primarily, as a result of increased user sophistication. We anticipate that similar events will take place during the next decade with regard to expert systems.

ACKNOWLEDGEMENT

This research was supported by the Dean's fund for Faculty Research of the Owen Graduate School of Management of Vanderbilt University.

REFERENCES

[1] Michaelson, Robert and Donald Michie, "Expert Systems in Business," *Datamation,* Vol. 29, No. 11, November 1983, pp. 240-246.

[2] Blanning, Robert W., "Management Applications of Fifth Generation Computers," *Business Forum,* Vol. 9, No. 4, Fall 1984, pp. 280-285.

[3] Miller, Richard K., *Artificial Intelligence Applications for Business Management.* Madison, Wis.: SEAI Technical Publications, 1984.

[4] Reitman, Walter, (ed.), *Artificial Intelligence Applications for Business.* Norwood, N.J.: Ablex, 1984.

[5] Winston, Patrick H. and Karen A. Pendergast, *The AI Business: The Commercial Uses of Artificial Intelligence.* Cambridge, Mass.: The MIT Press, 1984.

[6] Pau, L. F., *Artificial Intelligence in Economics and Management.* Amsterdam: North-Holland, 1986.

[7] Sviokla, John J., "Business Implications of Knowledge-Based Systems," *Data Base,* Vol. 17, No. 4, Summer 1986, pp. 5-19; Part II: Vol. 18, No. 1, Fall 1986, pp. 5-16.

[8] Holsapple, Clyde W. and Andrew B. Whinston, *Business Expert Systems.* Homewood, Ill.: Irwin, 1987.

[9] Silverman, Barry, (ed.), *Expert Systems for Business.* Reading, Mass.: Addison-Wesley, 1987.

[10] Blanning, Robert W., "Management Applications of Expert Systems," *Information & Management,* Vol. 7, No. 6, December 1984, pp. 311-316.

[11] Negoita, C. V., "Management Applications of Expert Systems," *Human Systems Management,* Vol. 4, No. 4, Autumn 1984, pp. 275-279.

[12] Dhar, Vasant, "On the Plausibility and Scope of Expert Systems in Management," in *Proceedings of the Nineteenth Hawaii International Conference on System Sciences,* January 1986, pp. 328-338.

[13] Harmon, Paul, "Inventory and Analysis of Existing Expert Systems," *Expert Systems Strategies,* August 1986, pp. 1-15.

[14] Keen, Peter G. W. and Michael S. Scott-Morton, *Decision Support Systems: An Organizational Perspective.* Reading, Mass.: Addison-Wesley, 1978.

[15] Alter, Steven L., *Decision Support Systems: Current Practice and Continuing Challenges.* Reading, Mass.: Addison-Wesley, 1980.

[16] Sprague, Ralph H., Jr. and Eric D. Carlson, *Building Effective Decision Support Systems.* Englewood Cliffs, N.J.: Prentice-Hall, 1982.

[17] House, William C., *Decision Support Systems: A Data-Based, Model-Oriented, User-Developed Discipline.* New York: Petrocelli, 1983.

[18] Blanning, Robert W., "Knowledge Acquisition and System Validation in Expert Systems for Management," *Human Systems Management,* Vol. 4, No. 4, Autumn 1984, pp. 280-285.

[19] Blanning, Robert W., "Expert Systems for Management: Possible Application Areas," *DSS-84 Transactions,* April 1984, pp. 69-77.

[20] Clarkson, Geoffrey P. E., "A Model of the Trust Investment Process." In *Computers and Thought,* edited by Edward A. Feigenbaum and Julian Feldman. New York: McGraw-Hill, 1963, pp. 347-371.

[21] Bohanek, M., Bratko, I., and Rajkovic, V., "An Expert System for Decision Making." In *Processes and Tools for Decision Support,* edited by Henk G. Sol. Amsterdam: North-Holland, 1983, pp. 235-248.

[22] Rychener, M.D., M.L. Farinacci, I. Hulthage, and M.S. Fox, "Integration of Multiple Knowledge Sources in ALADIN, an Alloy Design System," *Proceedings of the Fifth National Conference on Artificial Intelligence,* August 1986, pp. 878-882.

[23] Mittal, Sanjay, Clive L. Dym, and Mahesh Morjaria, "PRIDE: An Expert System for the Design of Paper Handling Systems," *IEEE Computer,* July 1986, pp. 102-114.

[24] Lu, S. C-Y., C.R. Blattner, and T.J. Lindem, "A Knowledge-Based Expert System for Drilling Station Design." In *Applications of AI in Engineering Problems,* edited by D. Srivam and R. Adey. New York: Springer-Verlag, 1986, pp. 423-443.

[25] Dungan, Chris W. and John S. Chandler, "AUDITOR: A Microcomputer-Based Expert System to Support Auditors in the Field," *Expert Systems,* Vol. 2, No. 4, October 1985, pp. 210-221.

[26] Bouwman, Marinus J., "Human Diagnostic Reasoning by Computer: An Illustration from Financial Analysis," *Management Science,* Vol. 29, No. 6, June 1983, pp. 653-672.

[27] Talukdar, Sarah N., Eleri Cardozo, and Luiz V. Leao, "Toast: The Power System Operator's Assistant," *IEEE Computer,* July 1986, pp. 53-60.

[28] Barber, Gerald A., "Supporting Organizational Problem Solving with a Work Station," *ACM Transactions on Office Information Systems,* Vol. 1, No. 1, January 1983, pp. 45-67.

[29] Fox, Mark S. and Stephen F. Smith, "ISIS - A Knowledge-Based System for Factory Scheduling." *Expert Systems,* Vol. 1, No. 1, July 1984, pp. 25-49.

[30] Smith, Steven F., Mark S. Fox, and Peng Si Ow, "Constructing and Maintaining Detailed Production Plans: Investigations into the Development of Knowledge-Based Factory Scheduling Systems," *AI Magazine,* Vol. 7, No. 3, Fall 1986, pp. 45-61.

[31] Fikes, Richard E., "Odyssey: A Knowledge-Based Assistant," *Artificial Intelligence,* Vol. 16, No. 3, July 1968, pp. 331-361.

[32] Goldstein, Ira P. and Bruce Roberts, "Using Frames in Scheduling." In *Artificial Intelligence: An MIT Perspective,* Vol. 1, edited by Patrick Henry Winston and Richard Henry Brown, Cambridge, Mass.: The MIT Press, 1982, pp. 255-284.

[33] Barkocy, Brian E. and William J. Zdelblick, "A Knowledge-Based System for Machining Production Planning," *Proceedings of the Autofact 6 Conference,* October 1984, pp. 2-11-2-25.

[34] Bruno, Giorgio, Antonio Elia, and Pietro Leface, "A Rule-Based System to Schedule Production," *IEEE Computer,* July 1986, pp. 32-39.

[35] Blanning, Robert W., (ed.), *Foundations of Expert Systems for Management.* Koln: Verlag Rheinland, (forthcoming - 1988).

[36] Blanning, Robert W., "Expert Systems for Management: Research and Applications," *Journal of Information Science,* Vol. 9, No. 2, March 1985, pp. 153-162.

[37] Turban, Efraim and Paul R. Watkins, "Integrating Expert Systems and Decision Support Systems," in *DSS-85 Transactions,* April 1985, pp. 52-63.

[38] Blanning, Robert W., "Issues in the Design of Expert Systems for Management," *Proceedings of the National Computer Conference,* July 1984, pp. 489-495.

[39] Green, Cordell, "Theorem-Proving by Resolution as a Basis for Question-Answering Systems." In *Machine Intelligence 4,* edited by Bernard Meltzer, Donald Michie, and Michael Swann. New York: American Elsevier, 1969, pp. 183-205.

[40] Bonczek, Robert H., Clyde W. Holsapple, and Andrew B. Whinston, *Foundations of Decision Support Systems.* New York: Academic Press, 1981.

[41] Schell, George Powell, "Knowledge Representation and Knowledge Manipulation in Decision Support Systems," Ph.D. Thesis, Purdue University, August 1983.

[42] Dutta, Amitava and Amit Basu, "An Artificial Intelligence Approach to Model Management in Decision Support Systems," *Computer,* September 1984, pp. 89-97.

[43] Chen, Michael C., Jane E. Fedorowicz, and Lawrence J. Henschen, "Deductive Processes in Databases and Decision Support Systems," *Proceedings of the North Central Regional ACM Conference,* November 1982, pp. 81-100.

[44] Chen, Michael C. and Lawrence J. Henschen, "On the Use and Internal Structure of Logic-based Decision Support Systems," *Decision Support Systems,* Vol. 1, No. 3, September 1985, pp. 205-219.

[45] Elam, Joyce J., John C. Henderson, and Louis W. Miller, "Model Management Systems: An Approach to Decision Support in Complex Organizations," *Proceedings of the First International Conference on Information Systems,* December 1980, pp. 98-110.

[46] McIntyre, Scott C., Benn R. Konsynski, and Jay F. Nunamaker, Jr., "Knowledge Integration and Model Scripting in PLEXPLAN: An Automated Environment for IS Planning," *Proceedings of the Nineteenth Annual Hawaii International Conference on System Sciences,* January 1986, pp. 397-404.

[47] Dolk, Daniel R. and Benn R. Konsynski, "Knowledge Representation for Model Management Systems," *IEEE Transactions on Software Engineering,* Vol. SE-1O, No. 6, November 1984, pp. 619-628.

[48] Applegate, Lynda M., Gary Klein, Benn R. Konsynski, and Jay F. Nunamaker, "Model Management Systems: Proposed Model Representations and Future Designs," *Proceedings of the Sixth International Conference on Information Systems,* December 1985, pp. 1-16.

[49] Blanning, Robert W., "Management Applications of Metaknowledge," *Human Systems Management,* Vol. 7, 1987, pp. 49-57.

[50] Kerschberg, Larry, *Proceedings of the First International Conference on Expert Database Systems,* April 1985.

[51] Kerschberg, Larry, *Proceedings of the First International Workshop on Expert Database Systems,* October 1984.

[52] Yasdi, Ramin, "A Conceptual Design Aid Environment for Expert Database Systems," *Data & Knowledge Engineering,* Vol. 1, No. 1, June 1985, pp. 31-73.

[53] Smith, John Miles, "Expert Database Systems: A Database Perspective," pp. K1-K22 of [51].

[54] Blanning, Robert W., "A Framework for Expert Modelbase Systems," *Proceedings of the National Computer Conference* June 1987, pp. 13-17.

[55] Blanning, Robert W., "A Relational Theory of Model Management." In *Decision Support Systems: Theory and Application,* edited by Clyde W. Holsapple and Andrew B. Whinston. Berlin: Springer-Verlag, 1987.

[56] Blanning, Robert W., "A Relational Framework for Information Management." In *Decision Support Systems: A Decade in Perspective,* edited by Ephraim R. McLean and Henk G. Sol. Amsterdam: North-Holland, 1986.

[57] Merrett, T. H., "First Steps to Algebraic Processing of Text." In New *Applications of Data Bases,* edited by Georges Gardarin and Erol Gelenbe. London: Academic Press, 1984.

[58] Kosy, Donald W. and Ben P. Wise, "Self-Explanatory Financial Planning Models," *Proceedings of the National Conference on Artificial Intelligence,* August 1984, pp. 176-181.

[59] King, David, "The ERGO Project: A Natural Language Query Facility for Explaining Financial Modeling Results, *DSS-86 Transactions,* April 1986, pp. 136-150.

[60] Greenberg, Harvey J., "ANALYZE: A Computer-Assisted Analysis System for Linear Programming Models," *ACM Transactions on Mathematical Software,* March 1983, pp. 18-56.

[61] Andriole, Stephen J., *Applications in Artificial Intelligence.* Princeton: Petrocelli, 1985.

[62] Schutzer, Daniel, "Artificial Intelligence-Based Very Large Data Base Organization and Management." *In Applications in Artificial Intelligence,* edited by Stephen Andriole. Princeton: Petrocelli, 1985.

[63] Hice, Gerald and Stephen J. Andriole, "Artificially Intelligent Videotex." In *Applications in Artificial Intelligence*, edited by Stephen Andriole. Princeton: Petrocelli, 1985.

[64] Madni, Azad, Michael Samet, and Denis Purcell, "Adaptive Models in Information Management." In *Applications in Artificial Intelligence*, edited by Stephen Andriole. Princeton: Petrocelli, 1985.

[65] Parsons, Gregory L., "Information Technology: A New Competitive Weapon," *Sloan Management Review,* Vol. 25, No. 1, Fall 1983, pp. 3-14.

[66] Porter, Michael E., and Victor E. Millar, "How Information Gives You Competitive Advantage," *Harvard Business Review,* Vol. 63, No. 4, July-August 1985, pp. 149-160.

[67] Ives, Blake, and Gerald P. Learmonth, "The Information System as a Competitive Weapon," *Communications of the ACM,* Volume 27, No. 12, December 1984, pp. 1193-1201.

[68] Hamilton, Joan O. C. and Catherine L. Harris, "Information Power: How Companies Are Using New Technologies to Gain a Competitive Edge," *Business Week*, October 14, 1985, pp. 108-114.

[69] Scown, Susan J., *The Artificial Intelligence Experience: An Introduction.* Maynard, Mass.: Digital Equipment Corporation, 1985 (Chapter 6: "Getting Started with Expert Systems: A Case Study," pp. 111-145).

[70] Manuel, Tom, "The Pell-Mell Rush Into Expert Systems Forces Integration Issue," *Electronics,* Vol. 58, No. 26, July 1 , 1985, pp. 54-59.

[71] Wynot, Mark, "Artificial Intelligence Provides Real-Time Control of DEC's Material Handling Process," *Industrial Engineering,* Volume 18, No. 4, April 1986, pp. 34-44.

[72] Smith, Emily T., "Turning An Expert's Skill Into Computer Software," *Business Week,* October 7, 1985, pp. 104-108.

[73] Krepchin, Ira P., "Artificial Intelligence Ups Warehouse Efficiency," *Modern Materials Handling,* May 1986, pp. 68-71.

[74] Myers, Edith, "Expert Systems: Not for Everyone," *Datamation*, Vol. 32, No. 10, May 15, 1986, pp. 28, 32.

[75] Harmon, Paul and David King, *Expert Systems: Artificial Intelligence in Business.* New York: Wiley, 1985, pp. 155-173.

[76] Bulkely, William M., "Computers Take On New Role As Experts In Financial Affairs," *The Wall Street Journal*, February 6, 1986, pp. 21.

[77] Rauch-Hindin, Wendy B., *Artificial Intelligence in Business, Science and Industry, Vol II: Applications*. Englewood Cliffs, N.J.: Prentice-Hall, 1985 pp. 79-90.

[78] Bonissone, Piero P. and Harold E. Johnson, Jr., "DELTA: An Expert System for Diesel Electric Locomotive Repair." In *Artificial Intelligence in Maintenance,* edited by J. Jeffrey Richardson. Park Ridge: Noyes Publications, 1985, pp. 391-405.

[79] Miller, Frederick D., David H. Copp, Gregg T. Vesonder, and John E. Zielinski, "The ACE Experiment: Initial Evaluation of an Expert System for Preventive Maintenance." In *Artificial Intelligence in Maintenance,* edited by J. Jeffrey Richardson. Park Ridge: Noyes Publications, 1985, pp. 406-413.

[80] Waterman, Donald A., *A Guide to Expert Systems,* Reading, Mass.: Addison-Wesley, 1986.

[81] Long, Robert, and Paul Recker, "'Rolls Royce' Expert Systems for Lending and Underwriting," *AI Financial Report,* Volume 1, No. 5, August 1985, pp. 1-10.

[82] Koflowitz, Lewis, "Finding Premium Use for Machines," *American Banker,* Vol. 40, No. 107, June 3, 1985, pp. 42-43.

[83] Garsson, Robert M., "The Gut Feeling Goes Electric," *American Banker,* June 3, 1985, pp. 20-22.

[84] Shpilberg, David, "A Promising New Frontier," *Best's Review, Property/Casualty Insurance Edition,* Volume 86, No. 1, May 1985.

[85] White, Dennis G., "Expert Systems to the Rescue," *Best's Review, Property/Casualty Insurance Edition,* Volume 86, No. 1, May, 1985.

[86] Shamoon, Sherrie, "AIG's Smart Software: The 'Expert' That Thinks Like An Underwriter," *Management Technology,* February 1985.

[87] Friis, M. William, "Artificial Intelligence Systems: Some Banks Have Them, Others Will," *ABA Banking Journal,* Vol. 77, No. 6, June 1985, pp. 203-208.

[88] Dyson, Esther, "Pragmatic Intelligence," *Release 1-0,* EDventure Holdings, Inc., New York, April 24, 1984.

[89] Miller, Richard K., *Artificial Intelligence Applications for Manufacturing,* Madison: SEAI Technical Publications, 1984.

[90] Freedman, Roy S. and Robert P. Frail, "OPGEN: The Evolution of an Expert System for Process Planning," *AI Magazine,* Vol. 7, No. 5, Winter 1986, pp. 58-70.

[91] D'Ambrosio, Bruce, Michael R. Fehling, Stephanie Forrest, Peter Raulefs, and B. Michael Wilber, "Real-Time Process Management for Materials Composition in Chemical Manufacturing," *IEEE Expert,* Vol. 2, No. 2, Summer 1987, pp. 80-93.

[92] McFarlan, F. Warren, "Information Technology Changes the Way You Compete," *Harvard Business Review,* Vol. 62, No. 3, May-June 1984, pp. 98-103.

[93] Cash, James I., Jr., and Benn R. Konsynski, "IS Redraws Competitive Boundaries," *Harvard Business Review,* Vol. 63, No. 2, March-April 1985, pp. 134-142.

[94] Mertens, Peter, "Computer Assisted Strategic Planning," Universitat Erlangen-Nurnberg, Nurnberg, West Germany, presented at the TIMS/ORSA Joint National Meeting, Atlanta, November, 1985.

[95] Silverman, Barry G., "Should a Manager 'Hire' an Expert System?" In *Expert Systems for Business,* edited by Barry Silverman. Reading, Mass.: Addison-Wesley, 1987.

[96] Millar, Victor E., "Decision Oriented Information," *Datamation,* Vol. 30, No. 1, January 1984, pp. 159-162.

[97] Long, Robert, and Paul Recker, "Sorting The Facts from Fancy: Will The Mechanical Mind Fly?", *American Banker,* Vol. 40, No. 107, June 3, 1985, pp. 16-18.

[98] Horwitt, Elizabeth, "Exploring Expert Systems," *Business Computer Systems,* March 1985, pp. 48-57.

[99] Hayes-Roth, Frederick, Donald A. Waterman, and Douglas B. Lenat, *Building Expert Systems,* Reading, Mass.: Addison-Wesley, 1983. (See Chapter 1).

[100] Davis, Randall and Karen A. Pendergast, eds., *The AI Business: The Commercial Uses of Artificial Intelligence,* Cambridge, Mass.: The MIT Press, 1984, (See Chapter 2).

[101] Richer, Mark H., "An Evaluation of Expert System Development Tools," *Expert Systems,* Vol. 3, No. 3, July 1986, pp. 166-183.

[102] Lehner, Paul E. and Stephen W. Barth, "Expert Systems on Microcomputers," *Expert Systems,* Vol. 2, No. 4, October 1985, pp. 198-208.

[103] Shafer, Daniel G., "Microcomputer-Based Expert Systems: Where we are, Where we are Headed," *Expert Systems,* Vol. 2, No. 4, October 1985, pp. 188-195.

[104] Bachant, Judith and John McDermott, "R1 Revisited: Four Years in the Trenches," *AI Magazine,* Vol. 5, No. 3, Fall 1984, pp. 21-32.

[105] Smith, Reid G., "On the Development of Commercial Expert Systems," *AI Magazine,* Vol.5, No. 3, Fall 1984, pp. 61-73.

[106] Herrod, Richard A. and Jeff Rieckel, "Knowledge-Based Simulation of a Glass Annealing Process: An AI Application in the Glass Industry," *Proceedings of the 5th National Conference on Artificial Intelligence,* August 1986, pp. 800-804.

[107] Sheil, Beau, "Thinking about Artificial Intelligence," *Harvard Business Review,* Vol. 65, No. 4, July-August 1987, pp. 91-97.

Applied Expert Systems, E. Turban and P.R. Watkins (Editors)
© Elsevier Science Publishers B.V. (North-Holland), 1988

EASIE: A KNOWLEDGE-BASED SYSTEM FOR ACADEMIC ADVISING

Dr. Abu S. M. Masud [*] *and Maliwan Sripanich*

Industrial Engineering Department
The Wichita State University
Wichita, KS 67208, USA

In academic advising, much of the information necessary for error free advising is scattered over in several sources; moreover, some of the information is not available to the students because they are informal rules used by the faculty members based on their experience. The faculty members also, on occasion, act as 'rule interpreters' regarding the applicability of university regulations and degree requirements. This often result in improper and inconsistent advising. In this paper, we describe EASIE - Expert Advisor for Students in Industrial Engineering, a microcomputer-based knowledge system developed for advising the undergraduate industrial engineering students in The Wichita State University. We also remark on some design issues faced during the development and how they have been resolved.

1. INTRODUCTION

Academic advising in a university environment usually consist of charting a student's academic progress and ensuring satisfaction of all university and degree requirements. Much of the required information is scattered over such sources as: university catalogs, advising worksheets, memos, and other university records. While a student is expected to observe all regulations and requirements, he/she may not have access to all the information nor may he/she know where to look for the information.

Academic advisors are supposed to be able to help a student in such matters. But, they may forget, misinterpret, or not know all the regulations and re-

---

* Current Address: Techno-Economics Division, Kuwait Institute for Scientific Research, P.O.Box 24885, 13109 Safat, Kuwait

quirements. In addition, advisors often use informal rules which they have developed based on their experience; these informal rules may not be widely shared with other advisors. Thus, academic advising possesses some of the classic characteristics of a problem where knowledge-based system may be a solution [1,2,3,4,5]: (1) a large amount of knowledge available in several documents, (2) use of human experience unique to advisors (experts), (3) a large number of feasible alternatives (set of courses to be taken and their sequence) which are reduced to a few using knowledge and experience, and (4) need for easy accessibility of advice in a timely manner. In addition, the faculty members of the industrial engineering (I.E.) department at The Wichita State University (WSU) were facing the following issues related to academic advising: advising was taking more time than could be reasonably made available and a concern about consistency because of changing rules as well as faculty turnover. These provided the motivations for the development of a prototype knowledge-based system (KBS) for academic advising of the undergraduate students in the department. The result is EASIE, Expert Advisor for Students in Industrial Engineering [6]. The decision to use a microcomputer based system was made because a large number of microcomputers were already available in the department as well as in the labs of the College of Engineering and the students had easy access to these computers.

The rest of the paper is organized as follows: the process of academic advising at WSU is described in section 2, section 3 gives an overview of M.1 the KBS tool used in EASIE, a description of the knowledge domain itself is in section 4, an overview of the system design is given in section 5, section 6 describes the prototype system's performance, and concluding remarks are in section 7.

2. ACADEMIC ADVISING AT WSU

The student advising process at WSU normally includes [7]:
a. exploration of life goals
b. exploration of career/educational goals
c. selection of an educational program
d. selection of courses
e. scheduling of classes

Academic advisors, with some exceptions, are usually involved with the last three functions. These functions are usually performed by the faculty members from the department of the student's chosen major or by special advisors if he/she has not yet been accepted into a specific academic program. The academic advice includes advising on selecting an academic program consistent with the student's interests and goals, selecting the courses to be taken in a particular semester, and planning of course patterns and curricular sequence in order to meet requirements for graduation. The graduation requirements usually consist of required courses within the student's major and minor, elective courses in related areas, and university general requirements.

Every semester, all degree-bound students are expected to develop academic plans with the assistance of their advisors. Students who have declared major fields of study are assigned to faculty members in the respective academic departments of the declared major field. Students who have not declared majors are assigned to the academic counselors in the University College (UC).

All degree-granting colleges maintain a file of academic records of all students currently accepted into the programs offered by the college. UC maintains the academic records for those students who have not chosen a major yet or not been accepted in one of the degree-granting colleges. In a normal advising process, a student obtains the academic records file before consulting with his/her advisor. The academic records in the files maintained in the College of Engineering consist of a program check sheet, advisor's notes, and semester grade reports. The program check sheet contains the graduation requirements for the degree which consist of the university requirements, the general engineering requirements, and the departmental requirements; Figure 1 shows such a check sheet of a particular I.E. student. With the listing of all the required courses with the corresponding hours of credits and the completed courses with the grades obtained, the check sheet is normally used for charting a student's academic plans and progress.

3. THE KNOWLEDGE DOMAIN

The application domain of EASIE is limited to the advisement offered by the I.E. faculty members only. It, therefore, includes: (1) the UC Students who have declared I.E. as their major field, (2) the students who have already been accepted in the I.E. program, and (3) the students from other departments (either in the College of Engineering or in other colleges) who intend to transfer into the I.E. program. EASIE is also limited in the scope of the advice provided. Its advice does not include the development of a feasible list of courses to be enrolled in a given semester based on that semester's course schedule.

EASIE's domain knowledge includes, among others, the degree requirements by various catalog years, the College of Engineering's admission requirements, ABET (Accreditation Board for Engineering and Technology) requirements, unit hours of courses, sequence of courses and some of the informal advising rules used by advisors. The degree requirements in I.E. are divided into 5 main areas of study: mathematics & natural sciences, communications, humanities & fine arts, social & behavioral sciences, and engineering requirements. The engineering requirements are further divided into engineering core,

INDUSTRIAL ENGINEERING CHECK SHEET

134 Hrs. Min.   New Enrollments
for Graduation   to W.S.U.
                                                       Fall 1986

                    Name   Taylor, E. (444-53-2222)

MATHEMATICAL & NATURAL SCIENCES: 34 Hrs.

Math 242QC_5   Math 344 __3   Phys 313Q_C4   Phys 315Q or 316Q _B_1
Math 243 _A_5   Math 550 __3   Phys 314Q__4   +Nat. Science Elec __3
Math 311 __1   Chemistry 111Q   _B_5
               or approved calculus based math course.

COMMUNICATIONS: 9 Hrs.

English 101   _C_3   English 102   _C_3   Speech 111 (or Speech 112)   __5

HUMANITIES & FINE ARTS Div A   SOCIAL & BEHAVIORAL SCIENCE Div B + +18 Hrs.

_____ __   Economics 201Q   _C_3
_____ __   Economics 202Q   __3
_____ __   Sociology 211Q   _C_3
_____ __   Political S 103 G _C_3

          ENGINEERING COURSES: 73 Hrs.
              Engineering Core: 13 Hrs.

                  A.E. 323 ___ 3   E.E. 382 __ 4
                  I.E. 355 __ 3   M.E. 398 __ 3

Specific Courses Required by I.E. Department: 49 Hrs.

I.E. 110   _C_2   A.E. 373 __3   I.E. 556   __ 3
I.E. 213   _D_2   I.E. 452 __3   I.E. 558   __ 3
E.E. 199 __ 3   I.E. 549 __3   I.E. 570   __ 3
I.E. 354 __ 3   I.E. 550 __3   I.E. 590   __ 2
A.E. 333 __ 3   I.E. 553 __3   I.E. 665   __ 3
M.E. 350 __ 4   I.E. 554 __3

 +Technical Electives: 11 Hrs.
 A minimum of 6 Hrs. must be taken within the I.E. department and 1 Hr. from
 another Engineering Department.

   _____ __   _____ __   _____ __
   _____ __   _____ __   _____ __

NOTES:
    +   Chosen from approved list
   + +   At least 9 Hrs. must be taken in at least 3 Departments in Div. A.
         At least 3 additional Hrs. must be taken in non-Econ. div. B.
         At least 9 Hrs. of General Studies courses designated by G must be included
         within Divisions A and B.

Figure 1
The Degree Checklist

required I.E. courses, and technical electives. Each of these areas requires a specified number of hours. In the areas such as mathematics & natural sciences, communications, engineering core, and required I.E. courses, specific courses are given as the requirements. Whereas, in the areas such as humanities & fine arts, social & behavioral sciences, and technical electives, there are no specific required courses but the selected courses must be chosen from some approved lists. In addition, such chosen courses must also meet certain other distributional requirements.

The engineering admission requirements are applicable to the students who want to be accepted into the various degree programs offered through the College of Engineering. The requirements include, among other things, the completion of the following courses with a grade of 'C' or better : English 101; English 102 or Speech 111 or Speech 112; Math 242; and Chem 111 or Physics 313. The advisors must, however, have to consider that these are fundamental courses and they require certain levels of preparatory knowledge. For example, to take Math 242, a student must have had two units of high school algebra, a unit of high school geometry and one-half unit of trigonometry; otherwise, he/she may have to take appropriate preparatory course(s) before enrolling in Math 242.

Course prerequisites and corequisites are applied to constrain enrollment in a course. Prerequisites of a course must be satisfied before that course can be taken. Corequisites are to be taken before or concurrently with the course. Finally, the sequence of courses is significant in a sense that some courses should be given top priority because they are prerequisites for other higher-level courses. Also, not all courses are offered every semester and the offering of certain required courses follow an informal pattern (for example, the statics course is offered in fall and the dynamics course in spring; a day and an evening section of engineering economy is offered in fall but only a day section in spring). A suggested semester breakdown of the I.E. program as given in the university catalog is shown in Figure 2. Due to a variety of reasons, students can rarely follow this suggested schedule exactly.

Sources used for acquiring EASIE's domain knowledge were: the academic advisors (both in UC and in I.E.), the I.E. check sheets for various catalog years, the university catalog [8] and the advisor's handbook [7].

4. OVERVIEW OF M.1

Software tools are available from commercial and research sources to aid in the development of KBS. These tools provide [9]: (1) a substantial amount of computer codes that otherwise are needed to be written, tested, debugged and maintained and (2) specific techniques for knowledge representation, inference, and control for a particular class of problems. In this study, M.1 Version 2.0 by

Tecknowledge Inc. has been used. M.1 is a tool for developing and using knowledge-based system on the IBM PC/XT/AT (or 100% compatible) microcomputers. It is implemented in the C programming language. The knowledge based system developed by M.1 can contain as many as 1000 or more rules, limited only by the computer's memory. It is best used for developing a KBS that handles diagnosis/prescription type consultations. Brief descriptions of some of M.1's features are provided below; see M.1 reference manual [10] for additional information.

4.1. Knowledge Representation in M.1

The representation of knowledge within M.1 is through production rules and facts. The production rules represent heuristic knowledge and relationships by attribute-value pairs (attributes are called expressions). Rules link the values for expressions by testing the values of one expression and concluding values for another expression. Facts are also represented as attribute-value pairs. M.1 allows rules and facts to be written with symbolic variables. This special feature allows similar facts and rules to be written in one generic rule. In addition, uncertain knowledge is marked by certainty factors that range in value from -100 to 100. A certainty factor of 100 indicates complete certainty, a -100 indicates a negative certainty, and a 0 indicates complete uncertainty (not to be equated with unknown). This feature allows M.1 to conclude realistic solutions even with incomplete knowledge. In M.1, 'unknown' is always an acceptable answer in response to a query.

4.2. Inference Engine

The M.1 inference engine (or rule interpreter) uses a backward chaining reasoning process. The ordering of clauses in a rule and the ordering of the rules themselves influence how backchaining will proceed. M.1 also allows very limited forward chaining reasoning process by the use of such specific functions as 'whenfound' and 'presupposition'.

4.3. M.1 Facilities

One of the reasons for using a tool is to take advantage of its facilities that have been developed to support the system. These facilities normally include: debugging aids, knowledge base preparation aids, and user interface. M.1 knowledge base can be prepared by using any standard text editor in an English like language. It is then loaded into M.1 to solve specific problems using M.1's inference engine. M.1 also provides programming aids for debugging during the development of a KBS in a multi-window or interactive debugging environment. For example, each component of the system's reasoning process can be viewed through window based interface or the flow of reasoning and conclusions can be traced by an inference tracing mechanism. M.1's explanation facility allows the knowledge engineers to provide explanation about a path of reasoning in

Model Program

Freshman

Course	Hrs.
Eng. 101 and 102, College English I and II	
Chem 111Q, General Chemistry	6
Math 242Q and 243, Calculus I and II	5
Phys. 313Q, University Physics I	10
Phys. 315Q, University Physics Lab	5
Speech 111, Basic Public Speaking, or Speech 112, Basic Interpersonal Communication . .	1
Engr. 125, Introduction to Engineering Concepts	3
IE 110, Engineering Graphics I .	2
	2

Sophomore

Course	Hrs.
Math. 311, Introduction to Linear Algebra†	
Math. 344, Calculus III	1
Math. 550, Ordinary Differential Equations	3
Phys. 314Q, Classical College Physics Lectures II	3
AE 323, Engineering Mechanics: Statics*	4
EE 199, Engineering Computing Fundamentals	3
AE 373, Engineering Mechanics: Dynamics I*	3
EE 382, Electrical Dynamics* . .	3
IE 213, Engineering Graphics II .	4
ME 398, Thermodynamics 1* . .	2
Humanities and fine arts elective‡	3
Econ. 201Q, Principles of Economics I	7
Econ 202Q, Principles of Economics II	3
	3

Junior

Course	Hrs.
AE 333, Mechanics of Deformable Solids I*	
IE 354, Engineering Probability and Statistics	3
IE 355, Engineering Economy . .	3
IE 452, Work Measurement . . .	3
IE 460, Engineering Management	3
IE 549, Human Factor in Engineering Design	3
IE 550, Applied Operations Research I	3
ME 400, Fluid and Heat Flow* . .	3
Natural Sciences elective** . . .	4
Humanities and fine arts or social and behavioral sciences electives ‡	3
	3

Senior

Course	Hrs.
IE 553, Production Control . . .	3
IE 554, Statistical Quality Control	3
IE 556, Introduction to Information Systems	3
IE 558, Manufacturing Methods and Materials	3
IE 590, Senior Projects in Industrial Engineering	2
Social and behavioral sciences electives ‡	9
technical electives §	12

---

*Out-of-department engineering courses.
**Refer to general engineering requirements at beginning of this section for list of approved courses.
†Or any calculus-based mathematics course aipproved by the industrial engineering department.
At least nine hours must be taken in at least three departments in Division A. At least three additional hours must be taken in Division B outside of the Department of Economics. At least nine hours of general studies courses designated 'G' courses must be included within Division A and B. At least two courses are required in one department of Division A or B, and the two course sequence must include at least one course numbered 200 or above.
§Chosen from approved list. (A minimum of six hours must be taken within the Department of Industrial Engineering and must include a minimum of three hours of engineering science.)

Figure 2
A Model Program for I. E. Students

response to 'why' queries from the users. Finally, end-user systems can be built for delivery into application environments. An end-user system consists of the M.1 inference engine and a knowledge base in executable codes.

5. OVERVIEW OF EASIE'S SYSTEM DESIGN

The system design of EASIE is best described through its two structural modules: the functional structure and the operational structure. They are explained in the following sections.

5.1. The Functional Structure

The functional structure is composed of four sections: advising knowledge base, cache (working memory), user interface, and inference engine. Figure 3 shows the functional structure of EASIE.

Advising knowledge base: There are three types of knowledge base entries in M.1 that are used to represent EASIE's domain knowledge (both factual and heuristics) facts, meta-facts and rules.

Fact: A fact is used to directly assign values to an expression. An example of a 'fact' entry from EASIE is

prerequisite(engl102) = (engl101).

which reads "the prerequisite of engl102 is engl101." The prerequisites, corequisites, and minimum required grades for some prerequisites have been represented by facts. Meta-fact: A meta-fact provides information or directions about how to determine a value of an expression. For example, three meta-facts in EASIE that are used to determine a student's catalog year are

question(year) = 'Enter the year you first enrolled in W.S.U.
(select one from the following list).'.
legalvals(year) = ['1983','1984','1985','1986']. automaticmenu(year).

The legalvals meta-fact allows only one of the given four years to be selected, and the possible years are shown to the user by automaticmenu meta-fact. In general, the meta-facts are concerned with the consultation as opposed to the problem domain. Rule: A rule concludes one or more values for an expression according to the conditions set forth in it. Rules are of the form: if - then . Heuristics or rules of thumb and reasoning processes are represented by rules. For example, the following EASIE rule is used to find the eligible courses from the list of required courses:
    if courses-required = COURSE and

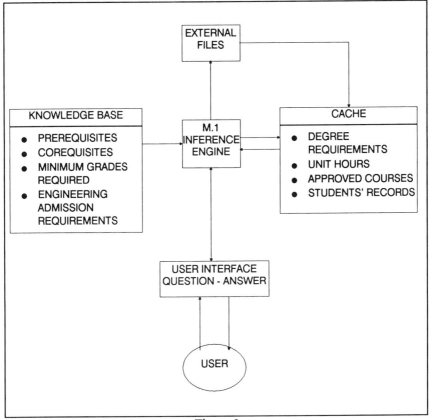

Figure 3
EASIE's Functional Structure

prerequisites-for-COURSE-satisfied and

corequisites-for-COURSE-satisfied then eligible-courses = COURSE.

Notice the use of variable 'COURSE' which can be instantiated to any specific course during the consultation. In EASIE, the knowledge about required courses for admission to the College of Engineering and their prerequisite courses are encoded in rules.

Additionally, the process of how to conclude the eligible courses, how to check for the completion of prerequisites, corequisites and areas of study, how to calculate 'grade point average' (GPA), etc., are also done by using rules. The rules also support the deductive process of backward chaining.

Cache: In M.1, the cache is used as a working memory (or global data base). It is repository of all information generated during the consultation. The cache stores information in the form:

EXPRESSION = VALUE cf CF because REASON.
where EXPRESSION is the expression term in M.1 that is equated to the value
VALUE with the certainty factor equal to CF and the REASON why the value
is concluded. The cache contents in any consultation with EASIE are created
by: the conclusions made during the consultation, user inputs, and the static information loaded directly from external disk files. The information loaded from
the external disk files include the degree requirements, unit hours of courses,
the lists of approved courses in humanities & fine arts (Div A) and social & behavioral sciences (Div B), and in some cases, the student's academic records
(courses taken, grades, catalog year, and the current GPA). Examples of some
of EASIE's cache entries are:

courses-required = phys313q because set by user.
hours(math242q) = 5 because set by user.
engineering-core = ae323 because set by user.

User interface: EASIE interacts with the users by asking questions as it
makes inferences based on the contents of the knowledge base. The user supplies the requested information and, in turn, may ask the system to explain the
reasoning process. In EASIE, the student records can be loaded from the student files or entered interactively during the consultation. The information in
student records consist of catalog year, courses taken, grades obtained, and the
current GPA. If a required information is not already in the cache or in one of
the files which can be loaded, the user enters that information through a
keyboard.

Inference engine: The inference engine reasons over the knowledge base
to arrive at conclusions, and initiates questions to the user to obtain more information. The inference engine in M.1 uses backward chaining and allows the in-
terruption of the backchaining by the use of a few meta-facts.

5.2. The Operational Structure

The operation of EASIE includes the performance of a number of tasks related to finding the eligible and recommended courses for a student. The operational structure of the system is shown in Figure 4. The consultation begins with
the following menu of three tasks, one of which is to be selected by the user : (1)
Regular consultation, (2) Creating a file, and (3) Updating a file. In the regular
consultation mode, the student identification a combination of name and social
security number (SSN) is checked against a student list to see whether a file for
that student exists or not. If the file exists, then the system proceeds with the advising process. If the file does not exist, then the system attempts to classify the
student into one of the following categories: (1) I.E. student, (2) other engineering student, or (3) non-engineering (UC and other college) student.

As part of the advising process, EASIE: (1) determines the eligible courses, (2) checks and verifies the completion of Division A, Division B and technical elective requirements, (3) determines the recommended courses to be taken corresponding to the number of hours the student plans to enroll in, and (4) displays an updated check sheet and a list of recommended courses. To determine the eligible courses, the complete list of required courses is matched against the courses that have been taken so far. The required courses are arranged in order relevant to the suggested sequence given in the university catalog. The list of courses, then, is invoked respectively from top to bottom. The unmatched courses from the list of required courses are checked for the completion of prerequisites and to determine the corequisites. If all the prerequisites and corequisites of a course are satisfied, that course is then marked as an eligible course. When this systematic verification is completed, the list of eligible courses is obtained. To check and verify the completion of Division A and Division B requirements, the approved lists of courses in humanities & fine arts (Div A) and social & behavioral sciences (Div B) are loaded into the cache. The courses that have already been taken are matched against courses in each list for the two divisions. The matched courses are checked for the total number of hours, the number of departments and the general studies (G) course designation. A specified number of unit hours and departments are required in each division, and a specified number of hours of G courses are required in both divisions. EASIE then determines whether or not the distributional requirements of two divisions have been satisfied. Next, it searches for courses that are applicable for technical electives from the remaining list of courses to be taken.

The advice given to the student by EASIE is in two forms: an updated check sheet and a list of recommended courses. It prints out, and displays on the CRT screen, the updated check sheet accompanied by one of the following comments against each of the required courses: 'taken', 'can take', or 'cannot take'. The list of recommended courses is developed from the identified eligible courses. EASIE inquires about the number of hours the student wants to take in courses other than those in Division A, Division B and the technical electives, and then lists the recommended courses such that total number of hours equal or exceed the desired hours. Next, the approved lists of natural science elective and general studies and general education distribution courses are displayed if desired by the student.

The other two tasks, creating and updating a file, allow a student to create a new file for his/her records or to update an existing file.

5.3. Some Design Issues

Several issues arose during EASIE's system design that merit some discussion. Most of them are specific to M.1 and some to the microcomputer environment.

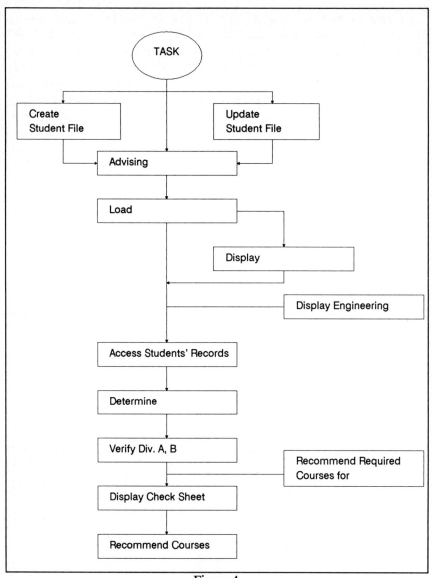

Figure 4
EASIE's Operational Structure

1. Memory: Even though the sales literature of M.1 says that it runs on microcomputers with 512KB memory, version 2.0 actually needs more than that. We did not encounter any problem with 640KB whereas we could not run programs with 512KB.

2. Size of knowledge base: The size of knowledge base is a function not only of the computer's memory but also of the number of rules, facts, and other cache contents. We could not run an earlier version of EASIE even when we had less than 200 rules because all the static facts were also loaded at the beginning of a consultation as part of the knowledge base instead of being in separate disk files as they currently are. The decision to put the static facts in disk files and load the necessary portions only when needed increased the performance time because of additional and frequent disk operations.

3. Cache management: For a data intensive system such as EASIE, active cache contents management is absolutely necessary; otherwise, one will encounter situations, as we did, where the cache space becomes full and the system crashes. We tackled this problem in two ways. One, not all the facts are loaded at the same time. Organizing and storing most of the static facts in disk files and loading the needed files reduces the cache contents dramatically. Two, selectively clear from cache contents all the facts which are no longer required after every major step of a consultation. In EASIE, both these steps free enough of cache space so that it can run without crashing but these steps slow down the consultation process by a significant amount. Using hard disk instead of floppy disks helps a little bit but not enough since the clearing of cache contents is a laborious and slow process.

4. Formatting of input/output: M.1 is case sensitive; the uppercase being reserved for variable names. As a result, we had to sacrifice elegance to some extent in much of the display operations. Moreover, frequently the information to be displayed is longer than one screen in which case we have had to devise rules and procedures for multi-screen display; M.1 does provide this automatically.

6. SYSTEM PERFORMANCE

EASIE has been designed to be used as an intelligent assistant to academic advisors. A student may consult with EASIE on his/her own and obtain an updated check sheet indicating courses that have been taken, courses that can be taken or can not be taken, and a list of recommended courses. Next, the student will develop his/her tentative schedule for enrollment based on the information given by EASIE and a semester's schedule of courses. Finally, the tentative schedule would be checked and approved by the advisor.

Figure 5 contains excerpts from a session with EASIE by a particular I.E. student. This particular student, whose check sheet is shown in Figure 1, had his/her academic records file maintained by EASIE. Figure 6 shows the results generated by the system including a check sheet and a list of recommended courses to be taken. The student's academic records file content, as maintained by EASIE, is shown in Figure 7. The records have the format of M.1 cache entry which is EXPRESSION = VALUE. The value for course enrolled is a character string consisting of the course number, course description and the course grade, separated by commas.

6.1. Limitations of the Prototype Version

Some of the observed limitations of EASIE's prototype version are discussed below.

1. The user input to EASIE must be in lower case because M.1 interprets all expressions starting with an upper case as a variable. And, course information need to be entered in exactly the same format as in the system's knowledge base.

2. Advice given by EASIE is unofficial and not complete for enrollment. It neither includes planning of courses for more than one semester nor the scheduling of the courses. The students, after consulting with EASIE, would have to work out the schedule from a semester schedule of courses and get it approved by the advisor.

3. EASIE performs at a relatively slow speed, especially during the process of finding eligible courses, and verifying and checking the completion of different requirements. These requirements contain a large number of courses that are processed by the system as possible conclusions. In finding the eligible courses, EASIE reasons backward from the list of required courses. It looks for the prerequisites and corequisites of each required course. Next, it checks for the completion of those prerequisites and corequisites. If the corequisites have not been taken already, it then checks one step backward for the completion of their prerequisites to determine whether the corequisites can be taken. When the pre- and co-requisites of a course are both satisfied, the course is concluded as an eligible course. This process is very time consuming because: (1) only backward chaining is permitted in M.1, (2) rules are invoked from the top every time a conclusion is desired, and (3) the lists of courses are quite lengthy .

The first two limitations are due primarily to the nature of M.1 which can be applied only to diagnosis type of problems and the way it is designed to operate. For the third limitation, the system can be modified by using a feature provided by M.1 the external function interface. For example, the list of courses may be stored and maintained in a dBASE III file. EASIE could then access the dBASE III file by external function interface prepared in C or Assembly language and conduct the search more efficiently in dBASE III. This is expected to reduce the

The advising system performs 3 principle tasks :

1. Regular consultation - to advise you in selecting courses required for a B.S. degree in I.E.
2. Create file - To help create an academic records file for you. If you are in the I.E. department, you should keep the information about courses you have completed in your own file.
3. Update file - To help you update your file.

Select a number corresponding to the task you want to perform:
        1.   regular consultation
        2.   update an existing file
        3.   create a new file
1

Do you want a print out of this session from now on?
        1.   yes
        2.   no
y

PLEASE TURN THE PRINTER ON.

Press 'c' when ready.
c

Please enter your lastname (first 8 characters in lower case) :
taylor

First initial (lower case) :
e

Your social security number (in quotation marks, e.g. '999999999') :
'444532222'

Do you want to view the list of degree requirements?
        1.   yes
        2.   no
n

.
.
.

Following is a display of the courses you have completed so far along with the grades received in those courses :
        math242q, Calculus I, c
        eng1101, College English I, c
        chem111q, General chemistry, b
        ie110, Engr. Graphics, c
        pols103q, Games Nations Play, c
        ie213, Engr. Graphics II, d
        econ201q, Principles of Econ. I, c
        math 243, Calculus II, a
        soc211q, Intro Sociology, c
        eng1102, College English II, c
        phys313q, Univ. Physics I, c
        phys315q, Univ. Physics lab I, b

        W.S.U. GPA = 2.27

Have you completed or are you currently enrolled in other courses at W.S.U.?
        1.   yes
        2.   no
y

Figure 5
An Example Session with EASIE

Enter the W.S.U. courses that you are currently enrolled in or received credit by exam or
   received transfer credit for equivalent W.S.U. courses as in the following example :
math311, eng1102, ie354, spch111, me350, \
ie355

(If the input does not fit in one line, USE '\' and continue on to the next line as shown
   above.)
engr125, math344

Enter grade received (or expected) in > engr125

(Enter: r if received credit by exam, t if received transfer credit)
        1.   a
        2.   b
        3.   c
        4.   d
        5.   f
        6.   r
        7.   t
b

        .

        .

        .

You can take either Speech 111 or Speech 112. However, it is recommended that
   engineering students should take Speech 111. What Speech course do you want to
   take?
        1.   spch111
        2.   spch112
1

Please wait for about 10 minutes !

Checking degree requirements . . .

Checking Natural Science Electives . . .

Checking Humanities and Fine Arts . . .

Checking Social and Behavioral Sciences . . .

Checking Technical Electives . . .

        .

        .

        .

Approximately how many hours do you want to take this semester?

(The indicated hours should be in addition to those you plan on enrolling in the areas of
   Humanities & Natural Sciences (Div. A), Social and Behavioral Sciences (Div. B), and
   technical electives)

Remember that the engineering students are not normally allowed to take a total of
   more than 20 hours per semester.
u

[Approximately 14 hours are assumed.]

        .

        .

        .

Figure 5
(Continued)

INDUSTRIAL ENGINEERING CHECK SHEET

134 Hrs. Min.   FALL 1985
NAME   taylor,e.
MATHEMATICS & NATURAL SCIENCES : 34 Hrs.

math242q	taken	(5)	math243	taken	(5)
math311	can take	(1)	math344	taken	(3)
math550	can take	(3)	phys313q	taken	(4)
phys314q	can take	(4)	phys315q	taken	(1)

[3 Hrs. of Natural Science Electives are to be taken.]

COMMUNICATIONS : 9 Hrs.

eng1101	taken	(3)	eng1102	taken	(3)
spch111	can take	(3)			

HUMANITIES & FINE ARTS Div A : 18 Hrs. (Div. A & B)

[3 department(s) in Div. A is(are) to be taken.]

SOCIAL & BEHAVIORAL SCIENCES Div B :

econ201q	taken	(3)	econ202q	can take	(3)
pols103q	taken	(3)	soc211q	taken	(3)

[6 hour(s) of courses designated by G is(are) to be taken in Divisions A and B.]

Notes :
1.   At least 9 Hrs. must be taken in at least 3 deaprtments in Div. A.
2.   At least 3 additional Hrs. must be taken in non-Econ.. Div. B.
3.   At least 9 Hrs. of General Studies courses designated by G must be included within Divisions A and B.

ENGINEERING COURSES : 73 Hrs.

Engineering Core : 13 Hrs.

engr125	taken	(2)	me398	cannot take	(3)
ae323	can take	(3)	ee382	cannot take	(4)

SPECIFIC COURSES REQUIRED BY I.E. DEPARTMENT : 49 Hrs.

ie110	taken	(2)	ie213	taken	(2)
ee199	can take	(3)	ie354	cannot take	(3)
ae333	cannot take	(3)	ie355	cannot take	(3)
ie452	cannot take	(3)	ie460	cannot take	(3)
ie549	cannot take	(3)	ie550	cannot take	(3)
ie553	cannot take	(3)	ie554	cannot take	(3)
ie556	cannot take	(3)	ie558	cannot take	(3)

[A.E. 327 may be substituted for E.E. 199 and in such case 1 more hr. of technical electives will be required.]

Figure 6
EASIE's Advice

TECHNICAL ELECTIVES : 11 Hrs.   (Chosen from approved list)

[At least 6 hour(s) is(are) to be taken within I.E. Dept.]
[At least 3 hour(s) is(are) to be taken from another Engineering Departments.]

THE LIST OF RECOMMENDED COURSES

I am recommending that you take the following courses this semester in addition to
any Div. A, Div. B, and technical electives that you plan to take :

spch111	(3)
math311	(1)
math550	(3)
phys314q	(4)
econ202q	(3)

Figure 6
(Continued)

course = 'math242q, Calculus I, c'.
course = 'eng1101, College English I, c'.
course = 'chem111q, General Chemistry, b'.
course = 'ie110, Engr. Graphics, c'.
course = 'pols103q, Games Nations Play, c'.
course = 'ie213, Engr. Graphics II, d'.
course = 'econ201q, Principles of Econ. I, c'.
course = 'math243, Calculus II, a'.
course = 'soc211q, Intro Sociology, c'.
course = 'eng1102, College English II, c'.
course = 'phys313q, Univ. Physics I, c'.
course = 'phys315q, Univ. Physics lab I, b'.
gpa = '2.27'.

Figure 7
Student Academic Records Maintained by EASIE

search time significantly and improve the performance time. Currently, it takes
about 30 minutes to complete an advising session, with much of the time waiting
for the processing to be completed. This time is approximately equal to an advising session without EASIE.